Borderland Dreams

Borderland Dreams

JUNE HEE KWON

The Transnational Lives of Korean Chinese Workers

DUKE UNIVERSITY PRESS   DURHAM AND LONDON   2023

© 2023 DUKE UNIVERSITY PRESS
All rights reserved
Project Editor: Livia Tenzer
Designed by Matthew Tauch
Typeset in Garamond Premier Pro
and ITC Avant Garde Gothic Std by
Westchester Publishing Services

Library of Congress Cataloging-in-Publication Data
Names: Kwon, June Hee, [date] author.
Title: Borderland dreams : the transnational lives of Korean Chi-
nese workers / June Hee Kwon.
Description: Durham : Duke University Press, 2023. | Includes
bibliographical references and index.
Identifiers: LCCN 2023001613 (print)
LCCN 2023001614 (ebook)
ISBN 9781478025337 (paperback)
ISBN 9781478020516 (hardcover)
ISBN 9781478027461 (ebook)
Subjects: LCSH: Koreans—China—Yanbian Chaoxianzu
Zizhizhou—History. | Foreign workers—Korea (South)—Social
conditions. | Borderlands—China—History. | Borderlands—Korea
(South)—History. | Group identity—China—Yanbian Chaoxianzu
Zizhizhou. | Korean diaspora. | Yanbian Chaoxianzu Zizhizhou
(China)—Emigration and immigration. | Korea (South)—
Emigration and immigration. | BISAC: SOCIAL SCIENCE /
Anthropology / Cultural & Social | SOCIAL SCIENCE /
Emigration & Immigration
Classification: LCC DS793.Y4835 K88 2023 (print) | LCC DS793.
Y4835 (ebook) | DDC 305.8957051/88—dc23/eng/20230614
LC record available at https://lccn.loc.gov/2023001613
LC ebook record available at https://lccn.loc.gov/2023001614

Cover art: Snowscape, Paektu Mountain, Yanbian Korean
Autonomous Prefecture, China. Imagechina Limited/
Alamy Stock Photo.

To my parents

CONTENTS

This book, having grown out of my long ethnographic engagement, marks the end of two parallel journeys, of movement accompanied by learning. Reflecting on these travels, I owe a deep debt of gratitude to many friends, family members, colleagues, and others both in the field and beyond. My profoundest thanks go to my Korean Chinese friends, migrant workers and their families who embraced my work and invited me into their everyday lives with hospitality, support, and wisdom. Despite the risks and political burdens, they were willing to accompany me to important field sites that helped me better understand the history of Yanbian Korean Chinese Autonomous Prefecture in Jilin, China, and the everyday lives of Korean Chinese. They were eager to become part of my study, teaching me the actual process of ethnographic collaboration every day. This book is the culmination of *our* enthusiasm for collaboratively understanding the history and meaning of Yanbian, both for them and the world. All the people I encountered were my teachers, and the field site was an indispensable anthropological school for me.

I reserve special thanks for the late Lee Woonhak *seonsaengnim* (리운학 선생님), who guided me from the initial stages of my dissertation fieldwork to the later follow-up research by taking me to different Longjing towns, arranging numerous introductions for me, and sharing his vast and deep knowledge about local history. I regret that I am unable to return his deep and sincere support. I am also very grateful to the late Ryu Yeonsan *seonsaengnim* (류연산 선생님), the renowned Yanbian writer with a kind and warm soul, who was always willing to tell me about his research and stories and share his files and photos. I was very sad to see his illness growing worse by the time I left Yanbian at the end of 2009. Both *seonsaengnim* would be very happy and proud to see this book about Yanbian in print, especially in English, because they believed it could be widely read and known to the "world." Their stories and lessons are deeply imprinted across the book. I am immensely thankful for their deep support and very much miss the time we spent in Yanbian.

My everyday life was enriched by my Korean Chinese friends who attended my English class in 2009: Kyungran, Woong, Mr. Parrot, the late Kyun, Boksoon, Bumsoo, and others who shared their stories, time, and lives. Despite our promise to meet again in Yanbian sometime soon, Kyun became ill and abruptly left this world. He introduced me to a new dimension of Korean Chinese art history by connecting me with a wider circle of Korean Chinese artists from Yanbian. The friendship and emotional support of this group made Yanbian my second home, and they opened my eyes to new horizons every day. I am also grateful to several Korean Chinese Communist Party members who want to remain anonymous. Their history lessons were priceless, and their life stories were a source of inspiration. I appreciated the hiking companions who gave me valuable geographical and cultural lessons, especially Mr. Baishan and Mr. Pine, along with numerous others. I appreciate Mr. Shin, owner of the café Happy Nara, who allowed me to use his shop as my meeting space. I am indebted to professors in the Sociology Department of Yanbian University and the staff at the Yanbian Science and Technology University. Their warmhearted welcome and continuous engagement with my research kept me alert to local voices and perspectives. I am thankful to the Korean Chinese writers and journalists at *Jilin Newspaper,* the *Yanbian Daily News*, and Yanbian TV and Radio. They sent me to the right places and put me in contact with people who helped expand and deepen my field research.

In South Korea, my deep gratitude goes to Lim Gwangbin, who gave me enormous support at the early stage of my research. His willingness to share his wisdom and his desire to expand the range of my scholarship have made me into a transnational ethnographer. I also truly appreciate Kim Youngpil, whose resourcefulness helped place me at the cutting edge amid rapid social changes in South Korea. My research would have been impossible to carry out without their help and support. I deeply thank the members of the Korean Chinese Association, who pushed me to think harder and write better about their stories with true integrity. The personal accounts they shared with me became the kernel of this book, and their persistent friendship gave it vitality.

Over many years, I have been very fortunate to have teachers and mentors who supported my research and career with consistent trust. I have deep gratitude for Anne Allison and Ralph Litzinger at Duke. Anne's insightful criticism and endless support have pushed me to become a better thinker and writer. Her continual challenges have connected my work with the diverse veins of anthropological discussion. Ralph's ethnographic sense and well-rounded theoretical knowledge helped me strike a balance between theory and ethnography. He did not allow me to forget that I am an ethnographer. I also appreciate the critical reading and warm cheer of

Leo Ching, who has been an excellent interlocutor beyond the discipline of anthropology. He taught me how to view different disciplines and geographies as connected and entangled, helping me become a well-rounded East Asianist. I thank Rebecca Stein for offering me a theoretical map and helping me hone my analytical skills at the beginning stages of graduate school. I am grateful to Orin Starn, who has generously supported my studies, and to Charlie Piot, who shared his insights on migration studies in a comparative perspective. I am also deeply thankful to the late Nancy Ablemann at UIUC, who read multiple chapters and provided sharp critiques as well as encouragement for my research. Nancy would have been very glad to see this book in print.

As I began my academic career and spent time at various institutions, I was fortunate to receive crucial support from numerous friends and colleagues. I am deeply appreciative of Nicole Constable, my mentor, who gave me her full and heartfelt support even after I became a postdoctoral fellow at the University of Pittsburgh. She is the model of an ethnographer, with a love of field research as well as writing. Gabriella Lukacs gave me great insights as an interlocutor, helping me generate new ideas and research directions. She has also been a steadfast and genuine friend with whom I can share my everyday life. I am also grateful to Thomas Looser, my mentor at New York University, where I was an assistant professor/faculty fellow. His friendship and mentorship sustained and brightened my bumpy time in New York City. The faculty in the Asian Studies Program at California State University, Sacramento, have created a new home for me by welcoming and embracing me as a scholar, teacher, and colleague. I am thankful to Pattaratorn Chirapravati, Eunmi Cho, Jeffery Dym, Greg Kim-Ju, and Raghu Trichur. James Rae has made a special effort to help me settle comfortably into my new position and invited me to develop a program together. His unceasing support was immensely helpful in finally completing this book.

I am thankful for my teachers and comrades in South Korea who nurtured my eagerness to know more about the world. Hae Joang Cho's innovative perspective, ahead of its time, opened my eyes to anthropology. Eun-Shil Kim's feminist critique made me critically aware of local and global power dynamics. Byung-Ho Chung sparked my interest in studying the Korean diaspora across different countries as an activist scholar. Hyun Mee Kim was the one who set me on the path to becoming a cultural anthropologist. She has always been my intellectual inspiration as an exemplary scholar in and beyond the field. Dukho Bae shared his expertise and persistence about activism on the rights of overseas Koreans. Jungsup Yeom showed me how one can be endlessly curious and passionate about the world. I thank him for pointing me toward who I am and where I am now.

This book was made possible by funding from diverse organizations. A fieldwork research grant from the Duke Cultural Anthropology Department enabled me to conduct my field research. An Evan Frenkel Dissertation Workshop at Duke University allowed me to focus on writing my dissertation. My postdoctoral fellowship in the Department of Anthropology at the University of Pittsburgh and my time as an assistant professor/faculty fellow at NYU allowed me to develop my dissertation chapters into three different journal articles. A Kyunjanggak Overseas Publication Grant from Seoul National University helped me complete the writing of my book's manuscript. Promotion and dissemination of this publication were supported by the 2023 Korean Studies Grant Program of the Academy of Korean Studies (AKS-2023-P-009).

Different parts of this book were formed by many different institutions. These are the James Joo-Jin Kim Center for Korean Studies at the University of Pennsylvania, the Department of Women's, Gender, and Sexuality Studies at Ohio State University, the Institute of Ethnology at Academia Sinica in Taiwan, the Asia Research Institute at National Singapore University, the Department of Anthropology at Johns Hopkins University, the Department of Anthropology at Stanford University, the Max Plank Society in Germany, the Department of Anthropology at the University of Toronto, the Department of Sociology and Anthropology at Fordham University, the Department of Sociology and Anthropology at the University of Mississippi, the Department of European and International Studies at King's College London, the Department of Languages and Cultures at Rutgers University, the Davis Center at Princeton University, the Department of Anthropology at Tulane University, the Institute for Korean Studies at Indiana University, the Center for Korean Studies at the University of Hawaii, the Center for Korean Studies at the University of California, Berkeley, and the Institute for Global Korean studies at Yonsei University. In particular, the SSRC Korean Studies Dissertation Workshop, the SSRC Korean Studies Junior Faculty Workshop, and the Korean Studies Junior Faculty Manuscript Workshop by the University of Michigan Nam Center for Korean Studies provided valuable feedback for me to revise and refine my manuscript. I am especially thankful for the solid and challenging comments from the late Nancy

Abelmann, Seungsook Moon, Nicole Constable, Nicholas Harkness, Eleana Kim, and Zhang Li. Following their suggestions made the book more consistent and approachable to readers. Ken Wissoker, with his bottomless support and encouragement, was the model of an academic editor who worked respectfully with me to keep the book's argument consistent and the supporting points clear. Ryan Kendall's editorial help ensured the book's swift move to production. Project editor Livia Tenzer made timely and professional arrangements throughout that process. They are truly the best editorial team.

I am fortunate to have made numerous friends who have been part of my writing journey. Our discussions have been critical for developing and revising my ideas and my writing. I thank the members of the Franklin Humanities Center Dissertation Writing Group (Eric Brandon, Christina Chia, Youngmi Cho, Patrick Alexander, Liz Shesko, and Sherali Tareen) and the Department of Cultural Anthropology's dissertation writing group (Katya Wesolowski, Lorien Olive, Jatin Dua, Erin Parish, and Juhyung Shim). Anru Lee has been my great writing partner with sharp criticism and warm encouragement. I also thank my smart and insightful friends who read part of the manuscript: Arianne Dorval, Brian Goldstone, Yidong Gong, Kevin Sobel-Read, Adra Rain, Alex Ruch, Eric Karchmer, John Cho, Haeyoung Kim, Cheehyung Kim, Jayoung Min, Myungji Yang, Seoyoung Park, Nan Kim, Christina Kim, Sungjo Kim, Joshua Howard, Angie Heo, Hyokyong Woo, Seungwhan Shin, Wonji Yoo, Hyeri Oh, Jeongmin Kim, Minjoo Oh, Jessie Schambers, Clara Lee, Joowhee Lee, Young Cheon Cho, and Michael Walker. I am grateful for the sharp commentary of Jesook Song and Caren Freeman. Gary Ashwill and Cheryl Nichitta provided fruitful editorial advice. Miree Ku helped me access archives in South Korea, overcoming geographical barriers. Loretta Kim's help with maps finalized the manuscript. My everyday interlocutors—Hyunseo Cho, Eunja Choi, Jayeon Jeong, Anne Pracila, Soonyi Lee, Chunmi Kim, Shine Shin, and Thomas Houfek—provided insights as well as downtime, which both supported me and kept me moving forward. I am grateful to the late Gihong Jeong and Songah Chae for restoring my health and vitality. Thanks also to Seunghyun Kim, Yonghyun Kim, and Jonianne Jeannette, who worked hard to heal my health issues. Because of them I have become a healthy and vibrant person again. My special thanks go to Boyeon Kim, who has remained my closest friend for all these decades, standing by my side and walking with me however far I go. My friends from New York progressive circles and the Sacramento Cabbage group, who have welcomed and supported me with good food and warm hearts, are another source of health and pleasure. Misook Chun's food, full of care and love, is a taste of home and always raises my spirits.

Finally, I owe a tremendous debt of gratitude to my family. My late grandmother, Kim Geumsun, with her fervor for education, would have been truly pleased to see my book in the world as the crystallization of my long-time efforts. My sister, Sohye Kwon, and brother, Juneyeop Kwon, continue to be my strong supporters. My foremost gratitude goes to my parents, Kwon Taeksung and Shim Insook. Their deep affection and confidence have sustained me on my long and bumpy journey away from home, and it is because of them that I can persist in my work. This book is dedicated to their patience and love.

Winds of Migration

I am a windflower floating without direction. I have been moving back and forth, not staying between where the wind is coming from and where the wind is going. I have flown here and there, continuously remembering and forgetting, blaming and missing the other world. I belong to both worlds, while at the same time I escape from both worlds. Who am I, the one who has flown all around? I am the wind.

—XU LIANSHUN, *Paramkkot* (The windflower)

On a hot July day in 2013, Sunhua and Taebong, a married Korean Chinese couple in their early forties, invited me to the opening party for their restaurant in Yanji, the capital of Yanbian, the Korean Chinese Autonomous Prefecture in northeast China that borders North Korea. Sunhua is the youngest of five daughters, all of whom (and all of whose husbands) have pursued the "Korean dream": leaving China and working in South Korea as transnational migrant workers, a practice that began in the early 1990s. Sunhua's husband, Taebong, had also gone to South Korea, following his hometown friends; they had all been swept up in what is known as the "Korean Wind" (*han'guk param* in Korean)—a nickname for the collective passion in Yanbian for the Korean dream. Sunhua and Taebong had met in South Korea and married there, and they had a five-year-old daughter. After fifteen years of working in South Korea, they had decided to come back to Yanbian, their hometown, and fulfill Taebong's longtime ambition: opening a restaurant. At the opening party, Taebong told me: "I could not live as a *dagong* ["manual laborer" in Chinese] working under South Koreans anymore. I am getting older. I want to have a more settled life. Most of all, I wanted to return to Yanbian for my daughter's education."[1] Taebong now considered himself an entrepreneur, someone who could hire and fire employees and run his own restaurant—the opposite of his status in South Korea.

On my first visit to the restaurant after the opening, Sunhua and Taebong were still very excited about their new business, which had enjoyed gradual but steady growth. Within a few months, however, I heard from them that the restaurant business had been a bit too "up and down" and could not give them the stable income that they needed to maintain their household, given the skyrocketing cost of living in Yanbian. As a result, they had decided that Sunhua would remain in Yanbian, running a scaled-down restaurant business and taking care of their daughter, while Taebong went back to work in a South Korean printing factory to secure a reliable salary—even though he had badly wanted to break out of the cycle of moving back and forth between China and South Korea as a *dagong*. In other words, Sunhua would stay in China in order to take advantage of the rising Chinese economy (the "Chinese dream"), while Taebong continued to pursue the Korean dream. This couple has, for the time being, settled on a diversified life strategy; they are now juggling both the Chinese dream and the Korean dream—or, as I call them, "borderland dreams."

This book examines this re/interpretation of the Korean dream that has haunted Korean Chinese and the region of Yanbian for the past three decades. It takes as its subject the collective craze for exodus to the homeland, South Korea, which, prior to the 1990s, had been long forbidden and branded as an "enemy homeland."[2] This collective haunting has been expressed in a common saying: "Everybody [any able body] who can walk is gone with the Korean Wind" (*kŏl ŭl su it nŭn saram ŭn Han'guke da katta* in Korean). Another common saying goes, "Whenever even two people get together, there is talk about South Korea." The Korean Wind has been indeed everywhere: imagined, spoken of, and acted on, in the context of financial successes and failures, fake (and real) marriages, new apartments and new businesses, thriving or disintegrating families. It has been analyzed and circulated via newspapers, academic journals, literary writings, and blogs, as well as in everyday talk. All this talk reflects widespread aspiration, yearning, and pride. It also hints at concerns and critiques about the sudden affluence that has accompanied the Korean Wind, about a prevailing attitude of obsessive materialism, and about the collapse of the Korean Chinese ethnic community and sustained family structure.

Korean Chinese have long believed labor migration to South Korea to be the most effective and powerful means of breaking the cycle they have been caught up in as farmers and workers in a rapidly privatizing China. In the early 1990s, the Korean dream was first visualized in Yanbian discourse as the "ten-thousand-yuan household" (*manwŏnho* in Korean), whose members went to South Korea, made 10,000 yuan (an amount that symbolized "a lot of money" at the time in China) in a short period of time, and then built a fancy new house with this "Korean money." The sudden wealth earned by the first migrant laborers in South Korea was envied and idolized by their neighbors, and it fed the aspirations of the Korean dream. These beliefs have led 726,000 Korean Chinese (out of around two million Korean Chinese living in China, mainly in the northeast) to emigrate to South Korea for work. According to recent statistics (as of 2020), Korean Chinese are the largest migrant group in South Korea.

The Korean Wind has brought significant changes to the lives of Korean Chinese immigrants over the last three decades. Yet it has also left deep marks on those who do not actually migrate, as well as on the place that is left behind—Yanbian. There are those who are waiting for someone's return, those who rely on money sent from South Korea, those who are waiting to migrate themselves, and those who take over the houses, lands, and jobs left vacant by migrants. Despite the high numbers of departing Korean Chinese, Yanbian has not been left empty by the Korean Wind, as those who have gone have left behind families, and new people have also migrated to Yanbian to fill the void the Korean Chinese emigrants have left. Under the influential, transformative power of the Korean Wind, Yanbian has become a migration-dominated borderland, subject to transnational rhythms of life and transnational flows of money.

What, then, has made this massive and persistent migratory craze possible over the past three decades? What established Korean Chinese as suitable migrant workers in the China-to-South Korea transnational labor market? What are the means of creating (or sometimes destroying) the transnational relationship between those who remain and those who go—the living and the leaving—in an environment where much of the population has gone with the Korean Wind? And what is (or will be) the afterlife of these Korean dreams?

Using bodies, money, and time as key ethnographic lenses through which to understand the persistent aspirations of labor migrants and everyone connected to them, this book analyzes the political economy of the enthusiasm fueling labor migration to South Korea, a migration that has formed Korean Chinese into a transnational ethnic working class. My argument is that the Korean dream is not only a collective myth that provoked individual anticipation of a better life, in part as a response to rapid privatization in China, but also a reflection of the new material realities that sprang from the intersection between post-socialist China and post–Cold War South Korea. In other words, the Korean Wind ushered in a unique era of transnational money and time between China and South Korea, leading to the ethnicization of Korean Chinese working bodies.

But this book also examines a new social imperative that has appeared, one that may break the cycle of the dominant Korean dream—a discourse urging Korean Chinese to stop working for and under South Korean employers and capital and to reembrace life in rapidly thriving Yanbian, as China emerges as a site for new economic opportunities. As seen in Sunhua and Taebong's story, which opens this introduction, Korean Chinese are struggling with competing and contentious dreams, the Korean dream and the Chinese dream. Moreover, in order to understand Korean Chinese migration, which appears predominantly transnational in the form of the Korean Wind, we also need to take a close look at all the migratory paths being followed on multiple scales (see chapter 5): from the countryside to the city, from small cities to larger cities, from cities in Yanbian to other parts of China—and many other migratory paths, multiplying the life choices beyond the Korean dream. Unraveling the various afterlives and reinterpretations of the Korean dream, we can see that the dream does not stand still but moves and changes. And sometimes dreams stop being dreams altogether. This book captures this complex array of borderland dreams: geopolitically sensitive and ethnically specific aspirations that are entangled with the new post–Korean Wind moment and buoyed by the hope of pursuing the Chinese dream and the Korean dream at the same time.

Gone with the Korean Wind

There are around two million Korean Chinese living in China nationwide, mostly concentrated in the northeastern provinces of Jilin, Liaoning, and Heilongjiang. Approximately 700,000 of them, 35 percent of the total, live in the borderland of Yanbian, an autonomous prefecture in southeastern Jilin province. The Korean Chinese, whose ancestors crossed the Tumen River from the Korean peninsula in search of better farming lands beginning in the late nineteenth century, are an ethnic minority group with Chinese nationality. Later, some Koreans moved to Manchuria to escape from poverty that was exacerbated by Japanese imperialism, and some were forced to move by Japanese plans for transplanting populations—what Hyun Ok Park calls "territorial osmosis" (H. O. Park 2005).[3] In addi-

Map I.1 Map showing the transnational commute between Yanbian, China, and South Korea.

tion, Koreans who opposed Japanese oppression moved to Manchuria in order to support the independence movement from relative safety outside Korea.

Korean Chinese in Yanbian are mostly the descendants of migrants from the northern part of Korea (Hamgyŏng-bukto, the northeast region of contemporary North Korea) who crossed over in the late nineteenth and early twentieth centuries. Most Korean Chinese in Yanbian speak a dialect similar to that of Hamgyŏng-bukto, which is right across the river, and they maintain the regional food culture and housing style. After the new China was established in 1949 and Yanbian was designated the Korean Chinese Autonomous Prefecture in 1952, these descendants of Korean migrants became Chinese nationals, "proud" to be one of fifty-five ethnic minorities officially recognized by the Chinese government.[4] Under the exigencies of Cold War politics, however, Korean Chinese were forbidden to contact or claim kinship ties to either of the two Koreas, especially South Korea, which was condemned as a hotbed of "devil capitalism" and "a bastard of imperial America" (*mi chabonjuŭi saekki* in Korean).[5]

Things dramatically changed, however, as China and South Korea normalized diplomatic relations in 1992 and Cold War hostilities faded away. Korean Chinese have since developed a close relationship with South Korea. They first recovered long-lost cultural and familial ties that had been forbidden under Cold War politics; soon after, Korean Chinese were recognized as "overseas Koreans," or ethnic compatriots (*tongp'o* in Korean), by the South Korean government (see chapters 2 and 3), and became persistent, even obsessive labor migrants, driven by the vast income gap between China and South Korea. The Korean Wind—with forces connecting Yanbian to South Korea, from family reunions to the labor market—has dominated the affect, materiality, and futurity of Korean Chinese across Yanbian, which I elucidate throughout the book.

The act of "going with the Korean Wind" has become widely accepted as an inevitable life phase for most Korean Chinese, marking a rapid cultural, economic, and political transition in Yanbian. Here, being "gone" does not simply mean to disappear or leave for South Korea or some other foreign country. Rather, it signifies a condition of living, of moving back and forth, a condition to which many Korean Chinese have become accustomed as a deep and essential part of their lives. However, some Korean Chinese intellectuals, journalists, and social critics consider the ubiquitous phenomenon of being gone as a pathological force that poses an ethnic crisis—a symptom of a spreading social "disease" that manifests in high divorce rates, deficiencies in childcare, juvenile delinquency, and extravagant spending. Critics of the Korean Wind believe that these factors threaten the stability of Yanbian's ethnic community by "contaminating" the consciousness of Korean Chinese with capitalism, creating within them a relentless desire to pursue "money-money-money" (*don-don-don* in Korean). Indeed, there is a tacit agreement that nobody is really immune to materialistic "contamination" by "Korean water" (*Han'guk mul* in Korean) since the money-money-money spirit has given rise to great economic achievement, dramatic urbanization, and rising aspirations—not only on the individual household level but also across and beyond the Korean Chinese community, and in Yanbian at large.

In this turbulent context, the concept of "wind" (*param* in Korean) connotes not only a fashion or temporary collective craze for migration but also the shifting politico-economic circumstances of specific eras—vernacularly circulated periodizations such as the North Korean Wind, the Soviet Wind, and the South Korean Wind. These winds are based on collective migrations, which occurred in accordance with the changing regional political economy between China, North Korea, Russia, and South Korea, as Korean Chinese have regained the freedom of mobility in the era of post–Cold War globalization and post-socialist China. In a more metaphorical sense, these winds can be understood as a symbol for the floating subjectivity of Korean Chinese as rootless, displaced, nomadic subjects, without clear sense of belonging to any one location—as in the passage from the Korean Chinese writer Xu Lianshun's novel quoted at the beginning of this introduction. The Korean *param* indicates the flow of air. But it also entails the fashions and collective obsessions shared by a society during a certain period of time. In the latter sense, *param* can cause people to "flow" in a certain direction, and sometimes people can get lost within the flow. Thus, *param* structures a vague but strong feeling of a specific moment in a given place, as well as creating a sense of a shared temporality (a periodization) that influences the attitudes and actions of contemporaries. For the last thirty years, the Korean Wind has been at once a condition of hope for the future and a destructive power that threatens to dissolve old ties. The Korean Wind is thus not only a material source of rapid economic betterment and modern life, but also a mythical medium through which Korean Chinese can articulate their relationships to the past and the future, politics and economy, socialism and capitalism. Korean Chinese have re/interpreted their Korean dreams—staging Yanbian as an ethnic borderland distinctive from, but integrated into, the transnational economy.

Winds of Migration

Yanbian's urbanization began with the end of the political turmoil of the Cultural Revolution, when Deng Xiaoping announced economic reforms in December 1978. This proclamation foresaw three stages of development: first, to end hunger and ensure food security (温饱 *wenbao*) from 1980 to 1990; second, to spread "decent affluence" (小康 *xiaokang*) throughout the whole population, from 1990 to 2000; and third, to achieve a socialist market economy through the mid-twenty-first century. Pragmatism was vital to this economic reform, as captured in the expression, "It does not matter whether the cat is black or white as long as it catches the mouse" (*baimao heimao lun* in Chinese). The reforms also allowed or even encouraged the enrichment of particular groups, admitting market competition and consequential social inequality as an inevitable rite of passage. Although Deng made this declaration in 1978, it took time for the reform policies to reach Yanbian and be put into practice. In the early 1980s, people in Yanbian were still confused about what it meant to take part in a market economy or to engage in profit making. During this time, privatization or selling was still officially forbidden, although it was growing gradually in secret. Due to Yanbian's geographical marginality as an ethnic enclave, its development has often been overlooked or deferred by the central government. Yet as Yanbian Korean Chinese began to experience the rise of a market economy, the markets helped to "open" their eyes through contact with the external world, including long-distance business trips to larger Chinese cities. Interaction with the world at large through travel generated an increased flow of things, people, and habits both into and out of Yanbian. This emergence and demise of collective fashions and yearnings for new or foreign experiences, opportunities, and goods can be understood in terms of four distinct phases, or winds.

The Market Wind (*Sijang Param*)

Beginning in the early 1980s, farmland was redistributed from collectives to individual families. This new system of production and distribution in the countryside encouraged farmers to increase their productivity and start selling surpluses on the market. The idea of profit making rapidly expanded to urbanites, and the consequent rise in all sorts of buying and selling caused Yanbian to be gradually connected to the external world.[6] While researching the history of markets in Yanbian, I attended a summer picnic organized by the Association of the Old (*Noin Hyŏphoe* in Korean). The association holds regular activities, such as dancing, singing, and hiking, for Korean Chinese retirees. At this picnic, I met several former businesspeople who in the late 1980s and early 1990s had taken part in what was known as *xiahai* ("the plunge into the ocean" in Chinese)— that is, the wave of private profit-making business activities. I talked at length with one of them, Mr. Hong, who was considered one of the most successful; he had reacted swiftly to the economic reforms and gained an advantage over his competitors.

In his late sixties, Mr. Hong had once worked for the post office in Yanji. In the early 1980s, he noticed some of his neighbors and other farmers selling simple things—tofu, sunflower seeds, tobacco—on the street and making profits, which began to bring in more income than their regular salaries. Their surreptitious activity made Mr. Hong interested in selling something. His wife, a factory worker, was also a talented cook and especially good at making *mahua* (a fried-dough snack with a twisted shape, popular in China). He and his wife soon started selling *mahua* as their secondary job, setting up a stand on a busy street corner. Since *mahua* was considered a morning food, they had to get up at 3 a.m. to prepare to start selling at 6 a.m. The *mahua* would be sold out by 7 a.m. Mr. Hong then would go to the post office for his regular job. As the business quickly picked up beyond their expectations, they had to prepare even more ingredients for more sales and started getting up at 2 a.m. As Mr. Hong described it: "We were physically tired, but that extra cash income made us forget about the exhaustion. It was much more than our combined incomes—more than four times."

He heard at one point that the local government would prohibit street vendors for the sake of preserving the city landscape. But he and his wife were not overly worried because they were not the only vendors. People—both Han Chinese and Korean Chinese—still sold things on the street regardless of the local government's ban. After realizing that the regulations were ineffective and the vendors' numbers were increasing by the day, the local government eventually decided to establish an "official market." The government acted as a landlord, selling or renting booths to individual sellers. Mr. Hong and his wife started by renting a booth in the new market, but soon their successful business allowed them to buy a booth. And they became the owners of a restaurant—*laoban* ("an owner of business" in Chinese).

The opening of this official market was a major event, one that dramatically transformed perspectives on money, profits, markets, and the larger world. In 1985, after the Yanji West Market (*Sŏsijang* in Korean) opened as the first and largest market in Yanbian, smaller cities—Longjing, Tumen, and Helong—also opened public markets that allowed sellers to run their own businesses as *laoban* within the markets. Mr. Hong's story is one of the numerous examples that can help us understand the growing mood of privatization at the time. He found a good niche in the marketplace by capitalizing on the talent of his wife. He also realized that the harder he worked, the more money he could make, in contrast to the collective farm and rigid socialist production system. Excitement about the emerging market and the profits it promised spread rapidly and widely. Whenever I interviewed businesspeople and government officials in their fifties or older, including the retired businesspeople I met at the picnic, they recollected the 1980s as a time of new energy, new experiences, and new ideas.

This was an exciting moment for Korean Chinese who were used to living in an insular ethnic zone.

Such eye-opening experiences occurred more frequently in businesses that required long-distance trips. While Mr. Hong's restaurant business was local, with not much need for travel, those who engaged in trading needed to buy products in larger cities. Until this time, most of these traders had never left Yanbian. When I talked to shopkeepers and former peddlers, at the heart of their memories of this time lay the fear and excitement they felt about making their first long-distance trips to other Chinese cities. Given the marginalized location of Yanbian in China, shopkeepers and purchasing agents (*caigouyuan* in Chinese) had to go to larger cities in order to buy new products, which they then carried back to Yanbian to sell in their stores.[7]

They had to repeat this cycle many times because Yanbian's economy was not big enough to create a high demand for consumer products. They took trains to closer cities in northeast China, such as Shenyang or Harbin—a three- to four-day round trip. But when they traveled to more commercialized southern cities, such as Shanghai or Guangzhou, it could take as many as three days just to get there because of the slow trains back then. The merchants remembered these trips as long, exhausting, and risky. Since they had to make purchases with cash, they were frequently the target of robbers. In order to protect themselves from being attacked, and to brighten up the long, dull trips, they took to traveling in small groups of three or four. Ms. Li, one of the Korean Chinese ladies I met at the picnic and a current seller in the Yanji West Market, said to me, "Whenever I took a trip, I felt that my eyes were opened to the bigger world and newer things. I learned how to do business in 'real' China with 'real' Chinese."

The rise of the market economy not only enabled goods to circulate but also transformed Korean Chinese culture. The business trips had a dual impact. They helped Korean Chinese who had grown up in a parochial ethnic enclave both to see a larger world and to realize more fully their status as an ethnic minority—as people who often spoke no fluent Chinese and had no knowledge of "real" China or Chinese culture (see chapter 5). As these ethnic subjects came face to face with the external world (*Oechi* in Korean) in the context of the market economy, they began to extend their geographical imagination and scope of their mobility beyond China to North Korea and the Soviet Union. North Korea, in particular, came to the fore as the first transnational business partner for Yanbian Korean Chinese due to geographical proximity, linguistic similarity, and kinship connectivity.

The North Korean Wind (*Pukchosŏn Param*)

Beginning in the mid-1980s, business travel expanded to North Korea. I heard about a variety of business experience with North Korea from Korean Chinese migrant workers whom I met both in South Korea and in Yanbian. The many stories they had to tell provide evidence of common business practices among Korean Chinese in the mid-1980s. Despite the geographical adjacency between Yanbian and North Korea, the business relationship between them had been limited for decades by political circumstances. Even though China and North Korea had been on reciprocal terms as neighboring socialist states, the diplomatic relationship became hostile during the Cultural Revolution because Kim Il Sung, the leader of North Korea, was critical of Mao's political strategies. Any possible tie to North Korea—familial, economic, or political—could be a pretext for political persecution. In order to avoid the emotional, political, and physical traumas connected to politics, Korean Chinese had to prove how faithful they were to China, and how fully Chinese they had become, by attenuating their ethnic identity. Yet as political tensions gradually eased in the mid-1980s, Korean Chinese were allowed to visit their families back in North Korea with less political burden. Some of them began to carry Chinese industrial products to exchange for North Korean seafood, which was known to be of high quality. Other Korean Chinese began to peddle their goods in North Korean markets at a high rate of profit, staying in North Korea for several days or weeks.[8]

One of these Korean Chinese migrant workers, Ms. Kang, was in her late fifties when I met her in Seoul in 2009. She told me about her trading experience in North Korea. She used to work in a furniture factory in Yanbian. But as the factory began to decline, she started her own business, selling fruit in the market. In addition, she began going to North Korea for extra income in the early 1990s.

> I carried as much stuff as I could all the way to North Korea. It was so heavy that my back and arms felt like they were going to break. Once I got there, I had to rely on a North Korean mediator who guided me to a large market that opened once a week. I put my products on sale there. There were a lot of thieves in the market. I got robbed once. It was very stressful to be alert all the time. Sometimes, I just passed the products on to the mediator and received seafood in exchange, right on the spot. The money I could earn from them was not bad—better than several months of salary at my factory.

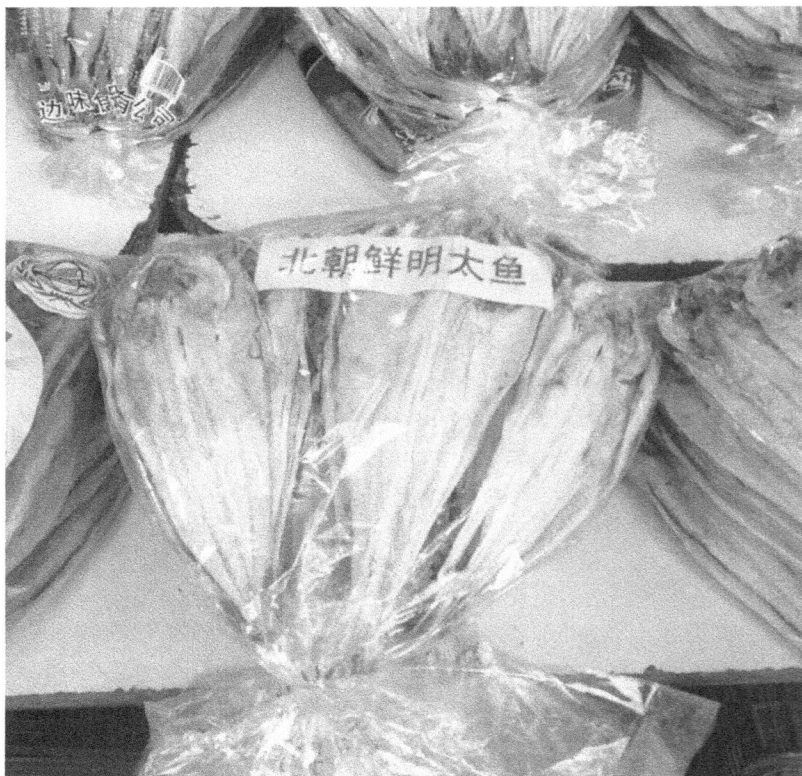

I.1 Dried cod from North Korea in the Yanji West Market, Yanbian, China, 2016. Photo by the author.

However, the trade with North Korea did not last long. Even though it became a popular extra source of income among farmers and factory workers, there were inherent limits. First, the profit margin could not increase because the Yanbian merchants could only carry a certain amount of goods to North Korea on each trip. Given that public transportation across the border was not reliable, the Korean Chinese business travelers had to hire personal vehicles to transport them and their goods to North Korea. They knew that the more they carried, the more they could sell and earn, because there was always high demand for Chinese products in North Korea. The Korean Chinese, who were individual street merchants and shopkeepers and not agents for large firms, could not amass much capital through business with North Korea. They realized that they were unable to turn their small-scale trading into big businesses. Most importantly, since Korean Chinese were unfamiliar with the market situation in North Korea, they had to rely on North Korean mediators, who were often distant relatives or newly minted business partners that they did not know well. It was not unusual for these mediators to turn out to be swindlers. Sometimes North Korean thieves robbed Korean Chinese merchants. In addition, since market regulations in North Korea—rules on where and when one was allowed to sell what to whom—were tight and subject to arbitrary changes, it was not easy for Korean Chinese to do business in the country. Under these high-risk, low-trust conditions, Korean Chinese merchants sometimes went bankrupt, even when their business had shown signs of success. The risky, unpredictable market conditions quickly exhausted Korean Chinese merchants, and the North Korean Wind began to flag. Then the Soviet Wind blew into Yanbian in the early 1990s.

The Soviet Wind (*Ssoryŏn Param*)

As China and the Soviet Union normalized diplomatic relations in 1991, many Chinese left for the former Soviet territories in order to introduce Chinese industrial products into suddenly open markets. In stark contrast to the small-scale, short-term, barter-style trade in North Korea, the Russian market was better organized and more profitable.[9] Since Soviet industrial development had been focused on heavy industry, the products of so-called light industry such as clothes, shoes, and daily goods were often scarce in Russia. In targeting this niche market, some Korean Chinese took long trips to Moscow or Ukraine, but the majority of Korean Chinese dealers left for the Russian Far East because it bordered northeast China—in particular, the eastern parts of Jilin and Heilongjiang. The items for sale were diverse, but these merchants mostly concentrated on selling clothes and shoes, which were in high demand in Russia.[10] The merchants dealt with a much wider range of products and often stayed for years—much longer than most Korean Chinese merchants stayed in North Korea.

Most of the merchants with experience in North Korea eventually went to Russia for business too. According to many I spoke with, business in Russia was organized for self-protection and profit-maximization; it was also known to be an extremely dangerous place to do business. It was said that "when people went to Russia for business, they put their lives on the line." I was told that Russian gangsters specifically targeted

Chinese merchants because they were believed to carry large amounts of cash. However, the high profit margins seemed to outweigh the fear and anxiety, and they kept the Soviet Wind blowing through Yanbian in the early 1990s.

The Soviet Wind seemed to dovetail with economic reform in China. Sometimes, government work units encouraged their workers to go to Russia by providing them with official vacations to do so—it was implicit but institutionalized support from the work units. Mr. Kim Hakman, in his early seventies, used to be the vice mayor of a Yanbian city. He recalled the Soviet Wind:

> When the Soviet Union collapsed in 1991, they needed many things. At that time, we Korean Chinese thought that it was a great opportunity to make money. Thus, in our work unit we encouraged our workers to take temporary vacations and do whatever they could to make money. They were allowed to return to the work unit within a couple of years, after making decent money. Since I was fairly high ranked in the city government, I could not stay away on my own business like that. But I did go to the Soviet Union a couple of times in 1991. I was very impressed with their higher level of "civilization" (*munmyŏng* in Korean) and development compared to China at that time. But doing business there was extremely dangerous. My brother-in-law, my wife's brother, went to the Soviet Union and made a lot of money. But Russian gangsters stabbed him. He was almost killed. Even with that risk, people went there until the early 1990s because of the profits they could make.

In response to the high risk, the merchants had to develop new methods to protect themselves. Mr. Kim and other former merchants who traded in Russia detailed what they did: before they left, they organized a team of Korean Chinese merchants doing business in Russia, or sometimes they formed a partnership with strangers after they got there. They also engaged in fake marriages in order to appear as if they were operating as a family, rather than as individual merchants. Many former merchants said that before they left for Russia or began to do business there, they would hold a wedding ceremony with another merchant. But the "couples" were not supposed to ask about each other's personal information, including their real names. The merchants lived under assumed identities throughout the period of their business in Russia. From the stories they told, it appears that there was a division of labor by gender. Women tended to take care of the store, while men were in charge of purchasing products from China and carrying them to Russia. In order to address the security issue, sometimes two couples joined together as business partners. These "married" merchants lived together as if they were a real couple for the common goal of safety. Sometimes they developed feelings for each other and engaged in actual love affairs. But the "official" agreement was that they were to keep up the fake couple relationship between themselves and would not meet again after they returned to China. Despite such agreements, the Soviet Wind posed a challenge to normative couples and family relationships among Korean Chinese merchants, with the embedded practice of "fake coupling" as a rite of passage. It was performed for business interests and self-protection, but it also evolved into a way of life, which led to actual affairs and increased divorces in Yanbian.

When I was collecting memories related to the Soviet Wind from various former Korean Chinese merchants, I could sense the anxiety and excitement of informants in recalling that time. The risk was high. The stakes were high. The potential benefit was high. It was the sort of chance that might come only once in a lifetime. But the Russian trade seemed to be so unpredictable that most merchants could not make more than one or two attempts unless they were able to put together a solid, well-organized support group—a network to provide financial help, security, and social support. In the end, the former merchants said it was difficult to maintain their businesses without support from gangster groups for security. Even though Korean Chinese merchants retain good memories of Russia as a developed and "civilized" Western country, Russia proved to be "too foreign" for them to live there for very long—not to mention that they found the language hard to master. The Soviet Wind peaked in the early 1990s, stimulating a flow of Korean Chinese merchants to Russia and bringing in large sums of Russian money. But it rapidly faded and was replaced with the Korean Wind after China normalized diplomatic relations with South Korea in 1992.

The South Korean Wind (Han'guk Param)

The diplomatic normalization between China and South Korea in 1992 was an epochal event for the Korean Chinese community in China, in the sense that it rejuvenated kinship ties forgotten and forbidden under

Cold War politics and created new population flows. South Koreans came to China to find new business partners and cheaper labor.[11] Meanwhile, Korean Chinese moved to South Korea to serve as cheaper labor. Korean Chinese often recalled their first encounter with South Korea as an experience of overwhelming anxiety and nervousness about their long-forbidden "home" country and impending reunions with long-lost family. The kinship reunions that the South Korean government began in the late 1980s as a humanitarian gesture became a channel for Korean Chinese to visit South Korea. The South Korean government issued "kinship visit visas" to Korean Chinese, which triggered an increased flow of Korean Chinese migration later in the 1990s. Many Korean Chinese brought Chinese medicine in bulk to South Korea, partially as gifts for relatives and partially to sell for profit. At the heart of stories I was told about traveling to South Korea was always the amount of money that could be made in several months by selling Chinese medicine. Through these repeated trips, South Korea emerged as a profitable marketplace for Korean Chinese. This sudden material achievement ignited a type of fantasy of South Korea as a capitalist dreamland. "If you go to South Korea," it was said, "your back will ache from gathering dollars in the street." South Korea, which Communist China had long portrayed as an impoverished capitalist enemy and "baby" subject of US imperialism, started becoming viewed as a destination that enabled an escape from long poverty in China. Korean Chinese emigration to South Korea started slowly in the late 1980s, as the South Korean economy expanded after hosting the Seoul Olympics in 1988, but then gathered dramatic momentum in 1992 with diplomatic normalization between the two countries.

The kinship visits evolved into full-fledged labor migration within a couple of years (see chapter 2). Starting in the early 1990s, many Korean Chinese who entered with family-visit visas began overstaying and working as cheap, illegal labor. However, despite the increasing numbers of undocumented Korean Chinese, the visa situation was not favorable to Korean Chinese from Yanbian. As I noted above, their ancestors had mostly moved to China from what is now North Korea, beginning in the late nineteenth century. Thus they had a harder time obtaining family-visit visas because the majority of them did not have actual kinship ties to South Koreans or registration records in South Korea.[12] As the suddenly well-off Korean Chinese returning from South Korea spurred a new Korean dream, illegal brokers developed methods to forge visas and passports by "making and faking kinship" via marriage (Freeman

2011) and putting into circulation fake documents as pricy commodities. Again, the stakes were high, as everything was illegal and the financial costs were extreme, which often put visa seekers into debt.[13] But there was a widely shared presumption that migrants could pay off the debt in a year or two, so the debt was not seen as an insurmountable obstacle. The illegal migration market expanded year by year, expedited by the brokers and by the high demand for visas to South Korea. The reliance on illegal brokers eventually became the most common route to get into South Korea. Within a far-flung black market advertised by word of mouth, those who wanted to enter South Korea searched for the best brokers with the highest success rates. The black market and its impact continued even after visa regulations were loosened to create a form of free movement (see chapters 2 and 3). The South Korean Wind greatly expanded the borderland dreams, driving unprecedented migration and economic development.

The Rise of the Korean Dream

In South Korea, the Korean diaspora had been long neglected, and acknowledgment of it even forbidden, under the Cold War regime. As the Cold War political mood gradually thawed in the early 1990s, the South Korean government began to pay attention to overseas Koreans (see chapters 1 and 2). Starting in the late nineteenth century, numerous natural disasters, as well as high taxes imposed by the corrupt government, displaced Koreans from the Korean peninsula, first to Russia and later to China, in search of farmland where they could put their diligence, work ethic, and productive rice-farming skills to good use (H. O. Park 2005, 2015; A. Park 2019). Later, poor Korean farmers displaced by Japanese colonization (1910–1945) left for Japanese cities to find better work opportunities, only to be confronted by harsh discrimination (Kawashima 2009). Koreans who migrated to Russia, China, and Japan during the colonial era commonly experienced ethnic discrimination and class exploitation as migrant farmers or workers, and their legal status remained unclear under ambiguous border controls.[14] Their marginalized status made them receptive to socialist movements that advocated for the landless and the exploited (Ryang 1997; Yun 2016).[15] Many ended up actively contributing to the communist revolutions in China and Russia and closely collaborating with the Japanese Communist Party.

I.2 Cover of *The Seoul Wind* (Yanji, China: Yŏnbyŏn Inmin Ch'ulp'ansa, 1996), an essay collection by Ryu Yeonsan. Photo by the author.

Following independence from Japan in 1945 and the Korean War (1950–1953), political tensions and military confrontation continued to characterize the relationship between North Korea and South Korea. One of the issues the two regimes competed over was embracing overseas Koreans. Before South Korea began recognizing or granting official status to overseas Koreans, North Korea initiated support mechanisms for them, especially after the Korean War.[16] In Japan, there was (and is) an ethnic Korean organization that explicitly supports North Korea. In addition, given that Kim Il Sung (the founder of North Korea) was deeply involved in the anti-Japanese movement as part of the Communist Revolution in northeast China (Manchuria), Koreans in China developed close ties to North Korea through kinship visits, as well as educational exchanges (such as when Yanbian University was established in 1949). During the Cold War, no "socialist" overseas Koreans were allowed to have any contact with South Koreans under the national security law.[17] South Korea's authoritarian regimes utilized anti-communism as a means of creating a unified "pure" nation completely free of communists. "Red-hunting" targeted not only Koreans within South Korea but also Koreans abroad—in particular, in Japan, Germany, and the United States—framing them as North Korean spies and, when possible, imposing draconian punishments, such as execution or life imprisonment (Hong 2020).[18]

As a result, overseas Koreans were considered potentially dangerous to South Korean national security, and many were falsely accused of being North Korean spies.[19] However, the issue of abandoned overseas Koreans gained new critical attention as South Korea experienced an intensive democratization movement in the 1980s and 1990s. Bringing a human rights perspective to bear, the more democratic South Korean governments, nongovernmental organizations, and media began to support recognition and reparations for overseas Koreans falsely accused of being communists.[20] For example, as a humanitarian gesture, the South Korean government organized overseas Korean family-visit programs in the 1980s to enable the renewal of kinship ties broken during the Korean War.[21] Moreover, the South Korean government came to increasingly take a neoliberal approach to understanding long-forgotten overseas Koreans by exploring "the methods of utilization of the overseas Korean" (*Chaeoe tongp'o hwaryong pangan* in Korean). Koreans in diaspora, previously feared and suspected as potential communists, appear to be included in the Korean national imaginary at the intersection of democratization with neoliberal South Korea, as Hyun Ok Park has shown (H. O. Park 2015).

Korean Chinese migration emerged in the early 1990s from this new political-economic context, which included South Korea's neoliberalism and democratization and China's rapid privatization. Over the past three decades, neoliberalism swept through and greatly transformed South Korea, especially as a result of the so-called International Monetary Fund crisis in the late 1990s (see chapters 2 and 3). This aggressive neoliberal restructuring, as many scholars have noted across the global context, aggravated economic inequality through "accumulation by dispossession" (Harvey 2005) and "economization" (Brown 2015), as market logic has encroached upon nearly all social domains, redesigning them to serve capital's interest.[22] During and after the restructuring process in South Korea, individuals have been forced to cultivate certain modes of behavior, bodily discipline, and personhood in order to properly cope with market logics (see chapters 5 and 6), including self-interest, self-responsibility, and self-sufficiency (Barry, Thomas, and Rose 1996; Binkley 2009; Foucault 2008; Ong 2006; Rose 1996). As seen in other neoliberal contexts, those who have lost a safety net, sense of community, and the state's protection have been exposed to extreme precariousness and insecurity, both materially and emotionally (Allison 2015; Berlant 2011; Butler 2010; Bourdieu 2000; M. Jung 2017; Standing 2011).[23] In the wake of the crisis that hit East Asia in the late 1990s, Korean Chinese, who were already experiencing rapid privatization and a growing need for self-responsibility in China, migrated to South Korea, where many aspects of life were subject to economic logic and where individuals were judged primarily in terms of economic value.

Korean Chinese transnational migration should also be contextualized with other contemporary transnational migrations arising from economic necessity and political turmoil that have uprooted large populations and put them in critically vulnerable situations.[24] The movement of Korean Chinese should be understood not simply in terms of mobility but as a form of "migration" (De Genova 2013)—a large-scale shift of population that has come to be highly regulated by nation-states (Mezzadra and Neilson 2013). In the neoliberalizing milieu, the state has emerged more and more as the power that determines who should be included or excluded, for how long and under what conditions (see chapters 2 and 3).[25] Korean Chinese migration, encouraged by the conditions of post-socialist, privatized China, exemplifies the unique state-market complex that has heavily promoted and implemented market logics and economization while preserving socialist and nationalist foundations under the name of "socialism with Chinese characteristics" (Meisner 1999; Rofel 2007).[26] Here, the migration of Korean Chinese, both domestic and transnational, has been considered an inevitable and influential means of building self-sufficient personhood and promoting urban lifestyles (Chu 2010; Hoffman 2010; Ngai 2005; Rofel 2007; Xiang 2005; H. Yan 2008; Zhang 2001).

Borderland Dreams

Yanbian, as an ethnic borderland, has been a site of negotiation for the different dreams of different groups of people in the wake of the Korean dream. Since the early 1990s, Korean Chinese have migrated from Yanbian, whereas Han Chinese have settled in to fill the void left behind. In the late 1990s, North Korean refugees crossed the Tumen River in order to escape from the food crisis—the so-called Arduous March—and North Korean women have married Chinese men (both Korean Chinese and Han Chinese) without being able to register their marriages in China.

Recently, more North Korean workers have worked in North Korean restaurants and factories located in the economic special zone in Yanbian. South Koreans also have flocked to Yanbian for the purpose of new business expansion and children's education. Because of proximity to Yanbian, Russians have visited, mainly from the east part of Russia to the city of Hunchun in order to purchase Chinese goods and sell them back in Russia. Indeed, Yanbian is a dynamic borderland in which different dreams have been competing for the last three decades.

Situating Yanbian among these competing desires, *Borderland Dreams* focuses on the new political economy of a neoliberal, democratic South Korea and a privatized China by using three lenses—ethnicized bodies, (South) Korean money (hereafter Korean money), and transnational time—to examine the mechanisms that have formed and transformed borderland dreams. First, by illustrating the detailed process of reconnection between Korean Chinese and South Korea, the long-forbidden homeland, this book offers a new understanding of the concept of ethnicity and ethnic bodies. I am particularly interested in what I call "ethnicized ethnic bodies," analyzing the process by which Korean Chineseness has been ethnicized and marketized within a transnational labor market.[27] I show how Korean Chinese ethnicity, repressed in China during the Cold War, has been revived, promoted, and transformed into a form of currency (see chapters 1 and 2) that has enabled Korean Chinese to enter the transnational labor market. I do not simply suggest that the authentic characteristics of Korean Chinese ethnicity or their ethnic similarities to South Koreans enabled Korean Chinese to wield competitive power or use their ethnic currency in the South Korean labor market. Rather, I argue that the particular relationality of Korean Chinese to South Korea—their status as *almost Korean, but not quite*—is precisely what has created a Korean Chinese niche in the South Korean economy.[28] I demonstrate how Korean Chinese have performed this ethnic relationality within a process of entry into and adjustment to South Korea—with the rising homeland functioning as a marketplace for Korean Chinese labor. I extend my analysis of ethnicity by drawing on theories of "articulation" (Laclau and Mouffe 1985) and "performativity" (Butler 1990, 1993), with a focus on how the Korean Chinese performance of ethnicity articulates with gender and class, as in fake marriages to South Koreans, and how the ethnic currency of Korean Chinese workers has rendered them as suitably cheap labor in certain service industries in South Korea.[29] In other words, Korean Chinese have shaped their labor migration into a site of value production and identity articulation, and have been made, and remade, into a transnational ethnic working class.

Second, *Borderland Dreams* illuminates the power of Korean money, a form of remittance that exerts a strong transformative power over material reality and also sparks anxiety about intimate lives. These remittances have induced rapid urbanization, bringing rural Korean Chinese to cities. They have also reshaped the ethnic composition of the region, as Han Chinese migrants have flocked into the city of Yanji in order to serve the newly thriving leisure industry—karaoke bars, saunas, and massage parlors—and into the Yanbian countryside, which is being vacated by the outflow of Korean Chinese to the cities and to South Korea. The influx of remittances has fundamentally restructured the landscape of and ethnic relationships in Yanbian. Any remittance-dependent economy is vulnerable to factors such as currency exchange rates and international economic conditions, regardless of the work ethic of individuals or their strength of purpose, as evidenced by what happened when the global financial crisis hit the Korean Chinese labor market in 2008 and 2009 (chapter 6). I highlight how remittance-dependent development is neither stable nor predictable, given the fluctuations of the global economy. More critically, remittance-driven development has shaped a new ethnic interdependency between Han Chinese and Korean Chinese, despite the long ethnic separations of the region. Han Chinese have not remained unaffected by the dramatic social changes generated by the Korean Wind, playing a critical role in remittance development as both investors and service workers. This growing ethnic interdependency can help us situate the Korean Wind as a transnational economic drive that reconfigures the ethnic and urban landscape across and beyond Yanbian.

I further view Korean money as entailing an attachment to a certain place and a certain time. In other words, Korean money, as distinct from Chinese money, is a powerful transnational emblem of what the time spent in South Korea means to Korean Chinese. Korean Chinese frequently told me, up until the late 2000s, "If I had worked in South Korea, I could have made ten times more than what I made in China." Or they said, "Taking on debt to go to South Korea via illegal migration brokers was worth trying because I could pay off the debt in a year or so—as long as I ended up getting to work in South Korea." For them, South Korean money signifies a speed and potency that Chinese money does not. At the same time, given that South Korean money is always remitted or relocated from South Korea to China, we can suppose an interdependency between those who are waiting for the money and those who are sending it—a connection, or in some cases a failure to connect, created by Korean money. Yet since Korean money requires an exchange into Chinese currency for actual use, the final amount in hand is subject to the whims and fluctuations of the exchange rate—and thus to general global economic circumstances. Korean money therefore embodies an anxiety stemming from the uneven and sometimes unpredictable chasms between when the money is made, when it is sent, and when it is spent. The days, weeks, and months of hard work are not directly translated into the final amount of Korean money that is remitted, since this money is affected along the way by so many external influences, including the currency exchange rate, diplomatic relationships, and the global economy. Exploring the ubiquitous stories of Korean money that I encountered in China and South Korea, I argue that Korean money is an affective currency that entails a division between time spent working and time spent waiting. It is also a powerful but vulnerable currency that has subtly transformed social bonds and material realities.

Third, whereas other migration studies raise the question of belongingness and out-of-placeness in relation to the state and culture, I explore the sense of belonging in relation to "transnational temporality" through examinations of visa regulations and regimes of waiting imposed on migrants and their families. Korean Chinese migrant workers have been subject to frequent and unpredictable legal changes imposed by the South Korean government. Most Korean Chinese who remained undocumented were granted amnesty in 2005, under a new regulation aimed at preventing Korean Chinese from permanently settling in South Korea (chapter 3). According to the new visa regulation, Korean Chinese migrants can only stay in South Korea for a limited number of consecutive years; they are required to return to China every three years. As a result, a spatial split has opened up, as Korean Chinese view South Korea as a place of work and China as a place of resting and waiting. During the "resting" period in China, migrant workers generally make no money; they can only spend, as anxiety about their unstable financial status increases. In addition, Korean Chinese migrants have in recent years come to feel that they have missed out on the Chinese boom and are lagging behind those who never left to work in South Korea (chapter 6).

I also examine transnational temporality through the lens of waiting (see chapter 4). I explore the lives of those who are waiting for remittances, for the return of family members, and for the opportunity to go to South Korea. They are supposed to maintain the household and manage the funds sent back by their partners, and yet their long wait is not always rewarded, as partners can be unfaithful or unreliable and the remittances may stop (chapter 4). Those who are waiting to leave for South Korea tend to stop working in Yanbian, as they often have to be ready to pick up and go at a moment's notice. Korean Chinese migrants face unpredictable rhythms of migration, interrupted by personal events and crises, aging bodies, financial developments, new visa regulations, and most of all, the fluctuations of the global economy. Instead of simply being controlled by these rhythms, migrants attempt to take their own control of time and transcend the regulatory rhythms that limit their transnational lives (see chapter 3). My argument is that state-imposed rhythms intersecting with market-driven rhythms reconfigure transnational time-space linkages and a transnational working class through the actual material force of transnational temporality.

Book Chapters

Borderland Dreams develops its archival and ethnographic analysis in three sections. Part I comprises chapters 1 and 2. This part stages Yanbian as an ethnic borderland and Korean Chinese as a mobile ethnicity to historicize the rise of the Korean dream. In particular, while exploring their encounters with the long-forbidden homeland of South Korea, I show the cultural, political, and legal process by which Korean Chinese have been ethnicized as a transnational working class moving between China and South Korea. The Korean dream rapidly spread across Yanbian, and Korean Chinese as cheap and capable migrant workers were largely welcomed in the South Korean labor market. But at the same time, the Korean dream was hindered by the South Korean government's legal constraints on the recognition of Korean Chinese (as not equal to that of other overseas Koreans) and often unwelcoming daily encounters at work.

In part II, I analyze the hopes and frustrations, rise and fall, mobility and stuckness in the fluctuation of the Korean dream through three ethnographic lenses: bodies, money, and time. Chapter 3, based on the stories of three Korean Chinese female workers, highlights the spatial division created by this repetitive migration: South Korea as a place for *making* money and Yanbian as a place for *spending* money. I argue that under these split spatial practices, migrants have internalized a rhythm (transnational temporality)—a back and forth—that serves as a governing force on the laboring body, thereby making care for the body more difficult and pro-longing its exploitation in intensive labor. Chapter 4 analyzes stuckness, another form of transnational temporality, through waiting practices. I argue that while waiting may begin as an act of love, it is susceptible to being transformed into a kind of work that requires the constant man-agement of monetary flows and remakes the expectations and realities of transnational spousal relationships. In other words, those who do not mi-grate may nonetheless sustain a critical dimension of migratory practice.

Part III comprises chapter 5 and chapter 6 and examines new reflec-tions and reevaluations of the Korean dream in the wake of the globally rising Chinese economy. Chapter 5 examines the hesitance that Korean Chinese, as well as Han Chinese, have demonstrated in response to the Korean dream—between living in Yanbian and leaving Yanbian. While exploring the differentiated but interrelated participation in Yanbian's remittance-driven economic development, I argue that the Korean dream has led not only to a desire for transnational migration but also to a newly defined interethnic relationship. Since the financial crisis of 2008 dramat-ically altered the terms of the Korean dream by greatly increasing Chinese economic clout, many Korean Chinese have turned their attention to a new dream: a Chinese dream. Chapter 6 elaborates on migrants' strug-gles with the new social imperative to "stop being a migrant, become an entrepreneur"—that is, to break the cycle of migration in the new era that has followed the Korean Wind.

Finally, the conclusion illuminates the afterlife of the thirty-year-old Korean dream as it loses the status of being the dominant dream in Yan-bian. The future is open-ended, with new dreams to dream, new actions to take, and new plans to make, as new generations arrive.

PART I

The Rising Korean Dream

Ethnic Borderland

YANBIAN 4: YANBIAN IS GOING

There are people who think Yanbian¹ is in Yanj
Or in Kuro Kongdan or Suwŏn²
But that is what people who do not know things say.
Yanbian came in a small basket carried by a cow (from Chosŏn)³
It once collapsed during the Cultural Revolution
Later, it was revived like vegetables in the Yanji West Market
And became famous along with kimchi in front of Changchun train station
Later, to Beijing, to Shanghai
It was stretched like noodles
Yanbian is everywhere in the big cities of China
Nowadays it goes to South Korea via ship and airplane
We can hear news from there, from restaurants and construction fields
But only a little
To the east, Tokyo, to the north, Khabarovsk
To Saipan, San Francisco, Paris, and London
There is no place without Yanbian in the world
Everybody is prepared to leave with fake passports or fake marriages
Someday, perhaps, we will find Yanbian on the moon (after everybody is gone)

—SUKHWA, *Yŏnbyŏn* (Yanbian)

On a sunny day in June 2009, I took advantage of the weather and went hiking with a group of Korean Chinese. Good health and quality of life have become widespread topics of interest in China in recent years, and hiking has become popular as a leisure activity in Yanbian, where there are ranges of beautiful mountains. Hiking with different groups became one of my best opportunities for participant observation, allowing me access to Korean Chinese everyday life; it enabled me to build friendships and hear personal life stories while exploring the geography of Yanbian.

1.1 The Tumen River, seen from Reguang Mountain in Tumen, Yanbian, China, 2009. Photo by the author.

On this day, we were headed to a mountain called Reguang. Standing on its peak, I could see the long ribbon of the Tumen River, which serves as a natural boundary between China and North Korea, and Yanbian's character as a border zone was vividly impressed on me. A small town on the North Korean side formed a distant backdrop: sparsely populated, its impoverished, dilapidated appearance stood in stark contrast to the more prosperous Chinese side. The members of the hiking club, who were for the most part well-off Korean Chinese, shared stories with me about how, long ago, their families crossed the Tumen River into Yanbian and how they have dealt with having relatives who live in both North and South Korea. All of them emphasized how proud they were of their citizenship in a globally rising China and what they saw as the economic triumph of Chinese socialism.

In these conversations, I found it notable that the Korean Chinese made a distinction between the economic success of Yanbian and that of China. Yanbian is considered both an integral part of Chinese territory and also a zone that is distinct from the rest of the country, as if it were not quite China. In addition, they understand the word "Chinese"

(*Chungguk Saram* in Korean) to mean Han Chinese, indicating the distance they felt, as Korean Chinese, from "real" Chinese. Korean Chinese call themselves *Chosŏnjok*, a word that conveys a sharp ethnic distinction from Han Chinese, despite their shared Chinese citizenship. This distinction identifies Korean Chinese as descendants of settler migrants from the Korean peninsula.

This chapter stages Yanbian as an ethnic borderland and Korean Chinese as a Chinese ethnic minority, a condition that has shaped them into a mobile ethnicity that has responded to social change via constant movement—through the winds of migration discussed in the introduction. I have witnessed repeatedly how the concepts of borders and borderlands function as core principles that construct Korean Chinese subjectivity— the subjectivity of an ethnic minority within the Chinese state, living adjacent to a divided homeland. The geography of Yanbian can, in this sense, be read as signifying the affective condition of its people, a constant reminder of their border location and settler migrant identity.

Yael Navaro-Yashin argues in her ethnography of the war-scarred borderland of Cyprus that "affect is a charge that has a part to play in the sociality of the human beings who inhabit a space" (Navaro-Yashin 2012, 20). Affect is not only a means for intersubjective connectivity but also a channel that mediates between subject and things/environment. Trying to go beyond the notion of affect as an inner energy of or between subjects, Navaro-Yashin focuses on the affect discharged by objects and environments, particularly ruins and other artifacts of war. In these terms, the Tumen River certainly "discharges affect," running as it does between North Korea and China as a geographical, natural, and political border that vividly evokes the migration history of the Koreans who crossed it into Yanbian a century ago. The river carries meanings of demarcation between *there* (where the ancestors moved from) and *here* (where their descendants now live), between poverty (in the Korean Peninsula long ago) and affluence (in the current China), and between an old homeland (in the northern part of Korea) and a new homeland (in China). The river also appears as an affective motif and backdrop in literary texts that depict the crossing of it as an entry into a new world, and the settlers as a new community with a strong sense of identity. Historical novels, especially, stage the Tumen River as a key trope, portraying river crossers as subjects who endured exploitation by their Chinese landlords for the sake of better lives, strove to maintain their Korean ethnic identity, and sacrificed themselves for filial piety and familial duty.[4] The river is seen as a source of life, turning poor Koreans into prosperous rice farmers. It is also a vital ethnic marker, identifying Korean Chinese as border crossers who have moved from one part of the world to another.

Yanbian can also be understood as a borderland that evokes anxiety over border control—especially over the frontier with North Korea. Korean Chinese stories and memories about North Koreans who were caught crossing the border, and who were persecuted, play a key role in creating a "border spectacle" (De Genova 2010) that highlights the naturalization of security and the criminalization of illegal crossings as transgressions against the state's authority (Squire 2010). Here, the Tumen River is a visible marker of the border that the sovereign power demarcates, inside and out. An increasing number of North Korean refugees have crossed the Tumen River to escape from dire poverty and political repression since the late 1990s, and border control on the Chinese side has become more militarized. In addition, North Korea has always been difficult to enter from South Korea because of the political division of the peninsula since the Korean War ended in 1953. These factors have made Yanbian the easiest and most reliable route into and out of North Korea, which has resulted in increased international and national political scrutiny of the province whenever regional tensions mount. Yanbian has become a channel, a link between North Korea and the outside world, especially South Korea, China, and other countries that need to engage with the unpredictable North Korean regime. This geopolitical border location means that Yanbian retains an element of Cold War anxiety, and it places the Korean Chinese who live there under the political influence of both Koreas, both directly and indirectly.

Recent critical border studies view borders not only as boundaries but also as "lines in the sand" that constantly change and perform. Instead of seeing the border as a fixed line between two states, these scholars see the border as a "suture" that connects two spheres of possibility and creates exceptionality to the general paradigm of sovereignty (Salter 2012). While noting the anxieties over sovereign demarcation embodied by the Tumen River, I also understand the river as a visual and affective suture that shapes the spatiality of the borderland—that discharges affect. By shifting our focus from line to suture, we can see the borderland as an interstice where different cultural values and intersubjective experiences are negotiated (Bhabha 1994). The borderland is an ambiguous space that links two worlds, imbuing its people with peripheral vision, a sense of marginalization, and a liminal feeling that "I am neither here nor there"

1.2 Iron fence that marks the Chinese border with North Korea in Tumen, Yanbian, 2016. Photo by the author.

(Zavella 2011). It is also an overlapping and layered space where people can see "double" worlds simultaneously and express both complex identities and resistance against the dominant social order (Anzaldúa 1987). Along with this intersectionality, hybridity, and multiplicity, borderlands also harbor the desolate, disconnected, and displaced feeling that Homi Bhabha calls "unhomeliness"—the condition of extraterritorial and cross-cultural initiation (Bhabha 1994, 13).[5]

This chapter illuminates the contradictory feelings of Korean Chinese toward their borderland within China as "a home" as well as "not a home." They feel both placed and displaced in Yanbian, which is at once an ethnic comfort zone and a parochial borderland that limits Korean Chinese interactions with the larger world—both ethnic hub and ethnic enclave. On the one hand, I find that Korean Chinese have tried hard to leave their parochial borderland in search of better life opportunities, while, on the other hand, they have valued it as an ethnic home. Yanbian's character as an ethnic borderland, one shaped and reshaped by Korean and Chinese economic reforms, has resulted in a pervasive unhomeliness, in Bhabha's sense of this term, and given its inhabitants a strong affinity with the winds of migration as a force that has gained them access to the outside world.

Crossing History

The theme of border crossing is deeply ingrained in both the oral histories I heard and in the Korean Chinese history books I collected about the region.[6] The narratives commonly begin with the ancestors of the Korean Chinese bravely and secretively crossing the Tumen River and enduring the biting cold to reclaim the barren wastes of the Qing Dynasty's "holy land."[7] Although it was forbidden for Koreans to cross the river and cultivate Qing land, in the late nineteenth century poor Korean farmers began to sneak into these territories, which had in some cases remained uninhabited for hundreds of years. They were inspired by the saying, "If you go to Manchuria, you will grow potatoes as big as a baby's head," as an eighty-five-year-old Korean Chinese lady put it to me in Yanbian.[8] In the mountainous northern part of the Korean peninsula bordering China, there was a lack of farming land. In addition, the Japanese occupation of the Korean peninsula had exacerbated poverty, which pushed many Koreans to cross the river into China.

A small textbook-like history book written by Korean Chinese historians in Yanbian summarizes what it views as the six phases of Korean Chinese migration history (Kim, Kang, and Kim 1998). First, in the late Ming and the early Qing era from 1620 to 1766, Koreans were captured as slaves in war.[9] Second, in the late Qing period from 1677 to 1881, just before the prohibition on entry into Manchuria was lifted, Koreans began to sneak across the Tumen River and cultivate land there. Third, between 1882 and 1910, the Qing government encouraged Han Chinese and Koreans to move to northeast China as a protective measure against Russian encroachment. Fourth, from 1911 to 1920, migration was freely allowed, and Koreans moved to China to escape the oppression and poverty of the Japanese occupation. Fifth, from 1921 to 1931, right before the Japanese invasion of Manchuria, China forced Korean migrants to adopt Chinese citizenship to forestall Japanese influence (since Japan considered Koreans to be subject to Japan). Sixth, from 1931 to 1945, Japan strongly encouraged Koreans to move to China as a means of territorial occupation. Most Korean Chinese and Korean historians consider the Korean Chinese migration to have begun during the third phase (from 1882 to 1910), after the Qing lifted the ban on entering the "holy land."

The distinction between migration phases and moments of settlement is a politically sensitive issue because this history can be used to define the affiliation of Korean Chinese to China in terms of ethnicity, nationality, and territoriality, and also to quantify how deeply and how long this migrant ethnic minority group has claimed association with the land of China. Although Yanbian—which used to be called Kando (located between China and Chosŏn)—is clearly Chinese territory, it has historically been the subject of disputes between China and Korea (H. O. Park 2005).[10] Even after the territorial settlement of 1909 (the Kando Treaty between China and Japan), the status of Yanbian's Korean migrants remained unclear. At various times they were considered citizens of China, Korea, and even Japan, which was the occupier of northeast China (Manchuria) from 1937 to 1945.[11] Koreans' border crossing to China continued until Korea (colonial Chosŏn) won independence from Japan in 1945. As the new China was established in 1949, Korean Chinese actively supported the Chinese Communist Party, and subsequently Korean Chinese became citizens of China as members of an officially recognized ethnic minority group (Jin Y. Lee 2002; G. Lim 2005). Some Koreans moved back to Korea following Korean national independence, while some remained in China, becoming settled farmers and Chinese nationals who received distributed lands as a result of the Communist Revolution.[12] Some Koreans were prevented from returning to Korea by the outbreak of the Korean War in 1950. Today, two million Korean Chinese—an officially recognized Korean ethnic group with Chinese nationality—are descendants of the settlers who crossed the Tumen River and reclaimed the land of what is now Yanbian. I have heard Korean Chinese in their seventies and eighties speak of these border crossings in their family histories, but most of them do not maintain family memories and active relationships with their distant relatives in North Korea.

The settler history of Yanbian turns on an ethnic distinction between Han Chinese and Korean Chinese. On one short trip to the countryside, I heard much about this ethnic comparison from my Korean Chinese companions: "Korean Chinese built their houses with shabby bush-clover fences," they said, "while Han Chinese built and rebuilt brick walls every year, expanding their territory little by little." This orally transmitted ethnic tale reveals how Korean Chinese seemed always to be ready to leave, whereas Han Chinese planned to stay put for longer periods. Many Korean Chinese, especially those over eighty years old, recount how they had moved continuously from one place to another in pursuit of better and more farming land, relying on kinship networks and friendship ties across northeast China.

Until Japan retreated from Manchuria in 1945, ethnic tensions between Chinese, Koreans, and Japanese were suppressed under the Manchukuo regime (H. O. Park 2005).[13] After the Japanese retreated and China established itself anew in 1949, the Chinese-ness of the Korean Chinese was especially important to Korean Chinese Communist Party members, who emphasize their contribution to the war of liberation against Japan and the Guomindang (the Chinese Nationalist Party) and their deep engagement in the socialist revolution. In fact, Korean Chinese devotion to the Communist Party enabled Yanbian to complete the class revolution and the redistribution of land by 1948, much earlier than other areas of China. The Chinese Communist Party gave credit to the Korean Chinese as a major revolutionary group by designating Yanbian an ethnic autonomous zone in 1952. Since then, Korean Chinese have been officially considered civic members of communist China, rather than temporary migrant farmers from the Korean peninsula.

However, even after Korean Chinese were recognized as an ethnic minority group with Chinese nationality, their ethnic identity seemed to supersede their (official) national identity. When I talked with elderly Communist Party members, they reminisced about their emotional and national attachment to the Korean Peninsula in the 1950s. For example, when filling out official documents and forms related to the registration of their houses, ethnic Koreans would enter North Korea as their "original" address or "birth" place. They also read, wrote, and sang in Korean; surrounded by other Korean Chinese, they had no need to be able to speak Chinese in everyday life.

Even though Han Chinese lived and worked in Yanbian, the main language was Korean in official meetings, while "small translation" (*xiaofanyi* in Chinese) from Korean to Chinese was provided for Han Chinese in a low voice. An old Communist Party member recalls Yanbian in that era as an "all Korean Chinese world" (*Chosŏnjok sesang* in Korean). Yet things changed dramatically, beginning in the late 1950s. The "national identity education program" (*Zuguoguan Jiaoyu* in Chinese) launched in 1958, emphasizing the idea that Korean Chinese were citizens of China, required Korean Chinese to break off their national ties to the two

1.3 Memorial site in Wangqing, Yanbian, commemorating the unit of the anti-Japanese movement stationed there from February to March 1933, photographed in 2016. Photo by the author.

Koreas—both North and South. Under this intensive program, Korean Chinese were taught that China was their only home country, and they were told that they were welcome members of the Chinese nation.

The Cultural Revolution was a particularly harsh period for Korean Chinese, as they became subject to random and continuous purges and persecutions. Their ethnicity—or more precisely, their ethnic affinity with North Korea and South Korea—came into play during the political tumult.[14] During this time, culture and discourse that could be considered "ethnic" were strictly prohibited and seen as a betrayal of China. Any possible tie to the two Koreas—familial, economic, or political—could provide a cause for political persecution. Kinship ties to North Korea were treated with suspicion, given the proximity of Korean Chinese to the North Korean border. Connections to South Korea—the capitalist enemy—were used as critical evidence for accusations. Many Korean Chinese were treated as political scapegoats, and some were killed, as they were caught up in unfair accusations and false reports. The overall turmoil left a deep scar across the community, as many members of the older generation of Korean Chinese testified to me, recounting their long silence and traumatic wounds (J. Kwon 2019a).

In order to avoid emotional, political, and physical trauma, Korean Chinese had to prove their loyalty to China as their home country and their full identity as Chinese by de-emphasizing their Korean ethnicity. Korean Chinese who endured the Cultural Revolution said that they had to eradicate their "ethnic color" by avoiding ethnic songs and dances, and they were not allowed to speak freely about anything related to their Korean ethnicity in public spaces. Politically, Korean Chinese had to avoid any association with North Korea or South Korea and defend themselves from political persecution by making overt declarations that they were "anti-capitalist" or "anti-South Korea," or by pledging firm allegiance to China. The period from the late 1950s to the late 1970s was culturally sterile and politically brutal for Korean Chinese. After the chaotic age of the Cultural Revolution eventually ended in the late 1970s, Yanbian, like other regions, entered a new era of economic reform.

The Rise of Ethnic Talk

China's economic reforms and open economy, beginning in the 1980s, brought the "ethnic question" to the fore across the Korean Chinese community, which responded by developing their ethnic identification in various ways. These can be understood as vernacular theories that attempt to explain what it means to be Korean Chinese. One theory is known as the "daughter-in-law" theory (*Minmyŏnŭrilon* in Korean). It was coined by a famous Korean Chinese literary intellectual, Zheng Panlong, who viewed the situation of Korean Chinese as parallel to that of a newlywed woman. According to the assumptions of Confucian gender patriarchy, the daughter-in-law (Korean Chinese) must obey the rule of the husband's family (China) and make a special effort to become a full family member. A common criticism of this theory is that it portrays Korean Chinese as a people without agency, mere subjects of the Chinese state. Another theory relies on the metaphor of "the apple-pear graft" (*sagwabaelon* in

Korean). This metaphor is derived from an ethnic tale about a farmer, newly arrived in China from the Korean peninsula, who decided to graft the Korean apple onto the Chinese pear. The graft turned out to be a great success, creating a new, delicious fruit, the "apple-pear," which combines the tastes of both parent fruits. The fruit has become a popular symbol of the doubleness of Korean Chinese, who have, in effect, grafted Korean culture onto the culture of China.

Yet alongside these theories emphasizing the dual characteristics of Korean Chinese culture runs another one: Korean Chinese should not be considered diasporic Koreans living in China. This theory views Korean Chinese as "100 percent Korean Chinese"—as civic members of and an ethnic minority within China, not migrants caught between China and Korea (Huang 2009). The first two theories assume "border-ness" as an essential part of Korean Chinese identity, whereas the third de-emphasizes and unmarks border-ness as an ethnic characteristic. What, then, constitutes this "100 percent"? Most importantly, in what ways do these vernacular theories shape or reshape the discussion of "ethnic minorities," a critical dimension that determines what it means to be Korean Chinese in the wake of an open economy?

Ethnicity, denoting both the peoplehood as well as the otherness of particular groups (Barth 1969; Sollors 1995), has been a major factor in producing and fixing "others" within and beyond the nation-state. Despite the flexibility and vagueness ingrained in the concept, ethnicity tends to be confined to "named human populations with shared ancestry myths, histories, and cultures, having an association with a specific territory and a sense of solidarity" (A. Smith 1986, 32). Ethnicity can function both as a term of exclusion, a clear boundary marker keeping out certain groups, and as a term of inclusion aimed at removing boundaries and discrimination against othered groups (Chow 2002, 25). But counter to the perspective that views "ethnicity as a group" runs another argument about "ethnicity without groups" (Brubaker 2004). Brubaker suggests that ethnicity does not merely mark out specific entities or groups but should rather be understood as defining "group-ness" in "relational, processual, dynamic, eventful, and disaggregated terms" (Brubaker 2004, 11). Ethnicity thus emerges not as an attribute of group identity bounded by biology, culture, and geography but as a process of ethnicization, forming and reforming the "human artifice" that maintains practical inequality (Wallerstein 1991).

The inequality entailed in the process of ethnicization is especially projected in the construction of the fifty-six ethno-national groups (*minzu*) scattered throughout China. Under the theme of the nation as "a plural singularity" (Mullaney 2011), anthropologists studying Chinese ethnic minorities have long emphasized the state's role in constructing "ethnic culture" and "ethnic identity" as a consequence of the perceived "backwardness" of remote zones (Dautcher 2009; Harrel 1995; Litzinger 2000; Mueggler 2001).[15] Characterizing the Chinese politics of ethnic minorities as a civilizing project, Harrell argues that the central government, dominated by Han Chinese, has engendered an ethnic periphery with a "stigmatized identity" as backward, uncivilized, dirty, and stupid (Harrell 1995). The arbitrary and simplified category of ethnicity devised by the communist state as a consequence of the ethnic classification project conducted in the 1950s ignores the complicated histories, cultures, and politics of ethnic groups and assimilates them under the rubric of "one China" (Friedman 2006; Harrel 1995; Litzinger 2000).

In the 1980s, however, the Chinese government began, in the wake of economic reform, to support the revival of the traditional cultures and rituals of ethnic minorities, recognizing cultural differences that were repressed during the Cultural Revolution. As part of a modernizing project, the state's past mistakes have been tacitly admitted, while forgotten or repressed traditions and cultures of ethnic minorities have been recovered and recuperated through "memory work" (Litzinger 1998). The recognition of ethnic others by the Chinese Communist Party has given rise to more openly displayed cultural differences and an appreciation of the uniqueness of each ethnic group. Deployed in the form of colorful attire or song and dance, cultural difference becomes the subject of ethnic tourism, and Chinese ethnic harmony is exhibited under the idealized "plural singularity." Chinese ethnic minorities take their place in the pageant of legitimate and official others that help constitute the long and grand history of China.

I take "the revival of the ethnic" (Litzinger 1998) as a key analytical turning point in understanding the new dynamics between ethnic others and the Chinese Communist Party, one that attempts to go beyond the simple dichotomy between domination and resistance, center and periphery (Harrell 1995), or internal orientalism (Schein 2000). Despite the constant and strong presence of the state in the governance of ethnic minorities, ethnic others emerge in the public and political domain as active agents who engage in deploying and promoting would-be proper ethnic elements and politics in order to define and redefine who they are and who they would like to be.

Map 1.1 Six cities and two counties of Yanbian, China.

A defining aspect of Korean Chinese ethnicity discourse is that it has been triggered not only by "the revival of the ethnic" in the economic reforms of China but also by the Korean Wind. Instead of dramatizing their ethnic cultural identity through attire, dance, food, and rituals for the benefit of tourists and state contests like other ethnic minority groups, Korean Chinese have actively promoted their assembled ethnic characteristics and associated values in the service of transnational labor migration. In other words, a new type of border crossing between China and South Korea has led Korean Chinese to undertake multiple redefinitions of their own ethnicity. As an ethnic survival tactic, Korean Chinese have appropriated their border-ness as an economic means of facilitating transnational migration to South Korea while simultaneously displaying their political affiliation to the state of China. An ethnic identity constructed in the borderland is repressed at certain points but revived at others (J. Kwon 2019a); some celebrate it, while others obscure or ignore it. But the key element of these redefinitions, especially since the Korean Wind years of the 1990s, is the fact that the Korean Chinese have become a transnational border-crossing ethnicity (*guojing minzu* in Chinese) leaving and living on the ethnic borderland.

Yanbian Zhou, the Korean Chinese Autonomous Prefecture, is a district composed of six cities (Yanji, the capital; Helong; Longjing; Tumen; Hunchun; and Wangqing) and two counties (Dunhua and Wanqing). The total population of Yanbian Zhou is around two million; ethnic Koreans comprise approximately 35 percent of the population, and Han Chinese 65 percent. Besides ethnic Koreans and Han Chinese, a small number of other ethnic minority groups also live in Yanbian, including Manzu and Mengguzu. Out of the six cities and two counties, Yanji has experienced the fastest population growth over the last thirty years, along with rapid urbanization and economic development, and is home to more than half a million people. Despite being designated the Korean Chinese ethnic autonomous prefecture, Yanbian has a majority Han Chinese population, and the Chinese language is essential to get by in everyday life. And yet many Korean Chinese told me that the increasing Han Chinese population and the emerging necessity of understanding the Chinese language are recent phenomena, which developed only after Korean Chinese started moving to South Korea and Han Chinese migrants arrived to fill their place in the remittance-driven economy.

Despite the growing dominance of "Chineseness," Yanbian still exhibits a strong Korean Chinese character through a series of ethnically focused organizations: the Yanbian Prefecture (Zhou) government, Yanbian University, the Yanbian newspaper, the Yanbian People's Publishing Company, and the Yanbian television and radio broadcasting. Ever since Yanbian was made an ethnic autonomous zone in 1952, these institutions have used Korean as their first language.[16] Street signs must be written bilingually, with Korean coming first and Chinese next. It is occasionally possible to find Han Chinese who can speak fluent Korean, although this is fairly rare. The ethnic minority policy is commonly credited with enabling Korean Chinese to maintain their identity while encouraging harmony with Han Chinese as well as other ethnic minorities and avoiding complete assimilation. Thanks to this policy, Korean Chinese tend to think that they live in China not as an "ethnic other" subject to "internal orientalism" (Schein 2000) or a "civilizing project" (Harrel 1995) but as a proud member of communist China—indeed, many Korean Chinese say they are the most highly educated and "civilized" ethnic minority in the country (*mofan minzu* in Chinese; *mobŏm minjok* in Korean).

Of the many Korean Chinese identity markers, the Korean language is commonly construed as the most critical. The majority of Korean Chinese children choose to go to Korean ethnic schools, where they are taught in Korean.[17] Korean Chinese speak a regional variant of Korean with an accent similar to that of the northern part of contemporary North Korea—Hamgyŏng-bukto, the original home of most ancestors of Yanbian Korean Chinese. When speaking Chinese, Yanbian Korean Chinese tend to have a certain accent, although many people in the younger generations speak fluent Chinese without much of an accent. But generally, in Yanbian, language is an easy way to distinguish Korean Chinese from Han Chinese.

For most of the years since Koreans first moved from the Korean peninsula to Yanbian in the late nineteenth century, Yanbian has been maintained as an ethnic comfort zone for Korean Chinese. Many of them, especially farmers and members of older generations, say that they did not need to speak Chinese or deal with Han Chinese people; an ethnic line divides living spaces and social networks. I sometimes saw Korean Chinese farmers or workers express annoyance and discomfort when they had to interact with Han Chinese or speak the Chinese language. With the rapid influx of Han Chinese in recent years, a lack of fluency in Chinese has become a definite hindrance living in a city like Yanji. But Korean Chinese are able to avoid overlapping spaces with Han Chinese if they want to because Yanbian, as an autonomous prefecture, still favors Korean Chinese in many ways, and Korean ethnicity and language are fairly dominant in daily life. Thus, a lack of fluent Chinese does not bring shame or make it difficult to live in Yanbian—even though interacting with Han Chinese has become increasingly inevitable.

Besides Yanbian's ethnic characteristics, its border location is a definitive factor in shaping its identity. A trip to the border is an essential part of the tourist itinerary. When I first visited Yanbian in 2006, a Korean Chinese friend of mine, Sun—whom I met through the Korean Chinese church in Seoul—took me to a border patrol zone under the authority of the Chinese military. She believed that this scene was uniquely characteristic of Yanbian. She also said it was Yanbian's most popular tourist spot. Border patrols range along the Tumen River looking to repel North Korean runaways. Some parts of the river are deeper and wider, while other parts are shallower and easier to cross; thus, border control is stricter in some places than others. A simple line on the bridge connecting China

1.4 A bilingual sign in alternating Korean and Chinese, Helong, Yanbian, 2016. Photo by the author.

1.5 "Let's build a Yanbian University that has a high quality and distinctive ethnic character"—banner (front) in Korean at Yanbian University, 2008. Photo by the author.

and North Korea indicates the border, but this simple line implies, both structurally and symbolically, the Chinese state's claim on security and sovereignty (Donnan and Wilson 1999) in that it signifies not only the physical extent of the Chinese state but also the prohibition on crossing into or from North Korea.

Although the border control that I observed looked fairly tight, tourists were enjoying themselves, taking pictures of the borderline and the border patrol. It was not a scene solely of anxiety or nervousness. Rather, the border almost resembled a theme park, with North Korea as backdrop. The long Tumen River, meandering as a natural and territorial border between the two countries, provided a walking trail for tourists. The trail allowed tourists to see the contrasting mountain views: the Chinese mountains were full of trees, whereas the North Korean mountains were naked because the trees had been cut down to make room for cultivation in the face of lengthy food shortages, especially in the late 1990s. Sun remarked that the differing mountain landscapes gave evidence of North Korean poverty contrasted with Chinese prosperity, echoing sentiments I heard from many other Korean Chinese. In this manner, the border zone, as a tourist spot, enables tourists to imagine the misery and poverty of North Korea across the Tumen River.

The sharp borderline separating the two countries seems to be constitutive of a borderscape with multiple overlapping cultures and hybrid identities (Gupta and Ferguson 1997) or "culture + culture" in a fusion of registers (Hannerz 1997). But at the same time, the newly built iron wall and public announcement that forbids anybody from speaking to North Koreans or crossing over to North Korea made me vividly realize that I was standing in a borderland divided by space but connected by anxiety.

Ethnic Feelings

Over the last thirty years, the Han Chinese population in Yanbian has increased sharply, reaching 70 percent of the total. This is one of the critical results of the rise in transnational labor migration to South Korea: Korean Chinese leave Yanbian to live a better life, and Han Chinese move into Yanbian also to find a better life. The various migratory flows—incoming and outgoing, living and leaving—have gradually reorganized the ethnic landscape. The daily conversations I had with Korean Chinese illustrated their complex feelings toward these rapid population changes.

1.6 "You are forbidden to take pictures of North Korea, to speak to North Koreans, and to throw trash in the river"—banner in Tumen, Yanbian, 2016. Photo by the author.

For example, I frequently heard Korean Chinese observe that before the Korean Wind hit Yanbian, most taxi drivers were Korean Chinese. But now that so many Korean Chinese have left, the taxi drivers are mostly Han Chinese migrants who moved from other regions. And that is not the only occupation that has been affected. Most service industries are overwhelmingly staffed by young Han Chinese workers (*fuwuyuan* in Chinese) who have moved from the countryside of Jilin and Heilongjiang in northeast China in order to work as waiters and waitresses in restaurants, karaoke bars, and saunas. Cashiers at supermarkets and shopping centers, bank tellers, and postal clerks are mostly Han Chinese. Sellers in markets and business owners are Han Chinese. In Yanbian, interacting with Han Chinese and speaking the Chinese language is now required on a daily basis—unlike decades ago.[18] The encroaching Han Chinese "occupation" of Yanbian has increased ethnic tensions and threatened the status of the Korean Chinese since the autonomous prefecture was officially established in 1952.

The tensions between Han Chinese and Korean Chinese are juxtaposed with a countervailing emphasis on "ethnic comfort." Ethnic comfort has been structured partly on the basis of a spatial division by ethnicity. First of all, schools are divided: Korean Chinese and Han Chinese go to different schools and are taught in different languages. Consequently, social networks tend to be ethnically differentiated. Except for those few who went to Han Chinese schools, Korean Chinese told me that they did not have many close Han Chinese friends. And the reverse is true as well, as I found from my interviews with Han Chinese. Most of all, marriage has played a crucial role in consolidating ethnic boundaries between the two ethnic groups. Even though Korean Chinese have lived in China for more than a century, most Korean Chinese I met in Yanbian and South Korea strongly discourage the interethnic marriage of their children, due to the language barrier and presumed cultural differences.[19] Although there have been growing ethnic and cultural interactions and interethnic marriages between Han Chinese and Korean Chinese in recent years, the "ethnic comfort" built upon social/ethnic separation causes Yanbian Korean Chinese to feel mostly detached from China's dominant Han culture and social networks.

Ethnic dis/comfort seems to be multilayered. The feeling emerges more obviously when Korean Chinese travel outside Yanbian, in what is called the *waidi* ("external world" in Chinese). Jielan, a college graduate in her late twenties (in 2010), insightfully explained the duality of "ethnic comfort":

> Whenever I take a train and stop seeing Korean signs—which means I'm leaving Yanbian—I feel as if I am in "real" China. Even when I go to Changchun, which is not the best or largest city in China, I feel ashamed that I am from a small ethnic town, and I feel myself not urban enough compared with these city people. In addition, I speak Chinese in an accent that sounds like a foreigner. Sometimes Chinese ask me if I am from Korea, thinking that I am Korean. Whenever I leave Yanbian, I feel disheartened because I am not Chinese enough.

Nevertheless, she stated that "despite its backwardness and marginal location, Yanji is the best city for me, because it has everything I need." Many other Korean Chinese friends of mine, in their twenties, thirties, and forties, expressed similar contradictory feelings regarding the "ethnic comfort" of Yanbian. Interestingly, the desirability of Yanbian as a home comes from ethnic comfort, while this same ethnic comfort forces Korean Chinese to realize that they are living within a parochial and insular ethnic enclave. In other words, the perception that "Yanbian is the best place to live" seems to be frequently accompanied by a disdain for Yanbian based on its small size, backwardness, and marginal border location. In fact, I often heard from non-Yanbian Korean Chinese that Yanbian Korean Chinese live "in a small pond," the assumption being that they have narrower minds and smaller worldviews.[20] Yanbian's cultural and political autonomy has helped Korean Chinese maintain or improve the quality of ethnic education, newspapers, and TV and radio stations. But Yanbian has also become a place where Korean Chinese interact less with Han Chinese and Chinese society at large.

The dual aspect of Yanbian—as both a comfortable home and parochial ethnic zone—might have helped to generate a particular receptivity to the Korean Wind. As recently as the 1990s, few Chinese traveled even within China, and even fewer traveled internationally. Most Korean Chinese had never been to any Chinese cities outside Yanbian before they visited Seoul. For the majority of Korean Chinese migrants to South Korea, Seoul was by far the largest city they had ever visited. In contrast to Chinese cities, toward which Korean Chinese often feel an ambiguous discomfort and fear, the city of Seoul provides some emotional comfort and familiarity. Linguistic similarity plays a critical role in creating the feeling of comfort; everything is written in Korean, and everybody speaks Korean. In addition, Korean Chinese commonly testify that things are more "civil" (*wenming* in Chinese) in South Korea, at least at first sight; everything is cleaner and better organized than in China. Along with the high demand for Korean Chinese as a cheap source of labor, this widely felt ethnic affinity has given Korean Chinese opportunities in fields that require especially close and interactive verbal communication, such as restaurant service, caring for the old and the sick, and construction. It is not only the vast income gap between South Korea and China but also the ethnic affinity that Korean Chinese feel for South Korea that has generated the massive, persistent, and sometimes reckless labor migration to South Korea.

Intersection: Yanbian Socialism and the Korean Wind

The reasons that motivated individual Korean Chinese to migrate to South Korea varied depending on personal trajectories and histories. But the testimonies I collected also showed some clear patterns and shared motivations. Some migrants needed to finance new apartment purchases or their children's education. Others had been laid off from their jobs. These reasons for migration reflect the transformations of post-socialist China and an increased emphasis on self-responsibility and self-sufficiency in the wake of privatization in China.

Recent studies of Chinese post-socialism explore recollections of the socialist past in order to historicize the subjectivities and material conditions rapidly emerging from Chinese urban migration and increasing global connections (Chu 2010; Ngai 2005; Rojas 2016; H. Yan 2008). These studies pay attention to contrasting experiences under socialism and post-socialism by focusing on the disparate relationships between the state, markets, and citizens-subjects. Neither the memory of socialism nor the current experience of post-socialism is clear-cut or simply continuous. Rather, individuals invoke the past differently and distinctively, depending on their social status and expectations—for instance, as government officers, entrepreneurs, or migrant workers (Rofel 2016). Strikingly, both recollections of the socialist past and post-socialist worldviews tend to be predicated on the idea that "you've got to rely on yourself" (Xiang 2016). However, as Xiang argues, the state is still commonly understood as a moral configuration and eventual protector of the people, based on the belief that not only do the people owe the state, but the state owes the people. In response to the growing importance of self-responsibility, the Korean Wind was generated on the basis of ethnic connection to the South Korean labor market, just as South Korea embarked on the rapid changes of its own post–Cold War political era.

The interconnection between the post-socialist and post–Cold War eras has been widely addressed in current scholarship (see Hann, Humphrey, and Verdery 2002; H. Kwon 2010; Whitfield 1991).[21] I construe the Cold War not as an "imaginary war" consisting of competition in economic development (and the avoidance of actual armed conflict) between the West and East or capitalism and socialism (H. Kwon 2010). Rather, it should be remembered that the Cold War, sometimes understood as a long, relatively peaceful era, was in fact accompanied by massive numbers of violent deaths, resulting in trauma that still persists, as we can see in historical cases such as the wars in Korea (North and South) and Vietnam. As Heonik Kwon argues, clear periodizations such as "after 1989" or "after the fall of communism" show a limited, Europe-centered understanding of the Cold War. They also impose coherence and unity on the Cold War, particularly the idea that it has "ended," without considering locally diverse regimes of ideas and practices. In the same manner, the widely used term "post-socialism" dismisses the radical diversities that have emerged in former socialist countries. The limbo or liminal state between socialism and capitalism, moral economy and market economy, past and future, has often been simply characterized by the umbrella term "post-socialist transition." Heonik Kwon's telling observation is that neither the Cold War nor socialism ended at a certain point but instead went through a "slow process of decomposition" (H. Kwon 2010, 32).

In the case of the Korean Chinese, the "decomposition" of the Cold War and the post-socialist transition were expedited through diplomatic normalization between China and South Korea. The Korean Wind has been a critical catalyst for this decomposition. Despite the long silence about, and deep vigilance toward, their ethnic identity and homeland during the Cold War, the Korean Wind has enabled Korean Chinese to speak about the long, unspeakable, traumatic past and to participate in a new ethnic politics in juxtaposition to the capitalist present (H. O. Park 2015).[22] In other words, I suggest that the Korean Wind is not only a source of rapid economic betterment and modern life but also a mythical medium through which Korean Chinese can rearticulate their ambivalence about the past and the future, politics and economy, socialism and capitalism. Restaging a deeply rooted, ongoing Cold War sensibility through encounters with transnational migration and related economic transformations, Korean Chinese began to reconcile their ethnic place in contemporary "Yanbian socialism," buffeted as it is by the Korean Wind emerging from the intersection between post-socialism and the post–Cold War era.

Conclusion

This chapter historicizes the ethnic borderland of Yanbian as a zone of traffic and translation in flux; it is a zone whose inhabitants show deep, contradictory desires both to confine themselves within its limits and to connect with the world beyond them—the desire both to leave and to live in Yanbian. Yanbian and Korean Chinese may seem flexible or vulnerable to the winds that have unsettled and destabilized the region. The Korean Wind can be understood as a particular style of economic reform and open economy, which Korean Chinese came to experience on the basis of their ethnic and cultural affinity with the South Korean labor market. The former capitalist enemy homeland, which once inspired fear and distrust, provides Korean Chinese with a doorway to better economic opportunities and resources that equip Korean Chinese to survive in a rapidly privatizing China.

Let me return to some of the contradictory statements commonly used by Korean Chinese. Han Chinese are called "Chinese" whereas Korean Chinese are "Chosŏnjok"; Yanbian is Yanbian whereas other parts of China are "the external world" (*waidi* in Chinese). The ethnic boundary between Yanbian and the rest of China means that Korean Chinese are Chinese—but not quite. The territorial boundary indicates that Yanbian is China, but not quite. Unhomeliness—a condition of extraterritorial and cross-cultural initiation—has taken root in Yanbian and, in large part, accounts for the responsiveness of Korean Chinese to the strong wind from South Korea. The next chapter illuminates how this Korean Wind has been imagined, practiced, and performed through the Korean dream: the actual and material encounter with the former capitalist enemy homeland, South Korea.

The Un/Welcoming Homeland

The problem is discrimination against Korean Chinese by the
South Korean government. Korean Americans and Korean
Japanese are free to enter South Korea. Why should the South
Korean government limit Korean Chinese? It is because they
are well off whereas we are poor—isn't it? Unlike Koreans who
left South Korea during the 1970s and 1980s, we Korean Chinese are descendants of those who left the Korean peninsula to
live a better life or to protect ourselves when we lost our country to Japan or to pursue the anti-Japanese movement in the
fight for independence. How can South Korea discriminate
against Korean Chinese simply because we are poor?
—XU LIANSHUN, *Paramkkot* (The windflower)

While anticipation and aspiration drove the Korean Chinese migration
to South Korea, the journey back to the homeland has often been fraught.
The recovery of forbidden and forgotten kinship ties with South Korean
relatives that emerged as a key method of entering South Korea, especially
in the 1990s, resulted in many Yanbian Korean Chinese, most of whom
had no familial records in South Korea, paying illegal brokers to acquire entry
documents to South Korea by faking kinship ties, arranging phony marriages
(Freeman 2011), or counterfeiting work visas. These illegal processes required
high fees, almost equivalent to a full year's income in South Korea, ranging
in value from US$5,000 to US$15,000 in the 2000s. The illegal migration
markets were also built on multilayered systems of brokers who took profits
from every step, and getting into South Korea was not always guaranteed; a
single unreliable or dishonest broker could destroy the entire process.

However, there was a strong belief among many Korean Chinese that
higher risk meant higher gain, and the illegal migration market rapidly expanded. Every rumor about a broker acquiring visas would attract some
interest from people eager to seize the opportunity. Some made it to South

Korea at the first attempt, but many failed to gain entry even after several tries, in the process incurring high debts. The miseries of cheated and indebted Korean Chinese became a pervasive and negative backdrop to the Korean dream. At the same time, the success stories of migrants who returned to China and were able to purchase an apartment or open a new business continued to inspire pursuit of the dream. As a result of these countervailing forces, the benefits of the Korean dream have materialized unevenly over the past three decades. The promises and betrayals, prosperity and bankruptcy of labor migration to South Korea have brought about rosy futures for some but also an "ethnic crisis" (*minjok wigi* in Korean) that disturbs and destabilizes Korean Chinese everyday life, as expressed in a local saying: "Yanbian has been contaminated by 'Korean water' [*han'gukmul* in Korean] and capitalism."

This chapter explores the journey that Korean Chinese have had to take to South Korea, which was both welcoming and unwelcoming to Korean Chinese as migrant workers. I focus particularly on legal changes and also capture the ethnographic moment of the summer of 2004, right before the amnesty was granted, when many undocumented Korean Chinese, in legal limbo, stayed on the edge of deportation. I examine the following questions: How did the encounter with the long-forbidden enemy homeland of South Korea change what it means to be Korean Chinese? What made a majority of Korean Chinese regard the illegal migration market as a necessary pathway to pursue the Korean dream? What kinds of legal regulations have sustained or shifted the Korean Wind? How have Korean Chinese dealt with the un/welcoming homeland?

As summarized in the introduction, Yanbian has cycled through various "winds" in the wake of Chinese economic reform, but the Korean Wind has critically reshaped the South Korean labor market and legal regulation for migrant workers. In the 1990s, it became common for South Koreans to encounter Korean Chinese in South Korea, especially working in restaurants, construction, and care support. However, despite the growing number of Korean Chinese migrant workers, the South Korean government was not fully prepared to accommodate them legally. As a result, almost all Korean Chinese became undocumented workers and faced years of persecution by government officers until the mid 2000s.

In what follows, I map out the Korean Chinese migration history to South Korea through different channels: kinship, marriage, and finally labor migration. Korean Chinese migration was initiated by a family/kinship visit program through which the South Korean government aimed to reunite families that had been pulled apart in the context of colonial migration following the Korean War. Those who visited South Korea through the reunion program often overstayed their visas and obtained employment without work permits. Since these kin-based visits served as the main legitimate route for Korean Chinese to go to South Korea, those who had no kinship ties would often engage in sham marriages or forge documents in order to travel there (Freeman 2005, 2011). Marriage also became a key method of creating new familial relationships. Once Korean Chinese brides gained legitimate legal status, they were able to invite parents, siblings, and close relatives, which could contribute to a dramatic increase in family income. The kin-based entry system gave rise to the expansion of illegal migration markets and a consequent large-scale influx of Korean Chinese undocumented workers.

When I first began my research on Korean Chinese migration in 2004, the miseries provoked by the illegal migration market, including indebtedness and related mental and physical stress, constituted a core of migrants' narratives. These sufferings were further aggravated by the South Korean government's passage of the Overseas Korean Act in 1999. The act defined overseas Koreans and outlined the benefits they could receive, but it excluded Korean Chinese on the basis of their socialist affiliations and the reluctance of the Chinese government to cooperate. In response, Korean Chinese, who were the single largest Korean diaspora group working and living in South Korea as migrant workers, joined with South Korean nongovernmental organizations (NGOs) to press for revision of the act to include Korean Chinese. The request for revision was finally accepted in 2004 and was a critical turning point in the history of Korean Chinese labor migration, ushering in a regime of "free" movement under a new work visa regime (see chapter 3).

This chapter illuminates a transformation in the meaning of kinship, from being grounds for political persecution, especially during the Cultural Revolution, to being a means of enabling transnational mobility. I analyze the processes and principles by which the Korean dream has systematically informed the categorization of Korean Chinese migrants—welcome, as well as unwelcome—as a cheap source of labor in South Korea. In addition to tracing the shifting political economy that China and South Korea had to go through and the legal changes that regulated the Korean Chinese entry to South Korea, I introduce individual stories of Korean Chinese who were on the edge of deportation, struggling in the un/welcoming homeland before they ended up becoming "free" subjects.

The Currency of Kin

Korean Chinese kinship ties to North Korea and South Korea were the subject of fear and caution due to the political consequences they had engendered during the Cold War. Despite proximity to North Korea, where the majority of Korean Chinese ancestors came from, reunions after several decades often did not result in many long-term relationships, with most ending up as one-time events.[1] The sharp economic disparity between North Korea and China has led many Korean Chinese to cut off North Korean relatives they perceive as financial drains. More importantly, since North Korean refugees have become a critical political concern in the border region, Korean Chinese try to avoid causing political trouble for themselves by minimizing those kinship ties. In contemporary China, where "money is more important than anything," as many Korean Chinese put it, they have focused their interest on South Korea, where they can work and make better money than in China. Thus, while kinship ties to North Korea have been forgotten, obscured, or denied over time, kinship ties to South Korea have been newly generated by the flow of migration and the emergence of a migration market.[2]

As the original kinship visits rapidly evolved into labor migration within a couple of years, both Korean Chinese and South Korean relatives soon discovered the mutually lucrative aspects of the kinship visa, which led to its commodification in the migration market. I encountered similar narrative patterns regarding the "visa deals" that Korean Chinese made with their South Korean relatives. A woman in her early fifties (in 2005) named Gumja, whom I met in South Korea, told me about her visa deal:

> We (my husband and I) were so happy to find that a cousin of my husband lived in South Korea. We felt as if we had gotten a lottery ticket since we could be invited to go to South Korea. Yet when they decided to invite us, they asked us to pay money for the visa application. They wanted five thousand dollars. That was fairly big money back in the early 1990s. We had to pay that amount to the cousin because we still thought it was a much better deal than going through illegal brokers. After we entered South Korea, there was no more business between the cousin and us. In South Korea, we could not get close to the cousin's family because they had been separated too long—the connection was broken even before the Korean War.

2.1 View of a North Korean town from Yanbian, China, 2008. Photo by the author.

This encounter between Korean Chinese and South Korean relatives does not much resemble the happy reunion of a family long ago split apart by the Korean War. Rather it looks like a business transaction, one that involved the actual exchange of money. In many cases, after making a "business-like" visa deal, the two parties simply turned their backs on each other—in the worst cases, completely breaking the relationship. However, since there are fewer Yanbian Korean Chinese who relied on kinship visit visas to enter South Korea than in other areas of northeast China (since most ancestors of Yanbian Korean Chinese originated in what is now North Korea), the relatively rare kinship ties to South Korean that existed came to be highly prized in Yanbian. Those who had such ties took full advantage of them, and their visits to South Korea resulted in rapid economic achievement. These suddenly well-off Korean Chinese greatly accelerated the Korean dream in Yanbian.

The South Korean policy toward Korean Chinese migration needs special attention. The kin-focused visa issued to Korean Chinese by the South Korean government shaped the pattern of Korean Chinese migration (Freeman 2011; J. Kim 2016), encouraging Korean Chinese to extend and manipulate kinship relations. Since Yanbian Korean Chinese have fewer biological kinship ties to South Koreans on the basis of geneal-ogy, marriage has become a major means of creating affinal kinship ties (that is, "in-laws"), usually between Korean Chinese women and South Korean men. The reasons for (and consequences of) these marriages vary greatly and cannot always be classed simply or easily as fake or real. Here, I do not mean to explore marriage patterns or the specific dynamics be-tween the two parties, South Korean and Korean Chinese. Rather, I focus on the way in which marriage plays a role in extending and transferring this invitation visa not only to close relatives, parents, and siblings but also to extended family members, such as uncles and aunts, and the way in which it contributed to work practices and overstaying in South Korea.

The history of the visa regulations runs as follows. At the start of Ko-rean Chinese migration in the 1990s, a Korean Chinese woman married to a South Korean man was able to invite her parents, who were allowed to stay for a year. However, it became common for family members to come and be allowed to stay for longer periods of time. The intention of the gov-ernment was to gradually increase the number of Korean Chinese while minimizing the number of undocumented subjects. Yet the South Korean government also resisted expanding the number of entry visas issued to Ko-rean Chinese in the name of protecting the domestic labor market. This meant that there was always an excess number of Korean Chinese waiting to go to South Korea. In these competitive circumstances, Korean Chinese who did not get visas relied on illegal brokers to expedite their entry into South Korea, and the brokers always found new loopholes in the system.

The visa regulations of the South Korean government are complicated and change frequently, depending on the government's position on mi-grant labor and overseas Koreans. I am often surprised to see how knowl-edgeable Korean Chinese are about South Korean visa policy trends and how swiftly they are able to adjust their plans in tandem with policy changes. I heard many details about the extended family invitation visa. During the hike I took to Reguang mountain (detailed in chapter 1), the youngest member of the hiking group, Jielan, told me a story that provides some insight into the economy of kinship. She was a daughter of farmers from a border town in Yanbian. Her parents were fairly well off compared with other farmers in her town, but they had a hard time paying for her college education solely with the income from farming. In order to relieve this financial burden, her father tried to go to South Korea many times via brokers, but his visa applications were denied for years. However, Jielan had a female cousin who married a South Korean man. The cousin was

2.2 "We are finding lost families for you"—advertisement in the magazine *Yanbian Women*, 1995. Photo by the author.

allowed to invite up to four relatives into South Korea. After the cousin's parents (Jielan's uncle and aunt) were invited, there were two spots left. A slight competition ensued between Jielan's father and his siblings. Two years before Jielan told me this story, the cousin's brother came back to China, and the spot became available to Jielan's father.[3]

Such stories are not uncommon in Yanbian. Once somebody has married a South Korean (usually a Korean Chinese woman marrying a South Korean man), the right of invitation can be transferred to other family members—both consanguineal and affinal kin. And if the invitation visa cannot be used directly by family members, the visa can go on the "market" and be sold to "customers" who want to go to South Korea. This "paper kinship," or kinship that is not only a product of relatedness but also the result of rights acquired as goods in the migration market, does not create communal feeling or affect.[4] Rather, it works as a potential currency that enables transnational migration and the pursuit of better economic futures. The ties that had once been seen as posing a threat during the Cold War era have become a valuable currency in the wake of the Korean Wind. At the same time, old kinship ties with communist North Korea were being forgotten or obscured.

This newly circulated currency attached to kinship does not lead Korean Chinese migrants to create or recuperate a sense of belonging to the "homeland"; rather, it facilitates border crossing for economic purposes. The role of kinship here is peculiar, in that it both implies the biological tie that brings about empathy and sociality and challenges its own biological basis, as it can be crafted and manipulated into an instrument that confers the ability to visit and work in South Korea.[5] The emergence of paper kinship also creates a kind of relatedness to strangers, who can use somebody else's visa and ID cards when faking kinship ties. Actual, biological kinship ties to North Korean relatives have worn thin and been downplayed due to the emotional, financial, and political burden they entail, despite sympathy for the impoverished state of North Korea. The links and ruptures facilitated by the economy of kinship have continuously rewired the connectivity of this borderland to the global economy, generating new flows of migration from China to South Korea, and from South Korea to China. The economy of kinship is driven less by familial intimacy than by a desire for this form of "enterprising-up" kinship.[6] Kinship-based entry has revealed the limits of the South Korean government's accommodation of the rapidly increasing Korean Chinese migrant population and expanded the illegal migration market. In response to the "Korean Chinese problem," the South Korean government had to diversify the qualifications for entry into South Korea, thus making and remaking Korean ethnicity in light of the Overseas Korean Act and work permit visas.

From Kin to Ethnicity: The Overseas Korean Act

The Overseas Korean Act was passed in 1999. It defined who belonged to the category of "overseas Korean" and what benefits they would get in the "home" country, benefits that included free entry and the ability to stay for up to two years with no need for a visa, along with medical insurance, the right to property ownership, and favorable conditions for capital investment. The act granted a sort of quasi-citizenship to overseas Koreans by providing them with almost the same rights as South Korean citizens (Park and Chang 2005). The category of overseas Korean, however, was limited to South Korean citizens who had lived in foreign countries, along with former South Korean citizens and their descendants. Since South Korea was established as a modern nation-state in 1948, South Korean citizenship only came into being at that time. Consequently, certain groups of overseas Koreans—Korean Chinese, Korean Russians, and Koreans in Japan, who had left the Korean peninsula during the colonial period (1909–1945), before the two Koreas were established in 1948—were excluded from the category of overseas Korean.

Here, let me briefly outline the history of Korean migration for a better understanding of the background from which the Overseas Korean Act emerged. Beginning in the 1950s, the South Korean government focused on rebuilding a new country out of the ruins of the Korean War. Modernization projects enabled rapid economic development during the 1960s and 1970s. During this compressed period of development, labor exports played a critical role in the dramatic rise of the South Korean economy (Athukorala and Manning 1999). Perhaps most importantly, the South Korean government promoted the transfer of South Korean nurses and miners to Germany, Korean soldiers to the Vietnam War, and South Korean construction workers to the Middle East from the 1960s to the 1980s. Remittances from these South Korean emigrants contributed significantly to South Korean economic development and the prosperity of individual households.

By the 1980s, however, the situation had changed dramatically, as South Korea had joined Hong Kong, Singapore, and Taiwan as one of the "dragons"—Asian countries that achieved rapid economic development led by strong and authoritarian states. South Korea became a net importer rather than a net exporter of labor under the promulgation of globalization (S. Kim 2000). In the early 1990s, the South Korean labor market even started suffering from labor shortages, especially in manufacturing. As the wages of South Korean workers went up, the search for cheap labor became more important in the struggle for competitive market power (G. Han 2003). In addition to declining fertility rates, the expansion of the service sector, and the improving education level of the overall population, younger South Koreans came to prefer to work in white-collar jobs rather than in manufacturing (Athukorala and Manning 1999).

In order to resolve this critical labor shortage, the South Korean government devised ways to import migrant workers with programs such as the Industrial Technical Training Program, which supplied the manufacturing sector with trainees, mainly from South and Southeast Asia, as cheap labor. A large number of migrants also came to South Korea to work. But the quotas on these workers were much lower than the number of people who wanted to enter South Korea, and as a result, most migrant workers entered South Korea by illegal means. Of these migrants, Korean Chinese quickly emerged as the most competitive group in the labor market, dominating construction and the service sector. Their advantage came from their geographical proximity and their Koreanness—most importantly, the fact that they could speak the Korean language. The sharp surge of undocumented Korean Chinese migrants into South Korea alarmed the South Korean government, and thus Korean Chinese were banned from having the right to permanent or long-term residence, even as they continued to flood the labor market.[7]

The financial crisis in 1997 was a critical turning point that dramatically changed the South Korean economy by accelerating the spread of neoliberalism in South Korea. At this time, the country underwent rigorous structural adjustments mandated by the International Monetary Fund (IMF). These structural adjustments were based on neoliberal economic models that emphasized labor flexibility, resulting in soaring numbers of irregular workers (Lim and Hwang 2002). The IMF sought market-centered policies by minimizing government control over the economy, and over finance, in particular (Stiglitz 2003). Less successful companies were merged into bigger corporations, and many people were fired without any safety net. Social welfare programs shrank, and the poverty levels and number of homeless surged in the late 1990s (J. Song 2009).

The South Korean government's response to the social problems caused by IMF policies was to pursue a number of structural reforms to attract foreign capital. The Overseas Korean Act was one of these measures. The South Korean government announced the rationale for the act, as follows: "We," as "global South Korea," should secure the free entry, residence, and business activity of diasporic (South) Koreans by recognizing overseas Koreans, not by ethnicity or blood, but by nationality—that is, citizenship (Park and Chang 2005; Seol 2002; Seol and Skrentny 2009). Therefore, the Overseas Korean Act embraced whoever had or used to have South Korean citizenship, a status that had only come into existence in 1948; the result was the exclusion of large numbers of overseas Koreans in China, Japan, and Russia.

The Overseas Korean Act was critiqued for its arbitrary rules of inclusion and selective exclusion, which resulted in a sense of "hierarchical nationality" (Seol and Skrentny 2009). "Rich cousins" from the United States and Japan were included but not "poor cousins" from China and the former Soviet Union (Park and Chang 2005). The act had a particularly strong effect on the legal status of Korean Chinese, many of whom had moved to China (to what was then known as Manchuria) during the colonial period (1909–1945) or even before and who had been granted Chinese citizenship after the People's Republic of China was established in 1949. By the 1990s these two million Korean Chinese constituted a large fraction of the six million overseas Koreans worldwide, and they had begun to enter the low-end, manual labor market in South Korea as the largest single migrant group. But they were not recognized under the Overseas Korean Act, and thus most of these Korean Chinese migrants ended up overstaying as undocumented workers. The South Korean government found it impossible to control the increasing number of undocumented Korean Chinese workers, and it gradually became a critical social issue.

A discourse of Korean ethnic solidarity among the Korean Chinese, as well as among NGO activists and churches, became the dominant counterargument against the Overseas Korean Act.[8] These groups emphasized colonial history and the Cold War context as critical factors in understanding the history of the Korean diaspora. They began to tell the personal and family histories of individual Korean Chinese to demonstrate the close kinship ties that existed with South Korea and that had been disrupted during the Korean War and the Cold War.[9] The stories varied: the ancestors of some Korean Chinese had been forced to go to Manchuria to escape severe poverty, which worsened under Japanese imperialism; others actively fought the Japanese in the cause of an independent Korea; some had wished to return to the Korean peninsula but were prevented by the Korean War and yearned for their homeland until they died. In the discourse of Korean ethnic solidarity, Korean Chinese were viewed through their history of colonialism and the Cold War but also as socialist subjects who were counterposed in various ways to South Koreans living under capitalism and liberal democracy. South Koreans knew very little about Korean Chinese people or culture until the diplomatic normalization between China and South Korea in 1992, as communist China (*Chunggong* in Korean) was something of a taboo subject under the anti-communist cultural and political environment of the so-called red complex.

The South Korean government had its own reasons for excluding Korean Chinese from the Overseas Korean Act. One reason was the fact that the Chinese government insisted that Korean Chinese be recognized as Chinese. Since neither China nor South Korea granted dual citizenship to their people, the Chinese government was concerned that the act could work as a medium through which Korean Chinese could convert themselves into South Korean citizens. This political concern was related to rumors about a possible separatist movement: China was worried that the geographical proximity and close ethnic ties between Yanbian and the Korean peninsula could lead Korean Chinese to demand some form of independence. A second reason was that the South Korean government was concerned that the current floating population of Korean Chinese under the Overseas Korean Act would grow and flood the South Korean labor market with too much cheap labor, even though undocumented Korean Chinese workers already made up a majority of the migrant workers in South Korea. A third reason was that Korean Chinese were associated with the aftereffects of the Cold War. Korean Russians and Korean Japanese, who were especially associated with North Korea or socialism, were also excluded from the act. It was feared that overseas Koreans with socialist affiliations could be a threat if they were granted unlimited free entry. Even as Cold War politics seemed to be coming to an end, their legacy remained in the Overseas Korean Act in treating people of the Korean diaspora differently depending on their host states.

Although the South Korean government was never explicit about its reasons for the selective exclusion of some overseas Koreans, the stakes were high, and the impact was far-reaching. The Overseas Korean Act stimulated heated political debate and demonstrations by human rights activists and churches that advocated for embracing Korean Chinese as fellow ethnic Koreans. These groups continued to organize demonstrations and raise their voices in support of revising the Overseas Korean Act, insisting that the South Korean government should not exclude and discriminate against Korean Chinese—sentiments very apparent in Xu Lianshun's novel *Paramkkot* (The windflower), quoted in the epigraph for this chapter (Xu 1996, 1).

A Camp for the Undocumented

Following lengthy demonstrations for the revision of the Overseas Korean Act, some Korean Chinese came to live in a church named Uijuro, run by Minister Lim Gwangbin, in a neighborhood of northern Seoul called Hongje-dong. Minister Lim had been a Christian activist in the pro-democracy movement of the 1980s. After the military government officially came to an end in 1993, his focus shifted toward issues of social inequality, and he led a year-long series of demonstrations to demand legal changes for undocumented Korean Chinese workers and reform of the Overseas Korean Act.

During the summer of 2004, I went to the church every weekday and also attended Sunday services. Most Korean Chinese were not Christians, but they continued to gather at the church to maintain social bonds as well as the political drive to keep their movement going. I helped Minister Lim counsel Korean Chinese workers regarding legal issues such as unpaid wages, industrial accidents and related insurance compensation, and marriage to and divorce from South Koreans (mostly South Korean men). But most problems derived from their undocumented status. Minister Lim wanted me to document these consultations to build an archive as a reference for the church, the public, and my research. The interviews helped me grasp the difficult circumstances under which undocumented Korean Chinese workers lived. Many of the testimonies were impossible to listen to without shedding tears. But the stories taught me much about the conflict and suffering that these workers had endured for years in what was supposed to be their ethnic homeland.

Uijuro Church was in some respects an ordinary church, offering services on Sundays and Wednesdays for South Koreans as well as Korean Chinese.[10] But it was also used as a refuge for dozens of Korean Chinese during the week. When I first entered the church in 2004, it felt almost like a camp.[11] Fifty or sixty undocumented Korean Chinese were staying there, sharing the space together, but were not free to go out to work or for any other reason. They were living exposed to the threat of deportation back to China. Stuck in the church, they were avoiding possible arrest while vaguely waiting for good things to happen to them, particularly a change of policy by the South Korean government, initiating more favorable treatment of Korean Chinese as ethnic Koreans.

Minister Lim and a hundred members of the Korean Chinese Association had fought to press the South Korean government to revise the Overseas Korean Act, sticking together through a three-month live-in demonstration—from November 2003 to February 2004—at the 100th Anniversary Memorial Church, located in the central part of Seoul. Eventually the South Korean government agreed that the act was flawed and accepted the need for revision. Although it was unclear when change would actually take place, the government's admission was accepted as a great victory for Minister Lim and the members of the association. Whenever I visited the church in July 2004, I heard stories from people about their demonstration experiences: "It's hard to express in words how much

we suffered during those three months of cold winter," one former dem-
onstrator told me. "We slept on the cold concrete floor, shared the room
with dozens of other Korean Chinese, ate only small amounts of distributed food, and rarely got to take a shower." During the demonstration,
some members got sick. Some left for work. Some returned to China or
got deported there. One person died in an accident. Most recalled how
tired they were and how frustrated they were afterward.

Since their legal status remained undocumented even after the demonstration, they still faced the risk of arrest and deportation. The Korean
Chinese members of the association all moved into the church in order to
find a community and sanctuary in case they were caught by the police.
During this liminal and uncertain period, the undocumented members
were included in, but also excluded from, South Korea. Inside the church,
they felt safe and did not worry about deportation, but outside it they
were still vulnerable to arrest. In effect, the church was treated as a zone in
which the law was suspended.

The church was also a voluntary community for these sixty people,
with a division of labor and special roles for each person: cooking, cleaning, grocery shopping, boiling water, and so on. The members were given
nicknames according to their task: Ms. Cook (*yorisa* in Korean) and
Mr. Boiling Water (*mul kkŭrinŭn Ajŏssi* in Korean), for example. Interestingly, since most of them entered South Korea under pseudonyms that they
had adopted on falsified visas and passports, some Korean Chinese used
two names—real and assumed—whereas others just used their fake names,
which had come to sound more familiar to them than their real names.

The church had to be reorganized to accommodate them. The main
hall was remodeled as a large dormitory, with separate spaces for women
and men. Dozens of Korean Chinese shared the hall as a sleeping place,
unfolding their own blankets on the floor at night. During daytime, the
hall served as a communal space where the members of the association
shared their anxieties and worried about their uncertain future. They
were strangers to one other, but at the same time, they were friends in the
same boat, undocumented and suffering from their fear of arrest. Only
when money began to run out did some people secretly go out to work.
But the working schedules they had to adopt did little to assuage their
anxiety since people's income was so irregular. The psychological pressure
made some of the residents physically sick, but they could not afford to
visit doctors. The anxiety also took its toll on community relationships.
Although the members generally thought of themselves as friends and

comrades, and often addressed each other in kinship terms, they also argued and quibbled, often about small issues. The community gradually dwindled as more people left to find jobs, regardless of the risk of deportation, but it endured until the amnesty of 2005, at which point the remaining members finally scattered.

On the Edge of Deportation

In the camp-like church, I talked with many undocumented Korean Chinese who were on the edge of deportation during the summer of 2004. Although Korean Chinese have become accustomed to life in South Korea, they still find it difficult to become legitimate members of society in many ways, no matter how long they stay. Despite the economic improvements that Korean Chinese have experienced, they feel they are unwelcome strangers in South Korea, serving as lower-class workers. Under constant threat of deportation, they are vulnerable in terms of lacking job security and subject to human rights violations. They have to work hard to make more money, but they also have to be prepared to leave South Korea at any time. A Korean Chinese lady from Yanbian named Bongja, who was in her early fifties at the time, told me that despite having been in South Korea for ten years, she did not feel that she fully fit in to South Korean society:

> Although my life got a lot better than in China, I have to say that I have worked myself to death. No eating, no spending money at all. Since I have more than 200,000,000 Korean won [US$200,000] in South Korea, there is no regret if I were to die right now. In addition, I have spent as much money as I have wanted. Yet whenever I buy something in South Korea, I ask myself why I have to buy this if I would leave or be deported from South Korea tomorrow. I would like to go back to China. I miss my mother who is getting old, and I dream of my siblings and my hometown in China. But I do not want to be "kicked out" by force.

Most Korean Chinese women I met in the church took it for granted that they were "illegals" who had to live with the fear of deportation. The otherness of the Korean Chinese could be observed in their lack of access to social services due to their illegality. Since Korean Chinese did not have access to medical care (before the new visa regulation of 2005), if they became sick, they depended on free medical services provided by churches or on their personal networks to obtain medication. For instance, a Korean

2.3 A group photo taken in the 100th Anniversary Memorial Church, Seoul, after the revised Overseas Korean Law was passed, January 8, 2004. Photo by Minister Lim Gwangbin.

Chinese lady from Yanbian named Chosuk, who was in her early fifties at the time, had a tumor in her uterus and needed an operation. Since she did not have medical insurance, she had to pay for the expensive surgery. After surgery, she received Chinese medication from a Chinese doctor, another Korean Chinese living in South Korea. Since the doctor was a member of the Korean Chinese community to which she belonged, it was cheaper and easier for her to receive the medication.

Oksu, a Korean Chinese lady in her mid-fifties who came from Yanbian, also had a tumor in her uterus. She heard that there was a minister who provided foreign workers with free medical service. She received support from the church for free. Oshil, a Korean Chinese lady in her late fifties from Yanbian, had chronic pain in her leg due to physically demanding work in South Korea. She had worked as a service woman in a restaurant, a domestic worker, and a cleaning lady in a motel, sometimes working for fourteen hours a day. She should have rested to cure herself but could not afford to stop working. Oshil thought of going back to China but could not afford to pay for medication there, so she remained in South Korea, earning low wages in order to afford her medicine.

Along with chronic health issues, Korean Chinese women testified that they had struggled with being isolated, excluded, and discriminated against in South Korea. Although they insisted on the ethnic connection between South Koreans and Korean Chinese, their Chinese citizenship did not allow them to be fully accepted members of South Korean society. One factor that reinforced the isolation of Korean Chinese was the deportation policy at the time, which had been modified since the beginning of 2004. While I was conducting fieldwork in August and September 2004, the South Korean government intensified its search for undocumented migrants and increased the rate of deportation. They wanted to uproot existing undocumented migrants and remove them from South Korea before the government could enforce new laws applying to incoming migrants starting in August 2004. As the search for undocumented migrant workers was pursued more vigorously, employers also began to fire these employees to avoid paying fines levied by the government. As a result, migrant workers found it harder to secure work. Many were afraid to seek employment for fear of being arrested and deported, and they were also vulnerable to economic and physical abuse if they were deported. Some people had such traumatic experiences during their deportation that they were unable to discuss them—they were too painful even to recall.

Faced with deportation, many Korean Chinese women that I met at the church complained about constant nervous agitation. To escape from the probability of deportation, Korean Chinese tended to avoid exposing themselves to public scrutiny—they either stayed at work as much as possible or they tried to leave Seoul to go to the countryside, where the regulation of migrants is less strict. Korean Chinese women who had worked in restaurants or motels tended to look for domestic work, feeling it safer from the eyes of the police. One woman named Bungi, a hotel worker in her late fifties who came from Yanbian, suffered from chronic insomnia and had to use sedatives to rest. Many other Korean Chinese women exhibited high levels of tension and nervousness, causing considerable health problems. In particular, the tension at work was far higher when they had to interact with South Korean coworkers and customers. To protect their identities, Korean Chinese attempted to maintain secrecy about their undocumented status by denying as much as possible their ethic identity at work and within their communities. Munil, a Korean Chinese lady in her mid-fifties from Shenyang, realized that her Korean Chineseness put her at a disadvantage in finding work, and she decided not to say that she came from China. This was possible for her given that she had been living in South Korea for fifteen years and did not speak Korean with a Korean Chinese accent. She was familiar enough with South

Korean culture and customs that she could pass as a native South Korean; she felt that since she was successful at displaying a South Korean identity, other South Koreans did not despise her at work.

But it is not always possible to hide one's identity. Often, Korean Chineseness can be detected from a person's accent or ignorance of detailed South Korean culture. Oksu, a Korean Chinese lady in her mid-fifties from Yanbian, had stayed in South Korea for eight years as a domestic worker and as a service woman in a restaurant. She was working in a public bathhouse providing massages and grooming services, and was satisfied with working there because it paid comparatively well. However, since the search for undocumented migrant workers constrained her options, she became increasingly anxious and her health deteriorated. She worried that she would be reported to the police by South Korean coworkers:

> I have to compete with other South Korean workers in the public bathhouse to gain more clients. To do this, I have to provide better services developing intimate relationships with the regular clients. However, when I have more clients than my South Korean coworkers, they get jealous. South Koreans don't share information about what's happening at work, and they tend to marginalize me from them. Sometimes, South Korean coworkers cheat me out of my tips given to me by my clients. However, even though I know I am being cheated by them, I can't complain to them about their wrong-doing. This is because they would report me to the police to get revenge. Even though they mistreat me, I can't tell them about my opinions. This is because I am an illegal migrant worker (*Bulboep Cheryuja* in Korean). But I don't want to be deported now. It is not time for me to go back to China since I have to make more money here.

Given the chance of deportation as a penalty, "illegality" made Korean Chinese vulnerable employees. Furthermore, Korean Chinese were not in a position to resist or negotiate over rates of pay or terms of employment. While competing with their South Korean coworkers, their illegal status created stratified relationships between South Korean and migrant workers. Simultaneously, the ethnic sameness provided Korean Chinese with advantages in finding jobs over non-Korean ethnic immigrants (Moon 2000). Sometimes, however, their Korean Chineseness could be exploited to dichotomize the "Korean Chinese" as the other, as the above stories show. Korean Chinese have been dually interpreted in the South Korean labor market, both as useful providers of cheap labor and as often unwelcome competitors with South Korean workers.

Given this dual attitude, it was difficult for Korean Chinese to understand the policy that led to deportation, given that they felt they shared Korean ethnicity. In particular, when they saw the South Korean government arresting or deporting undocumented migrants, they felt humiliated because they had become criminalized. Korean Chinese often complained about the way that the South Korean government treated "the same ethnic Koreans." The fear was intensified among the Korean Chinese community through rumors heard from friends and from media representation of deported undocumented migrants. In my interviews, I heard about deportation from several women who had directly experienced it. Their capture by immigration officers always happened unexpectedly, and the process of deportation was disrespectful and humiliating.

For example, when Munil was working in a restaurant in Seoul in 1992, the beginning stage of Korean Chinese migration, some Korean Chinese in her area were arrested en masse. Munil was not caught, but she was afraid to continue working in the restaurant. She left Seoul to go to Ulsan, in the southeast part of South Korea, but her salary was less than before and she felt lonely so far from Seoul, where she had many friends. She returned to Seoul and worked in a restaurant again, but somebody reported her, and a migration officer arrested her. She was upset as well as embarrassed:

> At that time, I did not have enough money and wanted to save money. So, by putting together several chairs, I slept on the chairs in the restaurant after work. Since I stayed in the restaurant days and nights, somebody noticed I was Korean Chinese who had nowhere to go. I don't know who reported me to the officer. When I was being sent to the place where "captured" illegal people are detained before real deportation, I said to the officer, a South Korean man, that I needed to arrange to take care of my work before I left, although I was being deported anyway. Speaking with very derogatory words, this South Korean man asked me to go with him right away. I strongly resisted him by pulling his arms. Then he said, "We are suffering because of fucking bitches (*Ssyangnyŏn*) from China." In China, we have never used those bad words. We were very angry at each other. Why do I have to hear these bad words from South Koreans? Even though I kept resisting him, eventually I was deported to China by ship.

Not only was deportation a humiliating experience for Munil, it also led to her realization that she no longer had livable circumstances in China. Her husband, who had come back to China from South Korea earlier than her, was now living with another woman. The remittances

Munil sent to her husband had been used for living expenses by her husband and his new girlfriend. After hearing about her husband's affair, she decided to return to South Korea by being smuggled on a ship. The process of smuggling was extremely dangerous, and she had to switch ships several times in the middle of the ocean not to be traced. She could not eat well for a week on the ship. Eventually, she arrived at a port in South Korea and became an illegal migrant again. But by performing and speaking like a South Korean, Munil has managed to hide her illegality since she came back to South Korea.

At the same time, arrest does not always lead to deportation. A migration officer also arrested Sun, a woman in her early forties from Yanbian, when she was working in a restaurant. A Korean male coworker, someone who had been fired due to his chronic sexual harassment of Korean Chinese women, reported her to a migration officer. She was detained in the migrant bureau for twenty-four days:

> When I was arrested, I strongly asserted I don't want to go back to China, and I can't go back to China. But who cares about what an illegal migrant says? I could not tell my family in China. I had to figure it out by myself. I still had a debt to pay off. It was not the right time for me to go back to China. When I was arrested, it was a very hot summer. There was only one bathroom for forty illegal migrant workers. I could not wash well. Since I have sort of sensitive skin, my skin went bad without washing, which caused me much suffering. In addition, I could not understand the fact that I was staying with other "colored" people, such as from the Philippines, Bangladesh, Pakistan, and Africa. How come, are we similar to them? We are all ethnic Koreans. Aren't we?

Sun was eventually released, thanks to a voucher from a trustworthy South Korean. She paid a fine equal to US$1,000 and agreed to go back to China by the promised date. But that date expired, and she became illegal again. Without making money, she could not go back to China. Under the relentless deportation rules, many Korean Chinese women came to think of deportation as a matter of luck. They felt that they were so powerless that there was nothing they could do except be cautious. At the same time, they felt they were being treated unfairly: they used racialized terms (such as "colored people") to make distinctions between Korean Chinese and other foreigners, and lamented the dismissal of their claims for special residential rights and of their sense of belonging to the homeland of South Korea.

Following years of aggressive deportation, the South Korean government began trying to devise a reasonable way to regulate migrant workers and address the shortage of labor in South Korea by decreasing the number of undocumented migrant workers in favor of documented migrants. The government encouraged undocumented Korean Chinese to leave South Korea without punishment and penalties between March and August 2005, with an understanding that they could come back to South Korea after one year. Since October 2004, tens of thousands of Korean Chinese returned to China with amnesty, and many came back to South Korea under this policy, this time with legal documentation to live and work there..

Post-Amnesty and the H-2 Visa: Back and Forth

In 2004, the Korean Constitutional Court found the Overseas Korean Act to be unconstitutional because it unjustly discriminated against some overseas Koreans on the basis of their host states and economic potential. The Overseas Korean Act was revised to include those who had previously been excluded, granting the same rights to all overseas Koreans (through the F-4 visa)—except those who engaged in simple physical labor, which was the kind of work that most Korean Chinese did. As a result, Korean Chinese who worked mostly in the service and construction sectors could not take advantage of the F-4 visa, which allowed free entry and long stays in South Korea. Instead, beginning in 2005, the South Korean government addressed Korean Chinese workers separately through the institution of the H-2 Overseas Korean Visit-Work Visa. Although this visa was designed for any overseas Koreans in low-skill jobs, in practice it has been used mostly by Korean Chinese and Koreans from the former Soviet Union.[12]

The revised Overseas Korean Act and the initiation of the H-2 visa is significant in two ways (see chapter 3). First, the H-2 visa was devised for Korean Chinese as a form of amnesty. In order to qualify, however, Korean Chinese workers have to leave South Korea and stay in China for a year before they can return to South Korea, at which point they are allowed to work there for three years. After the three years, they must leave South Korea again until the visa expires, and then they have to apply again. The visa allows Korean Chinese to work in South Korea legally but only for three years at a time. Despite this limitation, Korean Chinese migrant workers are no longer invisible and undocumented workers beyond the South Korean government's reach—they are officially recognized as particular groups of ethnic migrant workers governed under special visa regulations. This inclusion has enabled the government to track and predict the levels and patterns of Korean Chinese migration in and out of South Korea.[13] The governance of the Korean Chinese labor population no longer consists of relentlessly tracking down and deporting the undocumented but rather of subtly controlling and ordering individuals into specific visa categories (Mezzadra and Neilson 2013). Most importantly, the foreign identification card provided to documented Korean Chinese when they are granted H-2 visas constitutes symbolic proof that they are a special group of overseas Koreans. That is, Korean Chinese are now governed as legitimate foreigners working in their ethnic homeland.[14]

This special condition leads to another point. The new visa regulations for overseas Koreans have resulted in a sharp division between, and different treatment of, overseas Koreans according to the kind of visas they hold—F-4 for those who work in professional and business fields, and H-2 for unskilled laborers. The holders of H-2 visas became, in effect, officially recognized as a special migrant working class that is allowed to work only in fields designated as simple, physical labor. This articulation of ethnicity with migrant status and working-class subjectivity culminated in the enactment and implementation of the H-2 visa, which integrates Korean Chinese into the South Korean labor market as a transnational ethnic working class. The official categorization of Korean Chinese as a migrant working class has in turn reinforced discrimination toward Korean Chinese, not only in the labor market but also in South Korean society in general. The national mark of "China" or "socialism" inscribed in the very term Korean Chinese stamps a strong migrant working-class subjectivity on Korean Chinese that in some ways supersedes their Korean ethnic identity.[15]

The content, intention, and timing of the Overseas Korean Act (which codified the F-4 visa) and the H-2 Overseas Korean Work-Visit Visa reflect a particular historical entanglement within South Korean neoliberalism. These laws demonstrate how global South Korea has interpreted and situated the concept of ethnicity and built colonial history and Cold War politics into the logic of neoliberalism. They epitomize a type of neoliberal governmentality, distinguishing deserving overseas Koreans from non-deserving ones on the basis of the market potential that each national group is able to generate (Ong 1999, 2006). As John Comaroff and Jean Comaroff argue, "ethnicity has its origins in the asymmetric incorporation of structurally dissimilar groupings into a single political economy" (Comaroff and Comaroff 1992, 54). Each group of overseas Koreans has encountered the homeland of South Korea with a different political orientation and economic potential, and each has thereby been dissimilarly treated by the homeland (H. Lee 2018; H. O. Park 2015). Korean Chinese have become exclusively viewed as a migrant working class on the basis of their particular in-between-ness, their status as almost Korean, but not quite: the gap between their Koreanness and their Korean Chineseness.

Conclusion

This chapter reveals the process by which South Korea, a country that has been both welcoming and unwelcoming of Korean Chinese as a cheap source of labor, has been reconfigured from a former enemy homeland into a necessary marketplace for economic betterment, positioned at the intersection between post-socialist China and post–Cold War South Korea. My analysis also documents a significant transformation of the meaning of kinship, from a justification for political persecution at the peak of the Cold War to a means of transnational migration. Forbidden, interrupted, and discontinuous kinship ties were rejuvenated after several decades and quickly turned to the purpose of facilitating transnational mobility.

By focusing on a particular ethnographic moment that captures the legal limbo of Korean Chinese suffering on the edge of deportation during the summer of 2004, this chapter provides a contextualization for Korean Chinese ethnicization and marginalization in the un/welcoming homeland. Ethnicity has taken on a different meaning for Korean Chinese, as their encounter with South Korea has resulted in the emergence of a labor marketplace—an encounter that has created a site of value production. In addition, the ethnicization of Korean Chinese as a cheap source of labor from socialist China has become gradually articulated with a working-class subjectivity through the South Korean government's legal recognition, combined with transnational labor market demands. Indeed, as we have witnessed in this birth of a Korean Chinese migrant working class, ethnicity is not a mere category of human difference or simply a marker for exclusion of the other; rather, it is always situated in relation to other ethnicities. Part II illuminates how Korean Chinese have practiced and become frustrated with a Korean dream in flux, one that has, through transnational money and time, created a unique migrant working class.

PART II

Dreams in Flux

Rhythms of "Free" Movement

For Korean Chinese migrant workers who had been undocumented for years in South Korea, the year 2005 was life changing, as the South Korean government's new amnesty program made it possible for them to gain documented status. Most of the workers I had met in the camp-like church were able to move back and forth between China and South Korea as "free" migrants. This freedom created new rhythms of transnational life under the H-2 visa system, which was intended to "clean up" previous records of undocumented status. However, as noted in chapter 2, in exchange for amnesty and the right to free movement, undocumented migrants had to leave South Korea for one year before they were allowed to return and work for up to a total of five years. Upon their return they could initially stay and work for three consecutive years. After three years in South Korea, they had to return to China for a while; then they could use their last two years of work time in South Korea. After that, the H-2 visa expired, and the visa clock was reset. Since 2005, Korean Chinese migrant workers have lived with this one-three-two rhythm; they are also only permitted to work in designated service and physical labor sectors.[1] The new visa regime thereby relegates Korean Chinese labor to working-class fields—an "inclusion through exclusion" (De Genova 2013) that also serves as a means of discipline and control.[2]

This chapter captures the particular ethnographic moment of the post-amnesty period by highlighting the concept of rhythm as an emerging key principle in the ordering and reordering of the flow of migration and social belonging, and in the exercise of political control (Levin 2015, 50; Salter 2006).[3] Here, rhythm consists of repetition in movement—a new becoming with difference (Lefebvre 2004, 78–79). Lefebvre points out the contradictory aspects of rhythm—its capacity to order, as well as to disrupt, the everyday life of capitalism. This interference leads to an overlap and tension between the corporeal, social, and spatial regulations that control mobile subjects, who at times conform with authorized tempos and at times disrupt them (Lefebvre 2004; see also Edensor 2012). Especially when capitalism brings about destruction through its rhythms of accumulation, rhythm can carry with it the risk of a perpetual disruption of temporal order (Castree 2009; Edensor 2012, 12–13; Harvey 1989, 216).[4]

Under the newly liberalized migration regulations, the undocumented Korean Chinese female migrant workers discussed in the previous chapter can be understood as embodying the new era's sense of time and participating in its time-space making, with Yanbian as a resting place and South Korea as a working place. In this new era, Korean Chinese female workers have become visible as necessary and critical subjects who have sustained the South Korean care and service industries and perpetuated the Korean dream. Their stories reveal how Korean Chinese women have navigated between highly gendered workplaces (in South Korea) and gendered households (in Yanbian), and how they have constituted themselves as transnational migrant subjects by embodying the rhythm of migration, the power of Korean money, and their gendered and ethnicized subjectivities.

With a focus on three Korean Chinese female workers' stories, this chapter shows that the visa regime failed to create a coherent pattern of migration: these women continually face the need to build and rebuild their lives, as the rhythm of supposedly free migration is constantly interrupted by personal events, aging bodies, unpredictable illness, financial developments, new visa regulations, and most of all, the fluctuations of the global economy. At the same time, these women make an effort to seize control of time and exceed or escape the regulatory rhythms that limit their lives. Their stories contribute to our understanding of the material forces of transnational temporality, as well as the visceral dimensions of gendered transnational migration. This chapter shows how state-imposed rhythms and market-driven rhythms intersect and, in doing so, reconfigure transnational space-time linkages and transnational bodies, and thereby transnational subjectivities, through rhythms of free movement.

Rhythm / 1

One Year of an Unfamiliar Home

During 2006 and 2007, Yanbian was revitalized by Korean Chinese returning due to the South Korean change in migration policy described above. When I visited Yanbian in the summer during those years, I found reunions celebrating these homecomings taking place between long-separated families and friends in restaurants and hotels. Many of the un-documented migrants I had come to know through the church in Seoul told me about reunions with relatives they had not seen for years, recount-ing highly emotional moments at the airport. After more than a decade of separation, some did not recognize the dramatically aged faces of mothers and fathers, wives and husbands, daughters and sons.

While the amnesty transformed these Korean Chinese migrants from immobile undocumented workers to freely moving subjects, it also created feelings of unfamiliarity stemming from long absences from Yanbian.[5] Changes to the city alarmed many of them: the dramatic urbanization, intense consumption, skyrocketing cost of living, and especially the in-crease in the Han Chinese population. To Oksun Park, a Korean Chinese female migrant worker in her late fifties, returning home did not feel the way she had thought it would. "Home is not like home," she told me re-peatedly. "Yanbian is not like before, in many ways. I can't get by without speaking Chinese. Han Chinese are everywhere—bankers, sellers, workers (*dagong*), waiters and waitress (*fuwuyuan*). I don't like that." Most Ko-rean Chinese I had met in South Korea told me that their first impression of South Korea was that "it's like home," in part because everything was written in Korean, their mother tongue. Now they felt the opposite, as if Yanbian had become an unfamiliar home.

In a migration setting, home is a complex emotional and material locus in relation to the question of belonging and dwelling. One sees home as the place one comes from, to which one has an emotional attach-ment, the place one yearns to return to (Safran 1991). Beyond the limit of geographical boundaries, home might be reimagined through deterrito-rialized political engagement via new media (Appadurai 1996; Clifford 1994). To those who have been on the move for generations, home can be construed as either "where you are at" (Gilroy 1991) or "where you are going to" (Chu 2010). Home may appear as a creolized, hybridized, and impure site to migrants because their mobility has led them to reassess the seemingly absolute and essential link between territory and identity (Hall 1996) through a process of displacement and temporalization, in cor-respondence with specific histories and geopolitical dynamics (Axel 2004). On the other hand, those willing to leave their home in search of a better life may come to view home as an impoverished place lagging behind the present, held back by traditional culture (Chu 2010; Ngai 2005; H. Yan 2008; Zhang 2001).[6]

These definitions tend to assume that mobility is a condition of modernity, which emphasizes movement over settlement, urbanity over rurality, working over comforting, and moving forward over staying in place. Home is imagined as a static space of familiarity and repetition; it is thus a place to depart from, not return to—in fact, an impulse to return home might amount to a "regressive desire" (Felski 2000). To Korean Chinese, however, the locus of home is neither left behind nor static, given their current pattern of circulation between South Korea and China according to the one-three-two rhythm of the H-2 work visa. Moreover, since China has risen as a global economic power, creating a new "Chinese dream" among Korean Chinese, Yanbian is not seen as a regressive or backward place. Many Korean Chinese have begun to prosper in China's economic boom, especially after the Korean dream was fundamentally shaken by the global financial crisis of 2008 (see chapters 5 and 6). How have the migrants adjusted from the rhythm of work in South Korea to the rhythm of home in Yanbian, as well as vice versa, and how has this added complexity to their idea of home? In addition, how have their attempts to adjust to such sharp splits between working and non-working times and spaces reshaped their transnational subjectivity?

Yanbian Time

During my first visit to Yanbian in 2006, I was amazed by the open hospitality and relaxed time management I encountered, which was in direct contrast to my experience of meeting with Korean Chinese migrants in South Korea. The contrast initially caused me some confusion and embarrassment in scheduling. In Yanbian, there is a particular way of planning ahead in making an appointment. Eating and drinking together is believed to be a natural way to build a relationship, and meetings are commonly held at mealtimes, usually lunch or dinner. To arrange meals, I would call my contacts and ask if they could meet for a conversation and interview. They usually asked me to call them back in a few days, but it was not always specified when I was supposed to call. If I called in what I thought of as a few days, they often would say something along the lines of "Let's meet at 11:30 today." As I grew accustomed to the pattern of time arrangement in Yanbian, I tried to be more open to improvisation—to go with the flow. In South Korea, I was usually able to hold a large number of interviews and keep a tight schedule, but this did not work in Yanbian.

Schedules were less rigid, and people did not always clearly block out particular time periods for specific purposes. Sometimes a plan was made by spontaneously suggesting, "How about now?"

The flexible schedules became more obvious when I met someone for a meal, which was usually combined with drinks. It was quite common to drink multiple bottles of beer or strong Chinese alcohol (*baijiu* in Chinese) over lunch. The meetings generally lasted around from 11:30 a.m. to 2:00 p.m., which was, in fact, a normal lunch break. Sometimes lunch was prolonged to play card games and do "no work." Long lunch hours accompanied by drinking were often condemned as a violation of the Chinese work ethic, but the loose and relaxing use of time also evoked a feeling of freedom. This sense of "too much free time," as many Yanbian people called it, sometimes accompanied a sense of pride in socialism, as it showed there was no need always to be working under pressure, like in capitalist South Korea. At the same time, "too much free time" could also be regarded with a sense of shame—as a lazy and unproductive violation of the socialist work pattern. This ambivalent feeling about time was reinforced when Korean Chinese traveled to South Korea and directly observed the fast-paced life of South Korean time.

Korean Chinese who had recently visited or worked in South Korea mentioned two main points: first, the intensity of South Korean time has enabled South Korea to advance and develop in a relatively short period, and thus the Korean Chinese must learn from the strong work ethic of South Koreans; second, the stresses of South Korean time have made human beings inhumanly subject to "work-work" life, unlike in China, where there is an abundance of food, time, and hospitality. In the end, the sense of there being "too much free time" in China often led to the conclusion that China was the more comfortable country to live in. In particular, the Communist Party members I met in Yanbian tended to use current Chinese economic successes as clear evidence of the superiority of the Chinese way, one led by Chinese socialism and the Communist Party. These people also often assumed that going to South Korea for work was the result of failures to find success in China. Those Korean Chinese who have been able to benefit from the Chinese economic boom and have become better off than returnees/migrants have encouraged a belief that even though South Korea still offered a path to economic betterment for many Korean Chinese, the Korean dream was possibly waning, while the Chinese dream was on the rise.

Spending Anxieties

Given the unstable status of the Korean dream in Yanbian, returnees felt some anxiety and tension when they got together with friends who had achieved some measure of economic success without going to South Korea. This is partly because the returnees believed that life was not all about eating and drinking and otherwise enjoying one's free time. It was also because they had a difficult time adjusting to Yanbian rhythms, which seemed to them to involve spending large amounts of time as consumers rather than as earners. In general, they found it difficult to switch modes between South Korean "too little time" and Chinese "too much time."

I met Oksun in Yanbian again in 2009, and she emphasized, as many did, the difficulty of switching rhythms when she returned to Yanbian. She had gone to South Korea ten years previously, leaving behind her husband and two sons. While she worked in South Korea, her husband had taken care of their sons and maintained his job in Yanbian. Like many Korean Chinese, she had lived in South Korea undocumented for many years (seven, in her case). She had been arrested, detained for a month, and almost deported. Fortunately, the minister of the church (mentioned in chapter 2) sponsored her, and she was released from jail. When her family heard about her arrest, they wanted her to return to Yanbian, whether she had made money or not, but she insisted on staying in South Korea as long as possible, until she had made a substantial amount of money. In the midst of all this, the 2005 amnesty changed her undocumented status and allowed her to go back to China for a new visa, enabling her to return to South Korea. Of course, Oksun also wanted to return to China because she had not seen her family for years; in fact, she had been unable to attend the wedding ceremonies of her sons because she had been stuck in South Korea as an undocumented worker.

In 2006, Oksun returned to China to spend one year there in order to properly use the five-year work visa in South Korea. We became closer during this period, and she invited me to her home, even asking me to stay over from time to time. Her apartment was newly decorated and equipped with new furniture and home appliances. Her husband gave me a short tour, explaining to me how carefully he had selected decorations and appliances. "I chose quality materials from South Korea," he said with pride. "We spent more than other people in decorating. I try to decorate in an all–South Korean style." As I visited Korean Chinese returnee migrants in Yanbian, I realized the importance they placed on demonstrating how much they had spent purchasing and decorating their homes. Since Chinese apartments are sold unfurnished, décor is completely up to the homeowner and is an important sign of financial status and taste. The South Korean style of decoration, of which Oksun's husband was so proud, was prevalent in many newly decorated Yanbian houses.[7] Although the house had been purchased mostly with the remittances that Oksun had sent, she had not lived there much because she worked in South Korea for as long as her visa and her body allowed her to. Oksun had moved into the house after she returned to China, but she spent less than a year there before leaving for South Korea to work for another three years.

One evening when I stayed over at Oksun's place, we made dumplings together for dinner and she started sharing her disappointments about life in Yanbian. Despite the excitement of returning home, she was not completely happy. The changes that had taken place during her absence from Yanbian astonished her. Even though this was her native country, when she returned, she had trouble even finding her own home. The material conditions of Yanbian people had improved while she was in South Korea, and the cost of living had skyrocketed. "One hundred yuan [about 15 dollars] quickly disappears," she told me. "I cannot buy much with 100 yuan anymore—not like before I went to South Korea." Oksun was also worried that her savings from South Korea might run out quickly. She thought it would be hard to find the right kind of jobs, ones that would satisfy her needs and expectations. Aside from a small and reliable pension, there was essentially no social safety net. Oksun talked extensively, listing all the concerns that made her anxious.

She said that all her worries often made her want to go back to South Korea. In Yanbian, there was seemingly "too much life," much of it spent eating, drinking, and hanging out with long-separated family and friends. But returnees found themselves anxious about not working, not making money, and having too much time on their hands. They did not feel that they were leading an actual life—they were just spending money and marking time while waiting to go back to South Korea when the visa regulations allowed it. Moreover, "too much life" greatly burdened the returnees, particularly when they were invited to an event that was meant to show off the host's economic capacity and to consolidate their social network. In China, once invited, one is supposed to issue a return invitation and reciprocate to the same degree. Oksun regarded this cultural protocol with unease:

Another good thing about being in South Korea was that I didn't have to attend parties like weddings and birthdays, and so I didn't have to give monetary gifts. But here I can't avoid it. We all know each other because Yanbian is a very small society. If I don't go to my friend's parties and don't give them anything, they'd be pissed off and wouldn't come to my party. Then I'd lose my connections and my face [*mianzi* in Chinese]. If I were unlucky, I could end up with a bad reputation. People are afraid of the bad consequences of not going to parties. Also, it's not good to have too few guests at a party. The number of guests tells other people how big my network is and how good my relationships are with other people. It's kind of a mutual collaboration, whether we really want or need it or not. It's superficial. People are grumpy about going to parties. However, if I want to live life and have a business in Yanbian, it's essential to go to parties and manage relationships.

Although Oksun enjoyed these meeting and parties when she first returned, they quickly became a financial burden, as she had to attend several parties a month. Half of her monthly expenses went toward monetary gifts for weddings and birthday parties.[8] She thought the expenses were extravagant, and she could not afford to attend all the parties to which she was invited. "Since I've been in South Korea, I don't get 'back door money' from work units," she explained.[9] "Everything has to be paid out of my pocket. It's just too much. Life here is too expensive. I don't make anything, but I spend a lot." In Oksun's statement, we can find an interesting progression: "too much time" leads to "too much life," which turns into "too much cost"—and no productivity.

From Oksun and other returnees, I frequently heard about the disjointed and ruptured relationship between earning and spending in Yanbian because in Yanbian there is only consumption, or "too much life," springing from "too much time." Production (earning money) occurs in South Korea, whereas consumption (spending money) happens in Yanbian, creating a sharp geographical split between consumption and production.[10] In addition, we can witness different attitudes toward "too much free time" among different groups in Yanbian. In contrast to what Marx articulates—"He feels at home when he is not working, and when he is working he does not feel at home" (Marx 1988, 74)—free time does not feel free or like being at home to the returnees in the way that it does to well-off nonmigrants in Yanbian.[11] The Korean Chinese returnees may not enjoy free time with no work in Yanbian.[12]

Oksun and other returnees confessed that they had missed the congenial environment of Yanbian during their lonely sojourns in South Korea where they lived a "work-work" life. Yet when returnees have to live only on savings earned in South Korea, the cost of "too much life" turns out to be an economic and emotional burden that causes anxiety. Her friends and relatives tended to assume that she had earned a great deal of money in South Korea and thus expected her to spend generously when inviting them to meals and parties. These expectations were another burden, according to Oksun. "It's not just one invitation. There are so many to do once I start accepting all the invitations." "Too much life" exhausted the returnees, making them want to return to South Korea, where they could focus on working rather than spending. In South Korea they could live on a steady income without the burden of expenses for parties in order to maintain social networks. Korean Chinese migrants, including Oksun, said that they had gotten used to living as working individuals rather than as members of extensive and expensive social networks. In addition, they felt they could not keep up with the social tempo in Yanbian after growing accustomed to the "work-work" rhythm of South Korea.

Home as a place of spending without earning caused emotional and financial anxiety and made many of the returnees want to go back to work in South Korea as soon as possible. Home had become a place that made them feel backward, especially when they compared themselves with the increasingly wealthy work unit officers who had not gone to South Korea (see chapter 6). Here, again, home was not like home. Life has been split by the rhythm of one-three-two, making Yanbian a site of consumption and South Korea a site of accumulation.

Rhythm / 3

The Employment Agency

On a hot sunny day in August 2008, I called Chunja Lee, a Korean Chinese woman from Yanbian, to let her know I was back in Seoul for the next six months for my research. Chunja gladly answered my phone call, sounding out of breath, perhaps from being in the middle of work. Chunja, in her late fifties, had become my closest friend among the Korean Chinese women who had volunteered in the church, where she was called "Ms. Cook." Chunja and other members of the church had become free-moving subjects and were busy catching up on the time they had lost to

3.1 Employment agency boards displaying job opportunities in Taerim-dong, a district of Seoul in which Korean Chinese residents are concentrated, 2008. Photo by the author.

periods of enforced inactivity. There were many occasions where migrant workers were unable to meet with me due to the demands of their schedules, and there was little I could do except wait until they had time off, which happened once or twice a month. Their schedules were mainly a consequence of the kind of work that female Korean Chinese workers did, and they were sometimes occupied for more than twelve hours a day. Their schedules were also uncertain; they had to be on call, waiting for work to become available. Whatever particular situation they faced, most Korean Chinese workers tried to maximize their income in any given period and moved frequently in search of the best working conditions, the shortest hours, and the highest wages.

A few days later, Chunja wanted to meet me at an employment office to help manage her schedule and designated an agency in the Seoul Express Bus Terminal, where three lines of subways intersect and where the floating population and shopping stores are densely packed into the underground space. I asked why she chose this particular agency, and she said that it was because the agency had a wide selection of jobs with good wages, and it was situated in an area packed with restaurants—making it a good source for job openings. Chunja said that since she was not sure when she would go back to China, she did not want to work for a monthly salary, which would limit her mobility. Rather, she liked the freedom to move between jobs, in constant pursuit of better daily wages and nicer employers.

We arrived at the office—two desks, a couch, and two women busy answering phones. One of them, who seemed to be a manager, noticed Chunja and welcomed her with a big smile.

Chunja was a regular customer, but she first had a complaint about her last job. The pay wasn't bad, Chunja said, but the owner was "grumpy" and the restaurant "dirty." "You should pick a better job for me next time, okay?" The manager assured Chunja she would, and she suggested several new job openings, all cook or waitress positions in restaurants around the area. Chunja picked a cooking position near the office and received the address and phone number of the restaurant. I asked if there were generally more jobs than job seekers. The question triggered a conversation between the manager and Chunja.

AGENCY MANAGER: Of course, there are always a lot more jobs for good Korean Chinese workers like Ms. Lee [Chunja] than there are job seekers. The employers are always complaining about the working capacity and quality of Korean Chinese. Since the amnesty was granted, Korean Chinese don't work as hard as when they were illegal. They are not desperate anymore.

CHUNJA: You're right. The newly arrived Korean Chinese, they don't know how to work in South Korea. I have been in South Korea for ten years. I have become an expert at working in South Korean restaurants—almost like a South Korean. But the newcomers are just looking for money without knowing how to work. They are degrading the Korean Chinese reputation. The bad reputation seriously works against me.

AGENCY MANAGER: Yes, Korean Chinese are always looking for new jobs, asking for more money. What employers want to change their workers every day? These days Korean Chinese are spoiled and don't work hard. They spend money like South Koreans. They should save money and think of going back to China soon. Instead they buy expensive cell phones, drink a lot, eat out a lot, live in a nice house, and pay high rent. They're here to make money, not to live here forever.

CHUNJA: That's why there is the saying: the longer you stay in South Korea, the poorer you get. It's true that among my friends who've been in South Korea for as long as I have, nobody has made as much money as me. I control my money very tightly. My husband cannot use the money I send back without my permission, not at all. I'll go back to China after working in South Korea for a couple more years.

Behind Chunja, several more Korean Chinese women waited their turn. The agency manager had to go back to work. Phones in the office kept ringing, as people inquired about new daily jobs. As we left the office, Chunja spoke with some disdain about the attitude of the agency manager: "She pretends to be kind. But she's disrespectful of Korean Chinese. Look at what she said. She thinks Korean Chinese only know money-money, and we Korean Chinese are inferior to South Koreans. Don't South Koreans like money?" Chunja asked if I agreed, and I said I did. She was clearly dissatisfied with the conversation, even though she had portrayed herself as a "good" Korean Chinese, working hard without wasting money. At the same time, she made no attempt to avoid the stigma of being a money seeker. "We're here to make money, aren't we?"

I was struck by the conversation for several reasons. First, the agency manager shared assumptions about "good" Korean Chinese and "bad" Korean Chinese, as defined by their work ethic and the extent to which they save money. Good Korean Chinese do not move often between jobs, do not spend excessively, and have a plan to return eventually to China. This assumption leads to the idea that Korean Chinese should consider South Korea a temporary working place, not a permanent home. Thus, saving money—not wasting it like South Koreans—enables the good Korean Chinese to get back to China as soon as possible. Another assumption was that Korean Chinese have their own kind or level of consumption, in contrast to South Koreans. In fact, the wage gap between South Koreans and Korean Chinese in the service industries and physical labor is minimal. Korean Chinese with expertise as carpenters, electricians, or skilled construction workers could earn as much as their South Korean counterparts.[13] Overall, these assumptions have contributed to reinforcing or reproducing the representation of Korean Chinese—"almost Korean, yet not quite"—as temporary residents who should not be consuming as much as South Koreans.

The labor market, through institutions like the employment agency office, assesses the value of Korean Chinese as physical workers and service workers. Korean Chinese job seekers must tolerate the nuanced disrespect of South Korean agency workers and employers, while at the same time they must show a capacity to handle long hours and a demanding work-load. Workers who satisfy these two conditions can obtain better paid and less difficult or physically demanding jobs in the future. The agency is responsible not only for assigning workers to appropriate jobs but also for mediating work conditions and wages between employers and em-ployees, circulating the recognition and reputation of both parties in the labor market. In this manner, the agency is a crucial mediator for Korean Chinese, in the sense that it plays a role in sorting out "good" Korean Chi-nese from "bad" ones, based on their previous work experiences and repu-tation. That is why somebody like Chunja, who can work "almost like a South Korean," can get a good reference from the agency and be assigned to a well-paid and comfortable job, whereas newcomer Korean Chinese workers tend to keep moving from job to job until they build a certain level of recognition and reputation.

Despite the wide presence of Korean Chinese migrants in South Korea, mass media and public discourses have stigmatized Korean Chi-nese workers as "opportunistic," "immoral," "low quality," and "lacking in a work ethic." There seems to be an increasingly common tendency to think of Korean Chinese as job-jumping money seekers.[14] One Korean employ-ment agency worker, whose attitude seemed representative of many I spoke with, told me, "There are not so many Korean Chinese I would want to arrange for hiring." At the same time, however, Korean Chinese labor pervades the service sector, and is especially dominant among wait-resses and caregivers. It is almost impossible not to encounter Korean Chinese waitresses when eating out in Seoul. South Korean customers can tell that "they are from China" from the Yanbian accent mixed with a Seoul accent. The slight distinction tends to mark Korean Chinese as not fully South Korean. Regardless of the stigma attached to Korean Chinese, however, these workers, such as Chunja, often express their confidence as money seekers. "We are here to make money," they say. "What is wrong with seeking money-money?" Seeking money is the very reason they are in South Korea, and it provides them with a strong drive to get through their exhausting and stressful time there. Experienced Korean Chinese female workers often say that they have gotten used to and even come to like their tense and fast-paced "South Korean time." In particular, nostalgia for their "South Korean time" peaks when they return to China—where they "do nothing but spend money." Despite an earnest wish to return to Yanbian after living as long-term undocumented workers in South Korea, Chunja and many other Korean Chinese testified that once they got back to Yanbian, they missed the heavy—but regular—work schedule in South Korea.

Working Time

The population of Korean Chinese living in South Korea reached approximately 700,000 as of 2020. Over time, the occupational fields of Korean Chinese have gradually diversified and professionalized as younger generations of Korean Chinese have pursued higher education and become academics or entrepreneurs or have gone to work for globally well-known conglomerates such as Samsung and LG. A new generation of Korean Chinese—those who, since the 1992 opening, were born and raised in South Korea or moved there at a young age and do not speak with a Yanbian accent—are forming a larger part of the Korean Chinese community in South Korea. However, most Korean Chinese are still concentrated in the service sector and construction fields as migrant workers under the work-visa system. In these fields, there are broadly two kinds of wage systems: one is based on day-to-day employment, the other on month-to-month work, especially restaurant work. Once the wage system is determined—usually in the job announcement—the rhythm of work follows.

Oksun's everyday life followed a somewhat set pattern. She worked in many restaurants in Seoul as a cook or waitress, which are very common jobs for Korean Chinese women in South Korea. She told me that she worked mostly from 10 a.m. to 10 p.m. Although her work was supposed to end at 10 p.m., she rarely left on time, as she was often asked to clean up leftover dishes and prepare for tomorrow's orders by the owner of the restaurant. She did not have a moment of rest during working hours: "There was no time to open the eyes and nose [*nunko tteulsae eopda* in Korean]." Most nights she had to rush to catch the late subway back home, arriving around midnight, and falling asleep around 1 a.m. Then she had to get up at 7 a.m. to get ready for work in the morning. In other words, her time consists almost solely of "working time" and "sleeping time" (H. Kim 2008). She repeated the same pattern for ten years, except for the time when she was an undocumented worker and thus had to work secretively and irregularly. Since a day off meant she was "losing" (that is, not earning) her daily wage, Oksun tried not to take more than one or two days off a month, usually reserving those for special occasions, and would constantly remind herself, "I must be like a working machine." Although Oksun grew accustomed to the intensity and pace of working in South

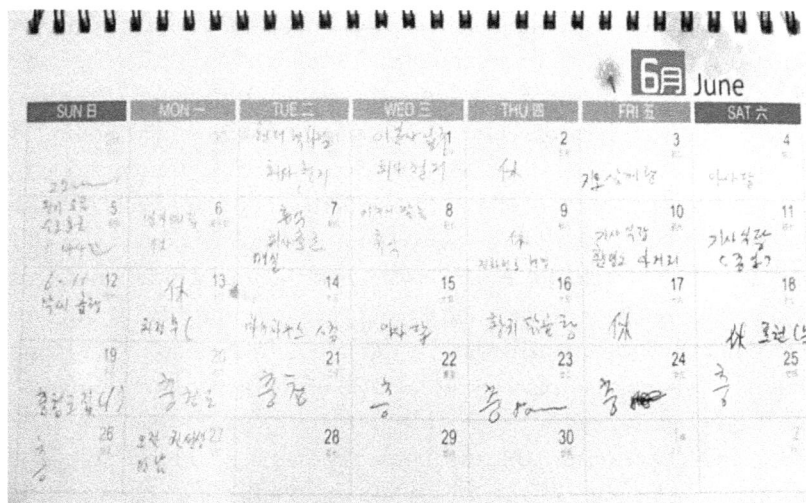

3.2 A work calendar filled out by Oksun Park, a Korean Chinese migrant in Seoul, 2009. Photo by the author.

Korean restaurants, the chronic lack of sleep exhausted her. On days with a heavy and demanding schedule, she took Chinese medicine and nutritional supplements to maintain her health, since being sick meant losing wages. She developed her own way of justifying the exhausting "work-work" life in South Korea, saying to me, "I forget my tiredness as soon as I get the cash in my hand at the end of the day. Then I get up and go to work the next day."

The power of earning money helped Oksun forget her fatigue and gave her the drive to go on. When I was doing field research in 2009, daily income in the service field ranged from the equivalents of US$50 to US$70 for women working in restaurants, and US$70 to US$90 for men working in construction.[15] This was often compensation for more than twelve hours' labor, depending on the kind of job and the worker's level of experience. The jobs are demanding compared to the work available in Chinese factories and offices, or even farms. South Korea is a country notorious for its speedy pace of life and the heavy workload heaped on migrants. Oksun and other Korean Chinese workers said that in the first two years it was extremely hard for their bodies to get used to the intensity of labor in South Korea. As time went on, however, heavy work became a "habit" (*inibakida* in Korean), and the pace was inscribed on the body.[16] Yet even under a disciplined working regime, proper compensation for labor was still the key motivation. As more than half a million Korean Chinese have occupied diverse sectors of the South Korean labor market over the past thirty years, they have developed a collective, informal understanding of the price of labor according to its duration, rhythm, and intensity—an intuitive measurement of labor value structured by many years of work experience. "If the work is too demanding or tiring," Oksun told me, "I will search for another job right away because there are a lot of restaurant jobs out there." Movement between jobs is so frequent that the migrant workers I knew were usually working different jobs whenever I saw them. It might be because wages are structured on a daily interval, making it easy for workers to quit or for the employer to fire them if expectations are not met. More critically, Korean Chinese workers (both women and men) have taken advantage of a churning, fast-paced job market to constantly seek better opportunities. This has become the usual pattern of job seeking among Korean Chinese migrants in South Korea. "Nowadays, what Korean Chinese would work in the same job for years under bad working conditions?" Oksun asked me rhetorically. Although there is no job security in daily restaurant wage labor, and the daily wage determines a large portion of her current and future economic life, Oksun does not consider herself simply subservient to her employers, as she can always respond to unfavorable conditions by moving on to a better-paid job. At the same time, Oksun is subject to the conditions of wage labor, as she places her trust in the power of the cash that sustains her while she is pursuing better opportunities.

Body Clock

Korean Chinese female workers value autonomy and friendly working conditions. For example, Maehua Kang, another worker in her late fifties from Yanbian (whom I also met at Uijuro Church), preferred not to change jobs often. A talented cook, she has enjoyed good relations with all her employers. For the last ten years, she has worked hard to be considered a "good" Korean Chinese while seeking jobs that offer flexibility as well as stability. As she explained:

> Once an owner recognizes my ability, she or he tries to keep me by giving me tips or a bonus from time to time. Also, as we become personally close, I might get a more flexible schedule. Then I can visit China for weeks for

some family events and still go back to the same job [in South Korea]. The restaurant owners would keep the position for me because they like me to work for them. It's still a daily wage, but there would be a little bit of a raise over time. I can have more stability in this way. Getting recognition from owners is the key to making money in a comfortable and stable way in South Korea. To me, freedom [the non-intervention of the owner in her work] is also important because I get nervous when the owner is watching and grumpy about what I'm doing. I don't like to work as a nanny or caregiver for the sick or the old. Doing those jobs, I'd be stuck someplace without being able to come and go freely. I'd be required to constantly serve the people in need. However good the money, it wouldn't be worth the work.

Whenever I talked to Maehua, she told me about the owner of the restaurant she was working in at the time, which was the most important factor in deciding whether she continued to stay in a job or not. She loved the freedom of flexible labor, in the sense that she could easily quit and find another, better job. But she considered freedom to be more than simply the ability to change jobs. Freedom, for her, included the capacity to negotiate with her employer regarding wages and days off. She valued freedom from an overworked schedule and from an over-policing gaze. Maehua believed that she could make better money only when she had some kind of job stability in addition to flexibility. "If we move too much between jobs, we cannot make money," she said. "It's better to stay in one place rather than move around." When Maehua did not have a stable job, it made her nervous, which caused other health issues. If she was sick, she could not work. If she could not work, she believed, she would "lose" money. Maehua counted every day, every moment in South Korea as a money-making opportunity—time was literally money to her.

However, her body clock keeps ticking—she is aging. "When I was healthy and fairly young, I didn't worry much about my body," she told me. "I'm already in my late fifties. I know my time in South Korea won't last much longer, although the visa will allow me to stay. I feel I cannot push myself as much as before—like when I was in my forties." Maehua was very careful about her health. Whenever I visited her place—she lived in a small room with a kitchen and an outside toilet, located in a soon-to-be developed area in the northern part of Seoul—she showed me multiple Chinese medicines she was taking for her health. Her husband in Yanbian sent some, and she brought some from China herself. Maehua also explained how she ate food that was good for certain organs and specific symptoms. She was knowledgeable and proud of her methods for caring for herself. "No health, no money in South Korea. If I'm sick, my time in South Korea ends." Over and over again, my conversations with Maehua reinforced the entangled relationship between the body, money, and time.

Along with the structural constraints imposed by the visa regulations that assign Korean Chinese to a specific kind of flexible labor, I take into critical consideration the female worker's bodily capacity for laboring. Despite the constant care for their bodies that these workers engage in, the working body has definite limits. Korean Chinese migrant workers, whose bodies are usually their only means of production, have to rely on those bodies to produce the same amount of labor, day after day. In order to have "tomorrow as today," as Marx elaborates in the chapter called "Working Days" in *Capital*, the body must be rested, fed, and clothed, so as to reproduce today's labor for tomorrow. For physical laborers, a healthy body is the fundamental factor that determines whether they can keep working in South Korea or not. As Maehua said, "What I'm the most afraid of is to be sick." Illness was her worst enemy, one that could ruin her time in South Korea along with her financial plans. However, Maehua and other workers who relied heavily on their own bodies for work did not know when they would be sick. Both Oksun and Maehua worried about their unpredictable bodies, often qualifying statements with phrases such as, "Before I get too old," or "As long as I am healthy"—their own ambiguous deadlines for their working time line in South Korea. Yet it is largely because of the intensive, long hours they have worked as cooks, day after day, that their bodies have deteriorated over the last ten years. Many of Maehua's friends returned to China unable to work because they had grown too sick or too weak from physical labor. "You remember when we were chased after by the police, right?" Maehua asked me once. "Look at us now. Everybody can come to South Korea to make money. Now time is good. We are completely free. We don't have to run away from the police anymore. But my body doesn't allow me to work here forever. I know the end is coming soon, in a few years. I should make as much as I can before then."

The stories of Oksun and Maehua show how Korean Chinese female migrants are constrained by the peculiar temporality of visa regulations, the types of work they do, and the body's capacity. This temporality has governed the Korean Chinese female working body and, in addition, the circulation of service labor. This limitation of migrant workers' time in South Korea pushes them to maximize their income during the time they have. As a result, the "surplus labor time" necessary to reproduce labor for tomorrow, as Marx describes, is shortened or deferred until around the one-year enforced return to China (in order to get the amnesty). The three-year intensive extraction of labor time in South Korea causes Korean Chinese female working bodies to burn out. Maehua wanted to take care of her body not for its own sake but rather to prolong her working time in South Korea, thus securing her money and future.

In fact, by the time I met Oksun and Maehua in Yanbian, after three years of intensive labor in South Korea, they were both exhausted and sick—their bodies were debilitated. Whether intended or not, the one-three-two rhythm had created a unique temporality of working and resting at both individual and collective levels. Additionally, it had resulted in entrenching its constantly moving subjects in certain habits and emotions. Korean Chinese migrant workers hope for predictability (that tomorrow will be the same as today) while, at the same time, seeking flexibility in the hope that tomorrow might be better than today. The future cannot be imagined in the long term but is rather renewed and repeated every day by the payment of daily wages.

Rhythm / 2

Hopes and Cares

On a summer night in 2009 in Yanbian, I received a phone call from Maehua, who was returning to China as compelled by visa regulations—she had used up her three years of work in South Korea. She suggested catching up by inviting me to stay at her place in Helong, one of Yanbian's cities, which is mostly populated by Korean Chinese farmers and located an hour away from Yanji. Maehua apologized for not being able to call me sooner, as she had been sick for a while after her return to China. She said she was feeling a bit better. I went to Helong a few days later to meet her. Maehua was staying with her husband, who had waited ten years for her to come back. He used to be a factory worker but had not been healthy enough to undertake heavy labor in South Korea, and thus Maehua had decided to go to South Korea alone. Since then, she had been the main breadwinner of the household, sending money home from South Korea. I remembered that she had often shown concern about her husband's addiction to mahjong, a traditional Chinese game often played for money. She had heard that it was common for Korean Chinese men with wives working in South Korea to become addicted to gambling and fall deeply into debt. Fortunately, Maehua's husband was not so deeply addicted that he gambled away the money that she sent, but he played often enough to worry her.

She told me how much she had missed her two sons when her status as an undocumented worker kept her from returning to China. She had been in South Korea since 1998, and both had grown up and graduated from college while she was in South Korea. Maehua was proud of her sons and also of the fact that she had been able to financially support their education. After college, both sons obtained respectable jobs and lived in Shenyang, an industrial city in northeast China. She considered her sons' achievements to be part of her life success, believing that "they are my hopes." While going through hardships in South Korea, Maehua had two dreams: sending her sons to college, and buying a new apartment in Yanji, the capital of Yanbian. The first dream had come true, but the second dream was still unrealized. Unlike other Korean Chinese migrants who earned enough to purchase cars and an apartment or two, Maehua had not saved enough money. Her earnings had mainly been used to pay for her sons' college education and to support her family's daily living costs. In fact, when Maehua invited me, she hesitated, and then warned: "My house is an old one. The toilet is outside. The kitchen is not modern. There's only one big room. If you're okay with this arrangement, you're more than welcome to stay with me."

When I saw her at her place, I noticed that she had lost a significant amount of weight. She seemed feeble, unlike in Seoul, where she had been full of energy. She appeared anxious and started listing all the problems she had with being at home. As she had warned, her house was an old-style Chinese house (*ttangjip* in Korean), one of four or five houses that were all tightly connected wall to wall. There was no indoor bathroom, only a public bathroom shared with dozens of neighbors. The outside toilet—the public bathroom—was even harder to use in winter. Maehua said that the kitchen without a sink or counter prevented her from standing up when she was cooking; she had to cook crouching on the floor, which caused her back pain. She didn't have a private room in her house all to herself, which put her in close quarters with her husband, who did nothing but watch TV or play card games by himself. Her savings were running out because the cost of living was higher than she had expected. She had a long list of inconveniences and discomforts.

In addition to her overall dissatisfaction with being at home, Mae-hua was ill, despite having been cautious about her physical well-being. Her symptoms ranged from stomachaches to insomnia, back pain, and sometimes pain in her joints. She had visited several well-known Chinese doctors (*mingyi* in Chinese) in Yanbian for acupuncture and herbal medicine. She went hiking or walking every morning, even with the chronic pain. She also received electronic massage treatment, which was becoming popular in Yanbian. She did not want to go out with her friends because she had to drink and eat with them, and she thought that was too expensive. Regardless of her attempts to feel better, Maehua still felt nervous and uncertain about her health. As she had told me in Seoul, "What I'm most afraid of is being sick." The state of her health would be pivotal when she decided whether she could return to work in South Korea in a year. During my visit, her anxieties seemed to peak.

> I should become stronger before I go back to South Korea. But I'm not sure if I can be healthier in a year. I am burnt out for ten years. I'm not as healthy and young as before. If I push myself too much, I could get sicker. I'm afraid of that. But I still have work to do. I want to move to a new apartment in Yanji. Also, my sons are waiting for me to return to open a restaurant in Shenyang. But I don't think we have enough money for that yet. I should save for a couple more years. So I need to stay strong.

Even though she had successfully realized one of her dreams in supporting her sons' college education, Maehua was desperate for more money, not only to move to an apartment in Yanji but also to pay for her sons' weddings. Maehua felt she needed to purchase homes for them too. She had been making fairly good money as a recognized cook in South Korea, but the rising cost of living in China seemed so hard to catch up with—for herself as well as for her husband, who could no longer work. Given her desperation, going back to South Korea felt like a necessary choice for her, although in the long run she would eventually return to China to live with her family. In making all her dreams happen, her body—in particular, her healthy body—was a key site because it was again her only means of production. But there was no doubt that her body was getting old and fragile. And even though she was a former factory worker (an occupation once represented as the ideal socialist subject who enjoyed total economic and social security), Maehua did not have a reliable social safety net for her retirement. Although she rigorously prepared for going back to South

Korea by taking special care of her health, her body remained vulnerable and unpredictable—she could not know when she would be sick again.

Oksun also was getting ready to go back to South Korea. After her experience spending but not making money in Yanbian, Oksun calculated that she would be better off going back to South Korea. To Oksun, China was a land of excessive expenses whereas South Korea was a place of earning and having too little time to spend on too much life. Oksun said: "If I'm stingy, my friends accuse me of being someone who seeks only money-money. Sometimes I just ache to leave everything behind and go to work in South Korea—although I hated to work when I was there." Oksun missed home very much when undergoing the risk of deportation in South Korea. At the same time, she became sick of Yanbian after returning: "Home is not like home." Unlike government officers with their pensions, Oksun could not draw on government or work-unit money for her retirement. She had nothing but daily wages to save for her old age. As she returned to the circuit of transnational migration, she promised herself, "I'll be in South Korea for two more years as the work visa allows. Then I'll see what to do."

Conclusion

During the years of my visits to Yanbian, I could see the attrition of the Korean dream being juxtaposed with the rise of the Chinese economy, making the Korean dream-seekers feel as if they had hit an impasse, where "one keeps moving but one moves paradoxically in the same space" (Berlant 2011, 199).[17] As one Korean Chinese Communist Party member aptly commented, "South Korean money has lost its pulse" (*Han'guk toni maeki ŏpta* in Korean). Korean Chinese migrants testified that the fading of the Korean dream stemmed from a shrinking income gap between China and South Korea, and an unfavorable exchange rate for South Korean currency. Although many Korean Chinese have remained in the circuit of migration and have come to enjoy the freedom of movement, the lost "pulse" of South Korean money shows the clear limits of the dream. The Korean dream is in crisis. The freedom of movement is caught in the circuit.

The three women highlighted in this chapter—Oksun, Chunja, and Maehua—like other Korean Chinese migrant women workers, emphasized "work time" as a crucial aspect of their life rhythm, one that gave them a sense of belonging.[18] These women firmly believed that there was no "life" for them in Yanbian, since they did not "work" there; they considered home to be a place where they could work. However, time spent resting is essential for migrant workers, in order to reproduce future work time. Especially for Korean Chinese female migrants, whose bodies have deteriorated due to the nature of care and service work in South Korea, their supposed resting time in Yanbian is, in fact, rather restless—because they are required to do the same kinds of work for their families at home, as mothers and wives in the highly gendered household. Resting time is not actually a "rest," but rather a temporary pause in "real" life. Caught between the competing temporal orientations of Yanbian and South Korea, Korean Chinese migrant workers attempt to envision new exits from this impasse, along with new definitions of "a better life" or "a better place," as the Korean dream falls into confusion and flux under the pressures of rhythms of free movement. In the next chapter, I explore the practice of waiting that constitutes another critical dimension of transnational temporality, in contrast to the rhythms of moving back and forth, in order to highlight the efforts of Korean Chinese migrants to deal with vulnerability in the midst of a Korean dream in flux.

The Work of Waiting

Wife is gone, husband is gone, uncle is gone
Everybody is gone, to South Korea, to Japan
To America, to Russia, to make more . . .
Everybody is separated and crying
What does life mean? We are all broken down
Why are we sick from missing each other?
We are waiting to be together again, someday.

—"Everybody Is Gone" (Yanbian popular song)

The Korean Wind has brought about multidimensional mobility—both physical and existential (Hage 2009)—as seen in Korean Chinese upward class mobility and unprecedented self-reinvention, from farmers to city dwellers to transnational migrant workers. But although it can seem as if "everybody is gone" to South Korea, there are, of course, many people left in Yanbian, waiting for those who have gone abroad. The single parent or waiting partner is called a *pot'ori*, a Yanbian term that connotes someone who is waiting and suffering from long-term loneliness amid the contemporary transnational, migratory landscape. As the numbers of *pot'ori* increase, many Yanbian residents have identified waiting as a source of social illness, exacerbating high divorce rates and juvenile delinquency. In response, many social groups—hiking clubs, writers' workshops, bowling teams—have formed to counter this loneliness, creating an emotional safety net. As noted earlier, hiking groups were especially popular, and I met many Korean Chinese *pot'ori* who joined to enjoy the company. A conversation I had in one of them is illustrative of their anxieties and concerns.

MR. HO: After my wife went to South Korea ten years ago, I became so lonely that I started drinking—almost every day. In Yanbian, there are so many lonely husbands without wives. What can we do? Nobody is at home waiting for us.

HIKER 1 (*enviously*): But your wife sends the remittances on a regular basis, right? How many houses do you own? Two or three?

HIKER 2: Nowadays, we should be happy if we're not divorced, if we own a house or two, if our kids have grown up without causing serious trouble, and if the remittances are still being sent.

MR. HO: You guys are right. But waiting for my wife for more than ten years is not an easy task. I don't hope for anything more except that my wife eventually returns. After waiting so long for my wife, I happen to believe that, as long as money is being sent back to China, there might still be love. (*He laughs.*)

This conversation captures the uncertainty and vulnerability many feel about living as *pot'ori*. It also makes clear the anxiety those waiting have about partners who might have an affair or try to obtain a divorce, which would cause remittances to come to a sudden halt. The temporality of everyday life, in general, entails not only the passing of time but also the necessity of waiting (Adam 1991, 121). To Korean Chinese migrants and their family members, waiting has emerged as an essential activity that requires the capacity to endure loneliness in order to maintain stable romantic relationships, as well as the flow of remittances. In Yanbian, "waiting properly" or heroically "waiting out," as Ghassan Hage (2009) highlights, comes into play as a valorized quality that shapes an orderly and self-governed subject within an uncertain context. What, then, makes waiting a necessary life condition for Korean Chinese transnational migration? What is the actual role of waiting as a link between intimate life and economic conditions? What pushes Korean Chinese to endure these long, lonely vigils?

This chapter examines "waiting" as an essential element that has shaped the afterlife of Korean dreams. As delineated in previous chapters, the Korean dream began with finding a way to enter South Korea. Yet once the dreamers got to South Korea, the dream took on unexpected dimensions. One of the first obstacles confronted was the counterfeited visas purchased from migration brokers, which often led to years of an undocumented status that disabled free movement not only between China and South Korea but also between different workplaces in South Korea. This widespread immobility within a larger cycle of mobility was long accepted as the normal and omnipresent condition of Korean Chinese transnational migration, both by migrants and their families. As noted in chapter 2, most Korean Chinese workers were waiting either for a grant of amnesty or for the chance, in some vague future, to return home. Nobody really knew whether or when they might get caught and deported by the South Korean police or immigration officers. This state of limbo, before the amnesty was officially granted in 2005, often caused migrant workers to defer taking care of themselves. They were constantly waiting for new jobs and new chances to make money in South Korea while, at the same time, waiting for opportunities to return to China, and this precariousness took a physical and emotional toll.

Korean Chinese transnational migration has been written about largely in the context of the instability, displacement, and other social issues affecting everyday Korean Chinese life (H. Kim 2008; Lee, Lee, and Kim 2008; G. Park 2006; Seol 2002). Studies describe such problems as "money fever" (Noh 2011) and "faking and making kinship" (Freeman 2011), and characterize "going to South Korea" as a phase that must be endured in order to arrive more quickly at the next stage of life. At least until the mid-2000s, when the rise of Chinese economic power was still inchoate, Korean Chinese accepted mobility as a necessary condition of a modernity that was more about movement than staying put, and more about work than leisure (Felski 2000).

During my research in both China and South Korea, I saw that the widespread phenomenon of waiting did not subside, however, even as the Korean Wind dwindled. I focused my attention on the increasingly tighter interconnections between those who were on the move and those who had been left behind. Waiting at home may seem like a passive activity, producing feelings of powerlessness, helplessness, and vulnerability (Crapanzano 1986). In this liminal temporality, those who are waiting experience an indeterminate boundary between the past, the present, and the future (Rundell 2009) while remaining in a state of repose or inaction until something happens (Gasparini 1995). Yet waiting also has the potential to create a new sociality and mutuality through "a mode of being attuned to others" with whom we have relationships (Mineggal 2009). Thus, waiting can also be understood as an active attempt to realize a collectively imagined future.

This chapter focuses on the stories of separated spouses by calling attention to dynamics of dependency and to the intersections between mobility and immobility, making money and waiting for money. Loretta Baldassar and Laura Merla (2013) have elaborated on the concept of the "circulation of care" as a new perspective to understand the connectedness

4.1 A hiking group in Yanbian, China, 2009. Photo by Baishan.

of people on the move. The transnational family, an increasingly common contemporary social form, has developed different ways to exchange asymmetrical, reciprocal care among family members and kin. This functions as a form of a moral economy of waiting for family members who are abroad and in motion. They bring themselves "together across distance" by dealing with the challenges posed by absence and separation (Baldassar and Merla 2013, 40). My focus is not only on connectedness and circulation of care between separated family members; I also highlight the vulnerability that connectedness entails in transnational families, especially in the case of spousal relationships that are susceptible to divorce and to the destabilization of the prior gender dynamics. Unlike waiting and caring for parents, children, and other family members, anticipating the return of a spouse is conditioned as a couple-oriented project. Especially as migrating and waiting are linked through the flow of remittances—expressed in the words of a common Yanbian saying, "where money goes, love is"—most separated couples would prefer to eventually be together in China, where precarity has increased in the wake of rapid economic reforms and the open economy. In other words, "waiting properly" for remittances and spousal return creates the possibility of mutual future economic welfare and preserves intimacy, by generating and sharing a deferred temporality. And yet the following stories also show that waiting can be met with betrayal or a partner's lessening appreciation, which can lead to elevated anxiety and further precariousness. We also can see that the dynamics of gendered labor and spousal expectations have become increasingly destabilized by long waits and transnational separations.

This chapter develops two interconnected arguments. First, waiting for love and money within migratory contexts constitutes a form of unwaged affective work that can generate not only a financial safety net but also a binding commitment between the divided parties. Yet I highlight waiting as a distinct kind of affective labor that can be distinguished from "productive" wage labor in the market economy.[1] I suggest that waiting is an immaterial, but nonetheless important, form of unwaged, profit-producing labor. Second, while waiting may begin as an act of love, it is susceptible to being transformed into a kind of work that requires the constant management of monetary flows, and in turn remakes the expectations and realities of transnational spousal relationships. By analyzing narratives of waiting, we are able to unravel the complex nature of remittances as promises of love and to see them as an affective medium that mitigates uncertain and vulnerable intimate relationships. My ethnography of waiting among the *pot'ori*, who could be romantically betrayed or treasured by their partners, or financially abandoned or taken care of, elaborates on the experiences of those who do not migrate but nonetheless sustain a critical dimension of migratory practice. The Korean Wind has required Korean Chinese families to endure times of waiting as an intrinsic part of realizing the Korean dream.

The Condition of Waiting

As in many other regions in China, economic reforms in Yanbian were expedited through the privatization of workplaces (*danwei* in Chinese) previously run by the government.[2] This resulted in many workers being laid off and leaving for larger cities in search of economic opportunities (see chapters 5 and 6).[3] For Korean Chinese, the idea of going to South Korea "in order to have a better life at a faster pace than in China" drove the aspirational, catch-up mentality of the Korean Wind.

Huasun Yang, a woman in her late fifties, had once worked in a Yanbian factory that made wooden tables and chairs, but she lost her job when the factory went bankrupt in the mid-1990s. I first met her in South Korea in 2004 at a church that advocated for Korean Chinese labor and residential rights. She was an accomplished cook who had worked in Seoul restaurants for a number of years, but she was anxious about the risks of being deported as an undocumented worker. Although Huasun wanted to return to China eventually, at that time she still needed to earn more income because the money she had acquired in her first three years had gone to pay off the debt to the illegal broker who had facilitated her migration. Huasun missed her family—her husband and one son—and communicated with them using international phone cards once every week or two during the mid-2000s. One day in 2005, she asked if I could help her with an instant messaging program with webcam capability (a technology she was unfamiliar with) so that she could actually see her family. I said yes, and she called to arrange for her family to gather in front of her son's computer at the arranged time. We used MSN Messenger, commonly used in the mid-2000s but at the time a previously inaccessible medium to her. I vividly remember how emotional the encounter was. She smiled broadly, her eyes moist with tears, through the whole conversation. Her son asked, "Mom, when are you coming back?" "As soon as I make enough money," she answered. Yet nobody seemed to know how much money would be enough or how long it would take to accumulate this unknown amount. Her husband said little on camera. But it was obvious that the family members wished to see each other, not virtually, but in person, and sometime soon.

Until 2005, the sort of waiting endured by Huasun's family prevailed among Korean Chinese, as detailed in chapter 2. The often undocumented legal status of Korean Chinese workers prevented them from freely moving back and forth between China and South Korea. Approximately 300,000 undocumented Korean Chinese were held in this limbo until the South Korean government granted them amnesty through revisions to the Overseas Korean Act.[4] Because of the exorbitant costs incurred in the previous regime of migration (before 2005), couples usually had to decide who would go and who would remain behind to take care of the children and the family's property. Under the pressures of South Korean migration law and the particular visa regime it engendered, couples increasingly separated so that they could send one spouse to South Korea. In this configuration, the waiting party became an essential contributor to Korean Chinese migration, enabling the constitution of new forms of intimate relationships and financial management that relied heavily on the flow of remittances.[5]

The waiting pattern changed during the post-amnesty era discussed in the previous chapter, and after obtaining an H-2 visa, Huasun was able to move back and forth between Yanbian and South Korea, still faithfully sending her remittances. Her husband, who earns no money himself, continues to seek out another apartment to buy so that he can secure rent as an extra source of income. The couple, now in their late fifties, onetime factory workers with very little in the way of pensions, are attempting to prepare for retirement the best way they can, given the precarity of their circumstances: one by making money and the other by waiting for money, but in two different countries—"together across distance."

Let the Blue River Run

In the South Korean entertainment industry, Korean Chinese are often portrayed as aggressive, brutal criminals and as "less Korean" than South Koreans.[6] The film *Let the Blue River Run* (*P'ŭrun kang ŭn hŭllŏra* in Korean), directed by Kang Mi-ja and released in 2009, is a noteworthy exception. An account of contemporary Korean Chinese migration, it was filmed in Yanbian, staging the prefecture as a "waiting room" where everybody is marking time until somebody returns. In the movie, Chul, a middle-school student in Yanbian, shows up one day at his school with a fancy motorbike. The motorbike makes him an object of flattery and envy among his friends and an object of attention among many girls. At the same time, the motorbike leads him to become "a bad boy," spending less time on schoolwork and more time eating out, drinking, and staying out late in nightclubs. Chul makes friends easily with his money and motorbike. He is well aware, however, that his lifestyle would be impossible without the money sent by his mother working in South Korea in order to support his studies and provide for his future.

Chul's mother, who was once a diligent farmer, had decided to go to South Korea after witnessing the sudden material affluence of Korean Chinese returnees. She had seen them move from old-fashioned countryside houses to clean and convenient urban apartments, dress their children in fancy clothes, and send them to larger cities for a better education, and she felt that her family was being left behind. Desperate to get to South Korea, she secretly prepared to migrate, using an illegal broker. She did not tell her family about her decision until the day before she left to be smuggled into South Korea. Although some Korean Chinese women choose the fake marriage route to South Korea, Chul's mother rejects this route. "I am going to South Korea," she says proudly, "not through marriage, but through smuggling. That way I do nothing shameful to my husband and son." Her awareness of the possibility of "going to South Korea through marriage" (*hanguge sijipgada* in Korean) evidences the sexual anxiety widely shared among Korean Chinese. She wants to portray herself as an honorable and brave wife and mother willing to confront the unknown dangers of a trip to South Korea on an old, shabby, and unsafe ship of the sort used by illegal brokers to minimize costs. People often die or disappear on the way; nothing is certain until the ship is safely anchored. These risks do not deter Chul's mother, who believes that smuggling represents a more honorable route than fake marriage.

After Chul's mother arrives in South Korea, she becomes an undocumented worker constantly beset by the police. Even under threat of deportation, however, she works hard day and night in construction as a plasterer and regularly sends letters and money to her family in China. Labor in South Korea is much more intense than farming in China, but she is happy with the higher income and the anticipation of a better future. Meanwhile in China, Chul's father, a quiet farmer, waits for his wife, still living their old life in the countryside. Sometimes, when he misses his wife, he ritualistically washes her clothes and dries them. There is little else he can do except wait for her money and wait for her return. The long-distance family relationship seems stable and peaceful but embedded within it is an unspeakable sadness. One day, as Chul's mother is running from the police, she falls off a cliff and dies. She never returns home to her husband and son. The movie captures the transformative power of money, the way in which it expands and transforms subjectivity; the boy can promote himself from a common nobody into the coolest and most popular figure in his school. Money from South Korea bought him the motorbike and, by extension, influence and status among his friends.[7]

In addition to depicting the achievement of material affluence, *Let the Blue River Run* highlights how money has transformed the intimate domain of Korean Chinese society in Yanbian. Conflicts over money cause separated couples to divorce or find better partners; a money-making wife can dominate the marriage relationship, upending the patriarchal Korean Chinese family structure; many cases of fake divorce turn into

4.2 A scene from the film *Let the Blue River Run* (2009). Hancinema Collection.

real breakups. Amid this turmoil, Chul's mother chooses to use smugglers to get to South Korea in order to avoid the stigma associated with fake marriages. However, her good intentions eventually come to nothing. Her family's long wait cannot be rewarded or reciprocated, leaving Chul and his father saddled with emotional debt and hopelessness. Chul's mother, fighting against the uncertainty of the future, sacrifices her time, labor, and body in the name of familial love—a deep moral obligation and material responsibility. But her death leaves the debt unredeemable and the desperate waiting unrewarded.

Waiting for Love

Beset by multiple forms of waiting, Yanbian is like a place of "dwelling-in-travel" (Clifford 1997, 2), with everyone always on the verge of relocating. In the stories I collected, I found that the most common fear among Korean Chinese migrant spouses who were waiting for their partner was, "What if my partner has an affair?" (*paramnada* in Korean), with either a South Korean or a fellow Korean Chinese migrant. In some cases, Korean Chinese migrants have stopped sending remittances and broken off contact after beginning another life with a new partner in South Korea. In this context, a breakup can be a critical, life-threatening event for the waiting partner, as it results not only in the loss of the relationship but also in economic vulnerability. This occurs regardless of gender, as both husbands and wives seem to be equally vulnerable to losing their partner to a possible affair.

In addition to the anxiety stemming from having an undocumented status in South Korea, moral and sexual anxiety can become intense, especially when love becomes a means of transaction and of transferring money. Marriages of convenience, primarily between South Korean men and Korean Chinese women, are used by illegal migration brokers to bring middle-aged Korean Chinese women to South Korea.[8] The manipulation of marriage has been characterized by anthropologists as a "global self-making" process that strengthens transnational ties through international marriages and remittances (Faier 2007, 2009), or, alternately, as "global hypergamy" (Constable 2005; Freeman 2005), with marriage being used to move up the social ladder. Both in China and South Korea, however, marriage has become a contentious topic not only because it enables entry into South Korea but also because it is stigmatized as an instrumentalization of women's bodies for the sake of monetary gain. Marriage as transaction serves as both a survival and an advancement strategy, allowing an escape from economic precariousness (Brennan 2004). Although there are many variations, the representative Korean Chinese international marriage tended to follow a pattern in the early stage of migration: marriages usually occured between lower-class South Korean men (rural farmers and urban lower working class) who could not find South Korean brides and Korean Chinese women seeking a way to enter and work in South Korea. In such marriages, "love" is a key term used to judge the nature of the marriage—whether it is real or fake—within and beyond legal definitions in both China and South Korea. Love becomes "the new gold" (Ehrenreich and Hochschild 2004), a means for the production of value and new conditions of possibility (Constable 2003, 2007, 2009; Faier 2007; Parrenas 2001; Yamamura 2020).

International marriage is ambivalently accepted as global self-making or global hypergamy, predicated on the ability "to eat and live," as one Yanbian expression puts it. Especially for those who have undertaken marriages of convenience by divorcing their "real" Korean Chinese husbands in order to marry "fake" South Korean husbands, the anxiety about the high divorce rate and the nasty endings of relationships has become more elevated in the wake of the Korean Wind. Although laments in Yanbian about the commodification of love are important to recognize, I want to push my questions in a different direction, to emphasize the conflation of money and love in remaking transnational couples. How have Korean Chinese couples who are separated developed ways to manage their anxiety about potentially losing their partner to transnational migration? What kinds of transactions have been made between the separated parties? And what is the reward for the couple that has successfully endured long periods of waiting, deferment, and isolation, in addition to the maintenance of a precarious relationship?

In March 2009, I had lunch with a number of "waiting people" whose partners had been working in South Korea for several years. In the midst of a lively conversation, I saw Bokja Kim looking depressed. Then in her late forties, she had been a farmer before her marriage to a Korean Chinese man. She was working in a Japanese plastic-bag factory in Yanbian, a job she disliked because of the long working hours and low wages. But she felt she had no better options. Unless she left for South Korea, she could expect little improvement in her financial life. Bokja's husband had gone to South Korea seven years earlier, promising he would return in three years. He was financially indebted to the illegal broker he had used to get to South Korea. Bokja and her husband had believed the debt would be a worthwhile investment in a better future for them both. The broker helped him secure a two-week business travel visa to South Korea, which meant that soon after he arrived, he became undocumented. His illegal status prevented him from moving back and forth between China and South Korea. He was determined to stay in South Korea until he had earned a satisfactory amount of money, and Bokja had been willing to wait, as long as her husband returned to China with the money he had promised her.

For the first two years of his stay, Bokja's husband sent money to her every other month, and she took good care of it, saving "every 10 won coin" in her bank account in order to purchase a modern apartment in the city of Yanji, Yanbian's capital, which is where many Yanbian Korean Chinese hope to end up living.[9] In her husband's third year abroad, however, the remittances began arriving later and less often, and the amounts became smaller and smaller, and eventually they stopped altogether. Her husband stopped contacting Bokja, and she could not reach him. There were rumors that he had met a new woman or had gone broke. She had been waiting seven years for his return, and the loss of contact made her feel as if she had wasted her life for nothing. Unlike her relatives and friends whose Korean dreams had come true, Bokja had neither a house nor financial resources, the typical visible reward for waiting for one's husband. She wanted to leave Yanbian and go to South Korea, even by means of a fake marriage if necessary. She told me that she would use whatever means she could to get to South Korea. And yet she was still married to her husband and could not divorce him, meaning that even a fake marriage to a South Korean man would not be an option. "I'm getting old and sick of waiting for my husband," she said. "I'm really stuck. There's no way out for me."

If we consider promises as an ordering of the future to make it predictable and reliable (Arendt 1972, 102), this broken promise disordered Bokja's future.[10] Her husband's disappearance all but destroyed her life and left her few options.

> I've been dying to go to South Korea—not only for money, but also to find my husband. At first, I worried about him so much when he didn't call me. But when I understood that he had intentionally cut off contact, I wanted to kill him! I'm just so exhausted from waiting for him, and then from hating him. I'm just one of a lot of unlucky people swept up by the Korean Wind. What's the use of revenge? Still, I need to divorce him officially so that I can start my life over again. I am really stuck.

Bokja's long-term, long-distance relationship with her husband started with a mutual promise, one that had a time limit: "I will return in three years." However, once her husband stopped sending money and calling her, their bond to each other and their commitment to a common future dissolved. Since then, her wait has been transformed into a chronic vigil. The longer it goes on, the more vulnerable she becomes. In fact, Bokja could have made ends meet in China without relying on the remittances sent by her husband. Although her wage was below what she could have made in South Korea, she could feed herself and her daughter on a tight budget. What made her more miserable, however, were her ceaseless attempts to get to South Korea and her ongoing hope to make more money there. "If I went to South Korea, I could get paid ten times more than now." But, as her visa requests were repeatedly rejected, her life seemed to float not in the present but in an imagined future somewhere else—perhaps South Korea.[11] The anticipation seemed poisonous, making her feel desperate to escape from the present. Furthermore, the discrepancy between her present life and her expected, anticipated future resulted in a suspended life that was much more painful, especially when she compared herself with someone who had realized the Korean dream.

Once she ceased to hope for a rosy future with her husband, her mental and physical health deteriorated remarkably. She was sick but still had to work. She was weak but still wanted to go to South Korea. Bokja told me at one point, "I'm no longer anxious because I've lost hope." She was becoming a mere spectator—she saw herself lagging behind in a rapidly changing Yanbian. She was not taking part in the prosperous part of Yanbian that was enjoying the fruits of the Korean dream. She could not brag to her friends and relatives who had seized their chance and whose husbands had not failed them. Her long, difficult wait appeared futile to her, plunging her life into a kind of suspended animation. Her prolonged waiting—promised in love—did not produce any value, and she felt that she had been left empty-handed. When I last met with her, Bokja was continuing to wait, not for her husband anymore, but for an imagined departure to South Korea.[12]

Remittances as Transformative Power

In Yanbian, talk of remittances is everywhere. Korean Chinese migrant families expect remittances to continue to flow to Yanbian even though they know there is always a risk that they might be interrupted—or cease altogether, as in Bokja's experience.[13] Remittances not only meet the economic needs of transnational families but also build connections and convey shared meanings between family members (Baldassar and Merla 2013).[14] Remittances are a personalized form of money dedicated to supporting the family back home in the name of love. Remittances are also a form of economic value used to buy houses and other material goods, such as new cars, flat-screen TVs, high-end refrigerators, and luxurious furniture. Remittances require special treatment; they need to be wisely saved, spent, and invested to create more wealth and a better future. Remittances transfer not only the actual value of their monetary equivalent but also an affective sense of care toward the partner and the relationship itself. Here we can see that, along with deferral and waiting, remittances emerge as a somewhat dubious medium of affection and support. They provide a way to practice moral responsibility for one's family, but they can also be a source of tension, forcing couples to separate for long periods of time. In what ways have senders and receivers negotiated their remittance transactions?

In numerous *pot'ori* waiting stories—full of frustrations, betrayals, and breakups—money and love become intermixed and interchangeable. The details of Mr. Ho's story, introduced above, exemplify the complex relationship between money and love in a context of transnational mobility. Mr. Ho was a dedicated Communist Party member in Yanbian. He was a factory worker in a printing unit, and he married and had a son in the mid-1980s. But when the Chinese government began privatizing both housing and education in the early 1990s, the cost of living soared, and his income quickly became insufficient to support his family. As part of the process of privatizing the housing market, Mr. Ho's work unit provided him with a new apartment below market price. He bought the apartment thinking it was a great deal but had to go into debt to do so. In 1992, the same year that Mr. Ho became an apartment owner, China normalized diplomatic relations with South Korea, and many of his friends and relatives left for South Korea to seek better economic futures. His wife, also a factory worker, quit her job and went to South Korea, while Mr. Ho concentrated on earning further promotions and extending his social network in Yanbian. Mr. Ho had a prestigious position in a good work unit, so the couple believed that his wife's departure for South Korea was a rational choice as a long-term plan.

However, Mr. Ho was reluctant to let his wife go. He was worried about the truth of a popular expression in Yanbian: "Once your wife is gone to South Korea, she will be lost in the Korean Wind." At the same time, he felt that she had to go in order to pay off the debt he had incurred when he purchased the family's new apartment. After she left for South Korea in 1993, Mr. Ho struggled to reconcile his feelings as a patriarchal male breadwinner whose wife was earning more money than he was. He filled his time with familial duties: taking care of his son, saving the remittances she sent, and transforming the money into tangible properties. His wise management of the remittances allowed his family to achieve material prosperity. Despite his and his wife's accomplishments, Mr. Ho remained anxious about her absence. "In order not to 'lose' my wife and manage our common future," he reflected once, "I have had to develop my 'secret method' to keep my wife for the last twenty years." This secret method was based on a belief that "taking care of money is more important than making money." Mr. Ho seemed to be afraid of both the constructive and destructive power of money as he gained material affluence from his wife's remittances.

These types of fears were prevalent in Yanbian, especially on the part of Korean Chinese husbands whose wives worked in South Korea. Mr. Ho's anxieties revealed how the creative power of money transformed his wife into a controlling figure. Because of her income, she gained power over many aspects of their marriage. For example, when Mr. Ho bought a new apartment with the remittances he had saved, his wife asked somebody else she knew to verify the actual price and condition of the place. Apparently, she did not fully trust him to spend her money. Although he felt horrible about his wife's suspiciousness, he believed that it was the consequence of her labors and the sacrifice of her body and youth. He also believed that the money, in fact, belonged to her, and there was little he could say against her. At the same time, he was anxious about his wife's growing freedom and worried that she might have affairs with Korean men, whom he imagined as cooler and more sophisticated than Korean Chinese men, based on his experience viewing South Korean soap operas. Despite his loneliness and frustration, however, he could not imagine having an affair with another woman. "If I had an affair, I would lose my wife, my money, and all that I have made. How could I dare think of such a thing?" After observing many cases where waiting partners' extravagant spending of remittances ended in divorce, Mr. Ho was convinced that his proper financial stewardship was the core element strengthening his long-distance marriage.

Mr. Ho's concerns crystalized when he visited his wife in South Korea after three years. He was eager to see the capitalist "home" country but even more eager to see his wife. He was excited about the trip, and he imagined how emotional, moving, and arousing the encounter would be. He repeatedly practiced the right words to express his love for his wife. However, when he met her in Seoul, he was disappointed. All she talked about was money: "My wife was very cold toward me. I had dreamt intensely about having sex with her. But she seemed to have no interest in me. She 'gave' herself to me only once and was in fact very reluctant. We had not seen each other in three years. I wondered what had happened. Is this because of capitalism?" His wife, Mr. Ho believed, had developed a strong attachment to money as a result of her long and harsh labors, more than twelve hours a day for years in exploitative conditions. All she seemed to be concerned about was money—the way in which her "blood money" should be spent, saved, and managed.

I think Mr. Ho's wife's obsession with money can be viewed from two different angles. First, it reflects a desperation to claim a hidden relationship between her work and its outcome. Money is an emblem of her investment of time, health, youth, and loneliness: a biography of her labor over the last twenty years. These financial objects act as her alter ego, a manifestation of herself that needs to be well managed and preserved in

4.3 Photograph from an article titled "Wife Gone to South Korea to Marry" in the magazine *Yanbian Women*, October 1995.

whatever form it takes. Second, money demonstrates its transformative power in reshaping the couple's relationship and subjectivity. Mr. Ho's wife converted herself from a docile wife working in a low-level factory job into a breadwinner who controlled the family's financial fortunes. At the same time, Mr. Ho—a self-defined patriarchal Korean Chinese man—dedicated himself to "caring work," normally considered the province of the wife, all the while catering to her directives. Despite the material affluence that he was able to achieve because of his wife's remittances, Mr. Ho had to develop a "secret method" to tame the transformative power of money and the unpredictable desires of his wife in more creative ways. He did this by overseeing the expansion of the family's wealth and the maintenance of their home to which his wife would (hopefully) want to return. In these competing goals and accumulating conflicts, we can see how remittances have acquired their own agency and act both as a means and as an end.

Remittances as Promises of Love

In Yanbian, I have witnessed different kinds of and strategies for waiting, but all of them demand the core trait of patience, which Giovanni Gasparini characterizes as "an ability to await events" and "the full acceptance of the other's time" (Gasparini 1995, 42).[15] Here, I would like to go beyond the meaning of waiting as a form of gift exchange—a relationship between a gift and its return—by thinking further about the role of the promise for a separated, transnational couple.[16] In reality, people must cope with broken promises, as we saw when Bokja's husband betrayed her both emotionally and economically. When waiting is conditioned by factors beyond individual control, such as state policy changes, evictions, or new housing developments, it becomes more oppressive because it undermines the individual's or the family's ability to plan economic and social activities (Harms 2013). An overabundance of unstructured waiting time indicates a form of precarity, social suffering, and social exclusion. As recent ethnographies on waiting have highlighted, those who are waiting experience boredom and suffer from high unemployment due to post-socialist development and neoliberal economic restructuring (Harms 2013; Jeffrey 2010; Mains 2007; Masquelier and Durham 2023; O'Neil 2014).[17] Yet waiting is not an entirely passive, powerless, and unproductive condition, or a mere consequence of structural violence. As Craig Jeffrey points out, waiting can be transformed into an opportunity to make social connections (Jeffrey 2010). Instead of anxiously waiting for something to end or to happen, those who wait can create economic value by producing not things but social connections that turn possibilities into realities (Harms 2013). In fact, "skillful waiting" produces a subject who is suited to the speed and contingency of late capitalism (Chua 2011).

I have heard many Korean Chinese migrants and their families accept long-term separation as a "necessary life phase for a better life."[18] The embrace of waiting in everyday life leads me to understand that waiting has resulted in an interpersonal and intersubjective temporality that binds two people, such as separated partners. I view the waiting caused by separation as a form of work practiced alongside a series of substitute meaningful jobs; for example, waiting for partners while taking care of children or investing remittances. Thus, waiting is a special domain that creates a particular affect and sense of temporality—the present of the future. Waiting is not, I would argue, the act of doing nothing in a void of time and space but rather consists in doing something special at a given time, creating new arrangements and new meanings.

Mr. Ho's story articulates how waiting and remittances represent a coeval embodiment of both promise and love, in support of a family's future through a deferral of togetherness in the fluctuation of the Korean dream. Mr. Ho had to effectively reimburse his wife by providing competent care for the money she sent; this was a way of showing his appreciation for her labor. As Mr. Ho told me, "I have always felt indebted to my wife. But I know my wife and I are mutually indebted to each other." The mutual debt between Mr. Ho and his wife must be repaid at a given time; this is because the debt, which generated waiting by manifesting the desire for possibility (C. Han 2012), provided the condition for continuing their marriage relationship. Mr. Ho was waiting for his wife's return home, and his wife was waiting to return to China. They had each endured distinct kinds of waiting in different places, and they had each engaged in particular forms of attending to financial resources. Waiting bound these two parties together, conditioning their interpersonal subjectivity.

Caring for money, however, did not prove to be sufficient for Mr. Ho to sustain his long-term, separated relationship. In part, this was due to the fungible quality of remittances: they are of ambiguous ownership, never fully belonging to anyone. Mr. Ho's wife's control over their money proved more powerful than he had imagined.

> One day I lent some money to my mother because she needed a security deposit to buy a new apartment. I did not tell my wife because I thought it was a trivial matter. Yet when she found out she became incredibly furious. She could not stop crying for several days and did not talk to me for a week. I had simply lent money to my mother! Wow! Since then I have realized how important the money is to her and also that I'm not supposed to touch the money under my control. I thought it was *our* money that needed my caring and management.

After discovering that the remittances could not be spent without her permission, Mr. Ho felt powerless because he felt as though he did not have any right to use the money, even though he was responsible for safeguarding it and increasing its value.

> I have never been selfish about the money. Thinking of her, I have done so much work here in Yanbian waiting for her to return. Is waiting easy work to do? I have had to play multiple roles to fill her absence as a

mother, father, and teacher. Waiting has killed me for the last twenty years. Loneliness has been the source of all my diseases. I say to myself, I deserve better than this!

Even though he managed their money and properties over the years, Mr. Ho's obligation seemed to remain unfulfilled. He felt cheated, in a sense, because his wife was never satisfied with his efforts. Waiting, for Mr. Ho, entailed the sensation of being stuck. But as he found, waiting is a kind of labor that often goes unappreciated. Mr. Ho believed that he had paid back the hardship of his wife's labor, but his wife apparently did not agree. In her view, the transaction was never fully completed, thus leaving both of them with a seemingly unpaid debt.

Mr. Ho kept emphasizing to me that his waiting as a *pot'ori* should be recognized in economic terms as well, because the remittances required his efforts to be transformed into property and wealth. He came to feel, though, that the insufficiently recognized labor of waiting undermined his masculinity and made him undervalued by his wife. Even though Mr. Ho was not the person earning the money, he was the one responsible for spending it, and yet his expenditures were subject to his wife's supervision. Their ability to imagine a common future was contingent on a mutual promise, one that turned out to be breakable and fragile. In the context of this uncertainty, Mr. Ho's "secret method" of preserving and investing their financial resources was the only technique that could demonstrate his love and appease his anxious waiting. Mr. Ho tried to believe that "where money is saved, my wife returns." At the same time, this bond was revealed as highly fragile, since the flow of money could stop whenever the love did. Money and love were thus connected as well as separated in a vulnerable spousal relationship navigating a transnational, migratory, and remittance-inspired setting.

Conclusion

This chapter has explored waiting as another critical dimension of transnational temporality that has sustained the Korean dream. Waiting for remittances, a form of money—a gift as well as commodity that entails a temporality of deferring the present togetherness of couples—has a transformative power that dramatically destabilizes the gendered roles and dynamics previously shared by Yanbian Korean Chinese couples.[19]

Analyzing the anxiety stemming from the uncertain futures and long waits for partners predominant in a context of transnational migration, I have shown how the anticipatory emotion of "not-yet-consciousness" cuts across the liminality between present and future time and produces a particular image of the future.[20]

Waiting is work. Korean Chinese who wait in Yanbian do not work directly for money but rather for the potential of making or receiving money, as they sustain the affective thread between mobility and immobility. Waiting is work because the act of waiting is a means of motivating two parties to remain together, committed as part of a larger circuit of migration and remittances. But the work of waiting is not always appreciated, nor is it necessarily monetarily rewarded as a form of waged labor. Waiting is part of an intersubjective project for couples, a kind of future-making strategy necessary to survive life in an increasingly competitive China. Here, I emphasize the future not as a stable temporality or psychological state but rather as a malleable set of possibilities that waiting partners actively manipulate in order to overcome uncertainty and despair. Two parties—sender and receiver—exchange and share not only economic value but also a particular responsibility for the future of their family in the name of love. Although the two parties may be eager to create a mutual futurity and sociality through the labor of waiting, their affinities may draw them into precarious conditions. This precarious condition extends beyond the personal level. As many Korean Chinese migrants have testified, "However much money I have earned in South Korea, my hands are still empty." China has rapidly become a much more expensive place than the country they left decades ago. The necessity to survive in China pulls Korean Chinese migrants back into the circuit of migration; they must return to South Korea in order to keep pace with economic development in Yanbian. The work of waiting continues not only under the pressures of visa regulation but also under the obligation to maintain new lifestyles and expectations in China. Thinking again of Mr. Ho's secret method, his proposition that "taking care of money is more important than making money," I believe that the essence of the work of waiting lies in this vulnerable interdependency between money and love, between waiting and working. As the Yanbian saying goes, "Where money goes, love is." Waiting is an im/mobile unwaged affective labor that continues to drive circuits of migration in the flux of the Korean dream. The next section, Part III, describes the rise of some competing dreams and a new interpretation of the Korean dream—dreaming anew.

Dreaming Anew

The Leaving and the Living

The force of the Korean wind is especially apparent across Yanji, the capital of Yanbian. One can often hear the sound of fireworks celebrating the opening of new businesses, as well as noise coming from the demolition of old buildings soon to be replaced by new high-rises (*diantilou*, "building with elevators" in Chinese). The lively streets of downtown are full of the high-pitched voices of sellers, haggling customers, and South Korean songs (which are widely enjoyed by Korean Chinese). On weekends, the restaurants, massage parlors, saunas, and karaoke bars are full. One often has to wait in long lines to find an empty room at the fancier karaoke bars or massage parlors. Taxis are lined up waiting to take home the nighttime customers. This small city is well set up for customers to spend money, twenty-four hours a day, on eating, drinking, singing, dancing, and massages. Within this landscape, there is a constant flow of Han Chinese and Korean Chinese flocking into Yanji, not only from the countryside of Yanbian but also from other Chinese cities, to serve the newly developing consumption industries and to enjoy the results of the rapid urbanization of the region. There is a strong local belief that this culture of consumption and migration would not have been possible without (South) Korean money, a development heavily dependent on the flow and temporality of remittances.

Although the migration-development nexus clearly enlivens Yanbian, an economy based primarily on remittances cannot be stable or predictable.[1] Until 2008, the equivalent of US$1 billion per year in remittances flowed from South Korea to Yanbian, according to unofficial Yanbian customs statistics. But the global financial crisis in 2008 caused the influx to drop to about US$700 million per year because of the sharp depreciation of the South Korean won, the country's currency. As the won recovered, Korean Chinese rushed to change won into yuan, the Chinese currency.[2] The flow of remittances is thus volatile, fluctuating with the contemporary interconnected global economy. The Yanbian economy is, in turn, highly sensitive to these unstable money flows and shifts in currency exchange rates.

5.1 Downtown district of Yanji, Yanbian, China 2009. Photo by the author.

A conversation I had with a Han Chinese taxi driver illustrates the volatile characteristics of remittance-driven development. The driver, a migrant from the countryside of Heilongjiang, emphasized the high levels of spending in Yanbian, particularly by Korean Chinese.

> Most of my customers are Korean Chinese. Korean Chinese spend money like water. When the South Korean economy is good, my business is good because Korean Chinese make more and spend more. They think that when it runs out, they can go back to South Korea to make more. I came to Yanbian to become a taxi driver because I heard that Korean Chinese are good at spending money like that. It's hard for us Han Chinese to go to South Korea. Thus, we have to make ends meet in China. We cannot spend money like Korean Chinese.

This taxi driver's comments exemplify certain ethnic stereotypes widely circulated in Yanbian. At the same time, his story demonstrates the interdependency and differentiated mobility between Korean Chinese and Han Chinese, accelerated by the Korean Wind and Korean money. The common trajectory of Yanji nightlife, which is usually dinner followed by karaoke, a massage, and lamb skewers over drinks, seems to be generated and maintained by different kinds and scales of migration. Remittance development occurs on multiple scales—transnational and internal, rural and urban, small city and large city—collapsed together and co-present in the complex migration narratives that produce the ethnic and financial cityscape of Yanji.

I cover three main points in this chapter. First, I explore the way that Korean Chinese have attempted to redefine Yanji in response to the Korean Wind. Yanji, which is considered an ethnic hub as well as ethnic enclave (see chapter 1), engenders mixed feelings in Korean Chinese as they interact more and more with the "external" world.[3] Focusing on multiscalar migration, I analyze the new ways in which Korean Chinese have related to Yanbian as the region is continuously remade, largely by the Korean Wind. Second, I examine how transnational migration has become intertwined with Han Chinese and Korean Chinese internal migration. In particular, my interest is centered on the ambivalence between "leaving and living" as a dominant structure of feeling among Korean Chinese. Third, I investigate the ripple effect caused by the Korean Wind. Here, I am attentive to "differentiated mobility" (Massey 1993, 61) by ethnicity (between Han and Korean Chinese) in transnational migration, a mobility driven by the uneven and unequal positioning of different groups and persons in relation to various flows and movements (Chu 2009, 10).[4] How have Han Chinese and Korean Chinese appropriated and reacted differently to the Korean Wind? In what ways have these two distinctive ethnic groups converged and diverged from each other in the context of remittance development? The following shows that the Korean Wind has stirred an ethnically specific mobility and created a deep interdependency between Han and Korean Chinese, both of whom have become distinctively connected to the flow of South Korean money and the remittance development of the region in conjunction with global economic changes.

An Ethnic Hub in Flux

One encounter with a Han Chinese businessman, Mr. Wang, whom I got to know through one of his Korean Chinese colleagues, was particularly informative about the shifting population composition of Yanbian. Mr. Wang was in his mid-forties and had moved from northern Heilongjiang to Yanji in search of better economic opportunities fifteen years earlier. Despite Yanji's small size, marginal location, and strong Korean Chinese culture, Mr. Wang was drawn to the city by its business potential due to the influx of remittances from South Korea. He and several friends moved around the same time, following the rumor of Yanbian's economic rise and related possibilities. He eventually ended up working in the interior decorating business, which has flourished in Yanji along with the increasing construction of modern apartments, mostly purchased by Korean Chinese migrants. Mr. Wang considered himself a success and had become well settled in the city. He was clearly proud of his knowledge of Korean Chinese culture as well as his ability to analyze Yanji's market conditions. During lunch together, he demonstrated his insight into Yanbian's economy with a joke about its "three industries." He told us that Yanbian's "heavy industry" is its *pulgogi* restaurants, because smoke comes out of the chimneys; the region's "light industry" is karaoke, because it is a service and leisure industry; and Yanbian's "handcrafting industry" is massage, because it involves work with the hands. Everyone at the lunch laughed at his joke, implicitly agreeing with him. The joke conveyed, of course, a keen understanding of the pleasure-centered consumption industries that have come to occupy a central position in the everyday life of Yanji. These leading industries—*pulgogi* restaurants, karaoke bars, massage parlors—are what keep the neon signs of the city lit up day and night, driving the main engine of the city's economy.

At the same time, I understood Mr. Wang's joke as poking fun at the city, implying that Yanji was a marginal place lacking in the "real" jobs that belong to stable and regular work units (*danwei*). In other words, the joke portrays Yanbian, and especially its capital, Yanji, as a place where people do not work to produce things but only consume and spend for immediate gratification. Most of all, the joke made fun of Korean Chinese who had developed a dependency on "Korean money." In this context, Korean money carries a double connotation: it is understood as a corrupting influence that can make Korean Chinese lazy and extravagant, unwilling to work hard in China as they instead dream of leaving for South Korea; and it is also understood as the "heart" of a regional economy that provides a livelihood to many people in Yanbian—not only migrant families but also newly arrived businesspeople and service workers, regardless of ethnicity.

Each ethnic group has reacted differently to Korean money, resulting in ethnic stereotypes built upon consumption patterns and methods of planning for the future. Ethnic stereotypes have been described as "brushing against that of the other" (Chow 2002), since stereotypes are grounded on fixed ideas that prevent actual understanding of complex ethnic dynamics and subjectivities.[5] For example, Mr. Wang and his friends at the lunch joked in a way that repeated stereotypes: "Korean Chinese are all customers

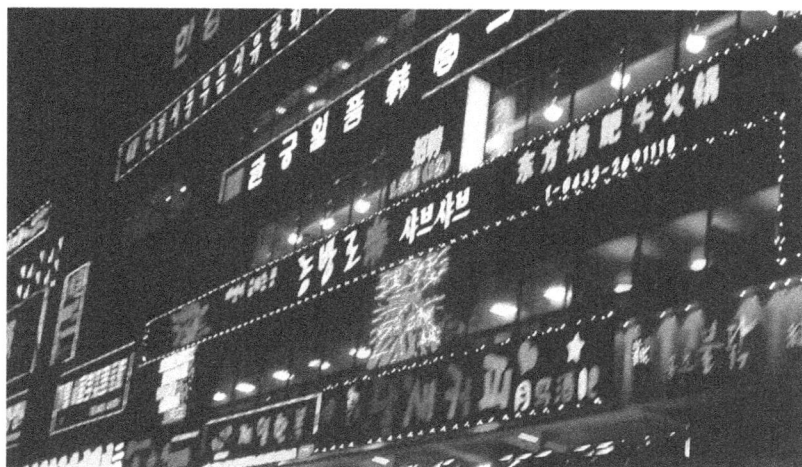

5.2 The neon lights of Yanji, a 24/7 city, 2009. Photo by the author.

who spend money for instant pleasure, whereas Han Chinese are business owners who make the money that Korean Chinese spend," and "Korean Chinese spend money without thinking of tomorrow, whereas Han Chinese save money without spending for today's pleasure." I heard versions of ethnic stereotypes regarding spending habits time and again, not only from Han Chinese but also from Korean Chinese—clearly a form of "ethnic contrast" (Sollors 1995) that solidifies the boundary between Korean Chinese and Han Chinese. Yet I would argue that, in contrast to the colonial context that Bhabha illuminates (Bhabha 1994, 112), these stereotypes are *not* simply an attempt to make "ethnic others" by essentializing each group in order to maintain an ethnic hierarchy. Instead, I view them in the context of "differentiated mobility" (Massey 1993, 61), as a demonstration of how each ethnic group has become differently related to the economy of trans/national migration and thus has created different routes and pathways to the future.

During my fieldwork, I noted strong patterns of mobility in Yanbian: Korean Chinese migration is primarily transnational, between Yanbian and South Korea, while Han Chinese migration is internal, into and across Yanbian. This means that Han Chinese are not immobile so much as differently mobile from Korean Chinese. In this respect, ethnic stereotypes, such as those voiced at the lunch discussed above, mirror differentiated mobilities by ethnicity that have developed in correspondence with the Korean Wind and Korean money. The latter phenomena did not cause or consolidate ethnic boundaries; rather, they have brought ripple effects to the lives of both Han and Korean Chinese in the wake of the "turbulence of migration" (Papastergiadis 2000), a turbulence that may seem chaotic but is actually well ordered through the interconnection and interdependence of various forces. Despite distinctively typified ethnic images—for instance, Korean Chinese customers versus Han Chinese workers—neither group is immune to the Korean Wind. Instead, both are subject to its influences, and ethnicities and broad economic and cultural forces together constitute a special ethnic and remittance landscape.[6]

I have underscored in previous chapters the way that the Korean Wind functions as an ethnically specific force among Korean Chinese who take advantage of ethnic similarities (linguistic and cultural affinities) to enter the South Korean labor market. This transnational mobility is not available to Han Chinese migrant laborers, who usually fail repeatedly if they attempt to get into South Korea through illegal brokers. As one Han Chinese worker glumly told me, "It is much harder for Han Chinese to get a visa to South Korea than Korean Chinese because we are not ethnic Korean, and thus less wanted in South Korea." Despite the far smaller chance of transnational migration to South Korea, Han Chinese do not remain exempt from the dramatic social changes generated by the Korean Wind.[7] The Yanbian Han Chinese who have not tried to migrate to South Korea have a different vision for their futures and have different responses to the influx of Korean money, which involves promoting their own businesses and chasing new possibilities in the domain developed and expanded by the influx of Korean money.

Jumping Scales

Korean money has enabled Korean Chinese migrant workers and families to move to larger cities, or even other countries, while also keeping their older houses in the countryside, to which they can return later in life. The migration routes that they follow are not always linear or coherent, in the sense that they do not always go to "better" or "larger" urban settings. Geographical scale matters, but so do politics, the economy, and culture. The multiple migrations that affect Yanbian encourage us to rethink scale and how we may take it for granted. Viewing scale as a social construct and "material artifact," Smith defines it in different ways: scale is the geographical organizer and expression of collective social action; scale is set or fixed amid the flux of social interaction; scale is the spatial resolution of contradictory social forces (N. Smith 2003, 228). The production of scale, expressed in terms such as rural, urban, region, and global, is both fluid and fixed (Jonas 1994). Scale is fixed (and politically charged), as in the case of national boundaries, tax issues, and identities attached to place. On the other hand, scale is fluid because it can be restructured by conflicts between opposing forces of competition and cooperation (N. Smith 1984). Social contention and interaction break the fixity of "given" scales, creating what Smith terms "jumping scale," a process and politics of uneven geographical development (N. Smith 2003, 229). Jumping scales could also involve a politics of representation, as local groups reshape contested political struggles across scale (Jones 1998, 27). Here, migration plays a pivotal role, as migrants appear to be "scale makers" (Çağlar and Schiller 2011, 12), engaged in readjusting and rescaling society according to the flux of mobility.[8]

The concept of scale and rescaling is especially useful in considering Chinese internal migration, a growing phenomenon that challenges fixed scales via deterritorialization and reterritorialization (Appadurai 1996). Since communist China was established in 1949, governance of its population has taken shape in three regards: location (household registration); quantity (the one-child policy); and quality (an emphasis on health, education, and welfare) (Greenhalgh and Winckler 2005). In China, population has become a terrain for the governmentalization and politicization of life, shaping a new social order and subjectivity. The system of location control, *hukou*, or family registration, is the most apt site to consider constraints on the rapidly increasing contemporary phenomenon of Chinese migration to cities.

Hukou has played a critical role in demarcating urbanites from rural people by restricting free movement and differentiating social benefits between cities and rural areas. When established in 1958, *hukou* represented the outcome of the social activity of people based on where they were and what they were doing, and yet eventually it became a precondition for social activity (Xikui 1998). It also resolidified caste and class, setting in stone the socioeconomic disparity between urbanites and rural people (Dutton 1998). Under the strict control of population movement, rural migrants who leave their registered homes to live in the city without city registration are called the "floating population" (Zhang 2001; Mackenzie 2002; Solinger 1999) and are treated as "outsiders," "second citizens," and "surplus beings" (Dutton 1998, 62–69). In contrast to nomads, an undifferentiated group detached from a place and posing a social threat as well as revolutionary social change, *mangliu*—literally meaning people "who have left, or been forced to leave, their own land"—are seen as engaging in no productive work, being out of place in the Chinese sense (Baoliang 1998, 63). The floating population is portrayed as an "amorphous flow" of laborers who can be expelled at any time after being used; they are considered internal others, stigmatized for being dirty, poor, and uncivil, and are seen as quite distinctive from "native" urbanites (Chu 2009; Zhang 2001).

Their vulnerability is exacerbated by "exclusive inclusion" (Agamben 1998, 7) and "forced flexibility" (M. Cho 2009). Deserting farming country for the city without an official *hukou*, these rural migrants, as "peasants," are excluded from state protection and market activity.[9] At the same time, they are included in the media and national narrative as the poorest, most miserable group that the state can embrace, thus establishing the right (however precarious) to be part of the city.[10] Under this regime of "exclusive inclusion" or "inclusive exclusion," migrants attempt to transform themselves into new urban subjects, inscribing civil, disciplined, productive, and responsible attitudes on their bodies and minds in order to improve their quality of life, or *suzhi* (see Anagnost 2004; Chu 2009; Kipnis 2006; Zhang 2001; Ngai 2005; H. Yan 2008).[11] The widening disparities between the poor and the rich, the rural and the urban, have come to be attributed to characterological traits, and it is argued that the achievement of a middle class position as an ideal consumer-citizen can be enabled by a transformation of consciousness (Anagnost 2004). The sharp distinction drawn between the urban and the rural has resonated at the heart of narratives of rural migrants adjusting to city life, as migration itself becomes a means of solidifying the migrant's role as "scale marker."

As I explored the turbulence of migration in the wake of the Korean Wind in Yanji, I found that scale markers—such as urban and rural—are determining forces deeply embedded in the subject-making process, governing who people are, where they are from, and what they are supposed to do. To this discussion, I bring an understanding of how transnational dimensions and perspectives intersect with internal migration, an intersection where scale jumping emerges as a dominant condition of living in Yanbian. In reality, scale markers are more fluid and flexible than simple registration distinctions, such as urban/rural, national/transnational, and Korean ethnic town/Han Chinese town. Migrants—both Han and Korean Chinese—are jumping between multiple scales, thereby blurring their *hukou* status, as well as the distinction between national and transnational.[12] I met many Korean Chinese transnational migrants who carry farmer's *hukou* identification cards but conduct lives that go way behind the farm; they may own a house and farmland in the countryside of Yanbian, but they also may own one or more modern apartments in Yanji, while also renting a small room in Seoul. If they are better off, some Korean Chinese purchase new apartments in major Chinese cities with rising property values, such as Beijing, Shanghai, and Qingdao, and rent them out as a source of extra income. These migrants frequently move between multiple places, regardless of their originally registered status. The scale marker—in this case, registration status—cannot fully capture who these migrants are, where they actually live, and what they really do. It is a new moment of mobility, as an old Communist Party member put it: "We [Korean Chinese] go to South Korea as we go to *our place* (*naechip* in Korean), unlike when we were afraid of going there several decades ago" (meaning under harsh Cold War circumstances or the tracking down of undocumented Korean Chinese). In other words, the Korean Wind has enabled something previously impossible—for example, farmers moving from rural areas to the city and owning apartments there without having actual urban *hukou* as a consequence of becoming transnational migrant workers in South Korea. They have embodied different scales by jumping different scales; they are migrant workers with rural *hukou* and metropolitan/transnational life experience.

What follows is an ethnography of the intersected traffic patterns and jumping scales of migrants who belong to multiple worlds in the post–Cold War, post-socialist moment. These stories are focused on those who conceive of themselves as living on the margins of Yanji, creating their own space with their own hands, often hesitating between leaving and living— the structure of feeling in Yanbian.[13]

Entrepreneur Farmer

While I lived in Yanbian, I rented a room from Ms. Ran, a woman in her late forties. Ms. Ran was a former rice farmer from a "pure" Korean Chinese city named Helong, one of several Korean Chinese condensed areas—along with Longjing and Tumen—long known for their vast and high-quality rice fields. When I met Ms. Ran, she was running a rental bookstore that sold comics. The store was located next to an ethnic Korean middle school in the city of Yanji, and Korean Chinese middle- and high-school students were her main customers. On the first day of each month, I would go to her store to pay my rent. As she gradually told me her story during my visits, I was struck by how little she matched the stereotype of farmers as uncivil, uneducated, and narrow minded. She had a sharp financial mind and admirable persistence, as witnessed by her determined attempts to make the difficult transition from life-long farmer to successful businesswoman and city dweller.

Ms. Ran had become an expert rice farmer while in Helong and had married another farmer from the same town some twenty years ago. The couple seemed talented in turning a profit—besides rice farming, they ran a store that mediated between rice farmers and wholesalers, collecting commissions by helping set up deals between the two parties. They were "getting rich first" indeed, as Deng had promulgated in 1978, economically surpassing most farmers in their town. Their financial stability allowed them to stay put even as the Korean Wind swept across the town in the late 1990s. Unfortunately, however, Ms. Ran suffered a life tragedy when her husband was killed in a car accident, leaving her a widow in her mid-thirties with a daughter and son to support. She was emotionally devastated by the loss, and her life as a farmer was affected, because she could not work the farm and run the store by herself. Farming is labor intensive, based on a gendered division of labor, and it is too much work for one person to take care of all the seasonal duties and chores in and out of the rice field. She made some decisions, as she explained to me: "I could not be lost all the time because I had to take care of my children. I had to put myself together. I had to get the farm and the rice store back on track. In order to live, I decided to remarry someone nice in town, although I knew my neighbors would whisper about my marriage behind my back. But I had to find a way out of the swamp."

After she got remarried, she started living in two houses, one in Yanji and one in the countryside, and so could send her children to the First Yanbian High School, which was considered the best high school in Yanbian for Korean Chinese. She also wanted to continue farming with her new husband. In order to live both in the city and the countryside, she said, "I had to become smarter about money." She rearranged her money, investing in real estate and buying a new apartment. It is unusual in Yanbian for farmers to buy a new apartment in the city without first going to South Korea to earn money. She soon bought two more apartments to rent out (including the one-bedroom apartment I was living in). She repeatedly warned me not to discuss the arrangement we had: "You should not talk about your apartment when we visit our town and meet my husband. He does not know anything about it." Apparently, the other apartments, and the rent she generated, belonged exclusively to her. She was also responsible for her children's care, without any help from her new husband.

Her income was gathered from different sources. The rental apartments helped her to run and pay the rent for the bookstore. The income from the store enabled her and her children to make ends meet in the city, though just barely. At the same time, her new husband was taking care of her land and rice store in the farming town. Her multiple jobs kept her busy. She moved back and forth between the countryside and city, as a farmer, landlady, and owner of a bookstore. During the busiest farming season, from June to August, she was in the farming town to help her husband. But the rest of the year she stayed in Yanji, supervising her children's studies while running the bookstore, with the hope that she would eventually be able to get her son into the right high school and a good college.

Although Ms. Ran was successfully multitasking, urban life was much more expensive than rural life. In her home village, she did not have to pay for food: she had enough vegetables and animals (pigs, chickens, and cows) on the farm to feed her family. She did not have to pay rent either, since the house and land (which are leased from the government for thirty years and renewable for another decade) belonged to her. But in the city, as a farmer with no work-unit benefit, food, rent, and everything else had to be paid for out of her own pocket. Most of all, the costs for her children's education heavily weighed on her. Even multiple sources of income did not seem sufficient for the soaring expenses of maintaining an urban life and supporting her children's education. She sometimes seemed to waver under the economic burden, saying, "If my younger son goes to college, I would like to go to South Korea to make money. I might be better off that way than being stuck here doing so many different things. But until then I need to stay here to look after my children."

Neither "poor" farmers nor relatively well-off urbanites have been immune to the Korean Wind in Yanbian. My landlady, a farmer with an exceptional entrepreneurial sense, had witnessed both successful and failed cases of people going to South Korea, and she continued to hesitate over whether she should go to South Korea herself. She knew there was nobody who would look after her children if she did; at the same time, whenever she felt that the cost of city life was too high, she would reconsider the possibility. Ms. Ran's story demonstrates the degree to which the boundaries between urban and rural life, and between transnational and

5.3 An empty rice-farming border town, Yanbian, 2009. Photo by the author.

5.4 An empty border town with dry fields, Yanbian, 2009. Photo by the author.

internal migration, are not static. She was jumping scales, yet her fluidity was not random, taking instead a particular, purposeful direction.

Ms. Ran had limited the scope of her actual and potential migration to Korean-speaking areas—to either Yanji or South Korea. Going to Chinese cities—"Han world"—was never an option for her. Her hometown was a Korean Chinese town without a single Han Chinese household. As a result, she had never had a chance to interact with Han Chinese or improve her Chinese language skills while growing up. She felt uncomfortable even in Yanji, where she frequently had to deal with Han Chinese when she went on errands or did business. When she needed to meet people who speak Chinese, she frequently would take her daughter, who read, wrote, and spoke Chinese fluently. Despite her successful real-estate ventures, she felt as if she were illiterate in Chinese and this, in turn, made her feel uncomfortable with city life. She often told me that "as soon as I am done with my children, I will move back to the countryside where I do not have to speak Chinese." Her background had limited her scope of migration due to linguistic boundaries. And yet her desire for an urban life had been boosted by the ethnic education that the city of Yanji could provide for her children. The condition of Korean ethnic schools in the countryside had deteriorated, as Korean Chinese moved out and Han Chinese moved in. As a result of the sharply decreasing Korean Chinese population in the countryside, Korean ethnic schools (*Chosŏn hakkyo* in Korean) have begun to close. Moving to the city for the sake of their children's education thus often felt like an inevitable life choice for many Korean Chinese farmers.

The city of Yanji posed an economic challenge to Ms. Ran, even though she had been successful in managing her properties and business. She explained her monthly income to me, to demonstrate how tight her monthly budget was in 2009: she collected the equivalent of about US$200 per month in rent (US$100 from my room, US$100 from the other room); her income from the bookstore was about US$200 per month; the income from farming was annual rather than monthly, so was more difficult to assess. But she calculated that her total reliable income from all sources was US$400 per month, without any extra social pension or benefits. This was a fairly low income, compared with government workers who then averaged US$450 per month or more in Yanbian, in addition to benefits and job security. If Ms. Ran had gone to South Korea, she could have made more than US$2,000 per month, based on the exchange rate between the Chinese yuan and the Korean won at the time (without taking into consideration the cost of living in South Korea). Despite rapid economic development in China, the income gap between Yanbian and South Korea remained large—in her case, equivalent to US$450 (plus farming) versus US$2,000. Farmers like Ms. Ran, as well as Korean Chinese factory and *danwei* workers who have moved from the countryside to Yanji, viewed going to South Korea as a route that offered the capacity to maintain the comforts of city life by overcoming the embedded discrimination against rural people.

These moves to the city have dramatically reshaped the ethnic composition of the Yanbian countryside. Many Korean ethnic towns have struggled with a critical shortage of labor, as vast stretches of land are left behind by migrating Korean Chinese. Although the land is not owned by individual farmers, but rather rented from the state for thirty years (according to Chinese law), it needs to be re-rented and cultivated by somebody when the original owners have left for the city or South Korea. Since so many Korean Chinese prefer to stop farming and go to South Korea as migrant workers, Han Chinese farmers—who have a much slimmer chance of getting to South Korea—have started moving into these Korean Chinese ethnic towns in order to cultivate land "abandoned" by Korean Chinese. Some of these places—including my landlady's hometown—have refused to accept any Han Chinese, in the name of cultural autonomy and to avoid potential ethnic conflicts. But the dwindling numbers of Korean Chinese farmers has made it highly unlikely that these towns can keep up this policy in the long term. The land needs to be taken care of, and Han Chinese are willing to do it. Ms. Ran, like other Korean Chinese I spoke with, constantly worried about the Han Chinese demographic threat. "We cannot hear a newborn Korean Chinese baby crying while Han Chinese are increasing," she said. "Korean Chinese land is taken over by Han Chinese. We may be losing *our* land."

Despite these concerns, the desire for urban life is widespread, and the rapidly decreasing Korean Chinese population in rural areas means that these Korean Chinese towns will not remain ethnically pure for much longer. Many Korean Chinese farmers had come to believe that the cultural and economic gap between urban and rural was bridgeable only as long as they could make it to South Korea. In an ethnic hub in flux, surrounded by a transnational fantasy and its seductive potential, Ms. Ran still hesitated, wondering whether or not she should leave for South Korea in search of a better life, leaving her children behind; her hesitation was rooted in the large monthly pay gap she had calculated, equaling US$400 versus US$2000.[14] It seemed that it could be a worthwhile sacrifice and investment for her children's future. But she was still hesitating when I left Yanbian in the winter of 2009.

Laid-Off Factory Worker

The ramifications of the Korean Wind loom large not only in its capital but also in the small industrial cities of Yanbian. A brief history of the border town of Yuejing (a pseudonym) reveals the impact of economic reform and the open economy.[15] In June 2009, I spent some time with local cadres (Communist Party members with an official rank) in Yuejing. Cadre Yang invited me to a huge banquet, with local dishes and strong alcohol (*baijiu* in Chinese) prepared by the female cooking staff working for the local government.[16] Over lunch, served in a backyard of the government buildings, the head cadre shared with me his thoughts about the town's history and contemporary circumstances, and expressed his excitement about having a guest from South Korea (meaning me).

According to him, Yuejing was once one of the most prosperous towns in Yanbian, with a pulp factory employing ten thousand factory workers. But when the impact of economic reform hit the area, the factory, full of outdated machinery, became less competitive and almost went bankrupt in 1997. As the town confronted the crisis, a wealthy Han Chinese businessman from southern China (vaguely indicated as *nanfang*, or "south" in Chinese) bought the factory at a low price from the local government and started reorganizing it, bringing in new machines and letting seven thousand workers go. In fact, these layoffs—people called it "privatization"— had already been planned before the factory was sold. The workforce had been half Korean Chinese and half Han Chinese, but in the whirlwind of rapid privatization, most of the Korean Chinese were laid off or quit, whereas the majority of the Han Chinese kept their positions. Some Korean Chinese workers who anticipated the approaching turmoil began to open their own businesses or prepared to leave for South Korea. "The factory has now become a Han Chinese world," said the head cadre.

Following these large-scale dismissals, or *xiagang*, Yuejing, formerly a prosperous border town proud of its large factory, rapidly declined, losing population and local businesses such as grocery stores and restaurants.[17] Many of the former factory workers left for Yanji, either for better job opportunities or in the hopes of getting to South Korea to make a larger amount of money in a shorter period of time. Either way was challenging to Yuejing Korean Chinese, as they came from a small border town. Furthermore, once the laid-off workers left Yuejing, they would never return to their hometown, which had become full of vacant houses. The head cadre lamented: "There was not much our government could do. There was nothing here to keep people from leaving." The cadres working for the local government received raises and better benefits every year, and thus he never personally considered going to South Korea for money. But most farmers and laid-off factory workers had few choices except to leave Yuejing to search for work in Yanji or elsewhere.

Hoping to examine the relationship between the mounting unemployment rate and migration to South Korea, I met with several former factory workers who had been laid off from the pulp factory in Yuejing. I became particularly close with a woman named Kim Meihua, who shared with me her insightful thoughts on China's economic reforms. Meihua, in her early forties, had worked in the pulp factory for fifteen years. She was the mother of a daughter who had just started middle school. I met Meihua at a social gathering in Yanji. Her family had lived in Yuejing for generations and her parents had also worked in the factory; in fact, she had inherited her mother's position.[18] Meihua considered her life as ordinary for a woman of her age: after graduating from her (Korean ethnic) high school, she got a reliable job, married, and gave birth to a daughter. But eventually she found that her husband was not as hardworking as she had thought, as he quit several jobs. Meihua decided to open a grocery store on the corner of their street, hoping that her husband would take care of the store during the day while she went to work. That way he could have a more stable job, and their income would be doubled, although she had to borrow money to open the store. Another reason that she wanted to open the grocery store was that she sensed that the factory would not last long, as her co-workers had begun talking about what they would do if the factory eventually went bankrupt. The business got off to a good start and did well for the first couple of months, but then Meihua discovered that her husband was having an affair with a neighbor. The affair led to their divorce, which made her want to leave for Yanji in order to start a new life and offer a better education to her daughter. I asked how she felt when she first moved to Yanji. Her answer was a bit unexpected.

> I really think it was great for the factory to go out of business. If the factory were still running, I would still be working in a small city on the

border. Now I have come to Yanji and can see a bigger and different world. I love being in Yanji. There are a lot more things to learn and more opportunities to pursue. My daughter has a much better education—Yanji has better Korean ethnic schools, better teachers than Yuejing. The collapse of the factory, caused by *gaigekaifang* (economic reforms and the open economy), turned out to be a great benefit to me.

Since coming to Yanji, Meihua had not been able to keep a stable job, because she did not have any special skills, and she tried different things in order to make ends meet. She thought of going to South Korea to make money but decided not to, because taking care of her young daughter was more important. Her sister—who had already gone to South Korea and had opened a restaurant in Seoul—let Meihua stay in her apartment for free in exchange for taking care of her son who was a freshman in high school at that time. Because of these commitments, going to South Korea felt out of the question for Meihua.

Since she did not have to pay for the cost of housing, Meihua started looking for jobs she could do while taking care of two children. A friend introduced Meihua to the Amway business, which was then becoming popular in Yanbian. Meihua also sold life insurance on a commission basis. Working as a salesperson suited her because of its flexibility, which allowed her to raise the children while having multiple jobs. In addition, these jobs did not require higher education, and they looked easy to tackle, at least to begin with. However, it turned out not to be so easy to sell Amway products and insurance to strangers as it was difficult to convince them to buy in the first place and even more difficult to keep them buying as returning customers. In order to foster her skills as a salesperson, Meihua regularly attended classes offered both by Amway and by the insurance company. The classes were about methods of persuasion, building self-confidence, and developing modes of self-management, as well as cultivating the correct attitudes and behaviors for person-to-person sales.

One day, she invited me to her place and showed the class materials to me, explaining the importance of having a positive attitude, citing her class lessons. She thought that if she really believed that "my business and the number of my customers will keep growing," that belief would become a reality. Meihua was devoted to expanding her social networks, a crucial factor in both Amway (a so-called pyramid scheme) and the insurance business. She became a member of many online communities and participated in numerous social gatherings. However, since she was a newcomer to the city, her business was not growing as fast as she wished. Even though she was barely making ends meet, Meihua continued to insist that she was "happy with being in Yanji. I am learning a lot. The quality of my life in Yanji is much better than when I was working at the factory." Most of all, Meihua was proud that she could give her daughter a better education in the city.

Meihua's move to Yanji illustrates the contradictory aspects of urban life after economic reform. She lost what was supposed to be lifelong security in her hometown; however, this loss and the consequent insecurity also represented an opportunity, one that enabled her to leave a small and dilapidated border town and move to the larger, more cosmopolitan setting of Yanji. As she pointed out, "The collapse of the factory turned out to be a great benefit." City life felt free, exciting, and unpredictable to her, compared with the "same old, same old" life in Yuejing. But her new life did not give her job security. Relying on Amway and insurance sales did not allow her to make any reliable future financial plans. In addition, unlike her life in Yuejing, Meihua had to pay for everything out of her own pocket (other than housing). Meihua badly wanted to be successful in business without going to South Korea and working under the notoriously exploitative employers there. As a single mother, she was devoted to the children she had to care for—yet eventually she could not help considering going to South Korea as a way to pay for the city life she enjoyed so much. She was seriously contemplating it by the time I left Yanbian in 2009. "I am not sure if I can support my daughter's college education without going to South Korea," she told me.

As discussed above, going to South Korea was for many years considered the most certain means of achieving prosperity, especially for those who prioritized educating their children and buying an apartment in Yanji and for those who had moved to Yanji without much social or financial support. It has become very common for Korean Chinese households to rely on Korean money sent by somebody working in South Korea. In the case of Meihua, her sister was able to send Korean money, which helped sustain her city life. But the influx of Korean money has also led to a surge in the cost of living and levels of consumption in Yanji; the city had become relatively expensive, given the income levels of its people. Many Korean Chinese migrants may wish to cut short the continuous cycle of migration between China and South Korea so they can rest from the exhausting grind of life as a transnational worker. But many also believe that they could not find equivalently well-paying jobs in Yanbian. These new urbanites, moving from rural or small-town Yanbian, find that they need quick, plentiful money in order to meet the expense of urban life in Yanji.

Surplus but Lacking Labor

Economic achievement via emigration exacts a "cultural price" that threatens a local culture and value system (Fitzgerald 2009, 128).[19] The cultural price is audible in local sayings such as "Someone drinking the Korean water [Han'guk mul mŏkta in Korean] would not want to work in China." The mockery contained in the phrase "drinking the Korean water" targets the small but significant behaviors and manners of Korean Chinese returnees. For example, those who "drink the Korean water" wear clothes and makeup like a South Korean but are not really South Korean. They mix a Yanbian accent with a Seoul accent, and thus they try to speak like South Koreans but cannot quite manage it. These failed attempts to imitate South Korean styles become an object of derision and taunting in Yanbian. Moreover, relentless imitation seems to be an evidential mark of "lacking." Those who "drink the Korean water" are believed to spend a lot of money to show off, regardless of their actual economic status. The common belief is that as soon as they run out of money, they will go back to South Korea because there is nothing they can do to make that much money in China.

Certainly, there is some hyperbole here, built on contempt for those who are seen as addicted to South Korean culture, style, and money. But the stereotyped image of Korean Chinese who return from South Korea as overconsuming is projected even onto their Korean Chinese children. A Korean Chinese college student whose father worked in South Korea for a decade recalled his time in elementary school: "We could tell kids whose parents went to South Korea from those who did not. Clothes, bags, shoes, and cell phones are the markers. They just look very different." A Han Chinese college student I met in Yanji, claimed that "Korean Chinese students spend money like water. They eat out all the time. They wear expensive clothes and shoes. Since there is no parent to control their behavior, they are spoiled and free to do what they want. A lot of them get in trouble. In contrast, we Han Chinese cannot afford to do that, and we grow up under our parents' protection, full of love." Stereotypes and perceptions of differing work ethics and future plans divide Yanbian along ethnic lines. Yet I also witnessed the consolidation of a certain ethnic interdependence and interconnection.

In contrast to some of my preconceptions, which were shaped by the Yanbian popular song "Everybody Is Gone" (see chapter 4, epigraph), Yanbian was quite lively when I first visited in 2006. The "three industries" about which Mr. Wang joked (mentioned above) were usually busy with customers. The amounts of money that young people spent every night on eating and drinking appeared to exceed the average income level in Yanbian. Interestingly, those who spent money "like water" were accused of having "backup money" that their parents or partners sent from South Korea, and they were expected to pay for the night. But this backup money was also considered a source of trouble for the Yanbian labor market, making Korean Chinese too lazy to work and unable to prepare for the future. The assumption was that Korean Chinese would not want to work in China, since they could not make nearly as much income as they could get in South Korea. David Fitzgerald explains how people assess their options in one labor market based on their experience in another, such as in the case of Mexico, where emigration is rampant and has great consequences for local economies (2009). The symptom is especially well exemplified by employers who rely on Korean Chinese labor. Mr. Cho, with whom I became a close friend, provides some sharp insights on this question.

Originally from South Korea, Mr. Cho was the owner of a coffee shop located in downtown Yanji, and he had become successful running several restaurants in Yanbian. Then in his early forties, Mr. Cho had decided back in 2000 that China would soon be a rising global economy and decided to come to Yanbian. Since Yanbian is a place where Korean is spoken as the first language, he thought that his broken Chinese would not be a great obstacle. He married a Korean Chinese woman, who also played a critical role in their restaurant businesses, and other Korean Chinese businesspeople call him "Yanbian son-in-law" (*yeonbyeonsawi* in Korean). Mr. Cho targeted Korean Chinese young people, the majority of whose parents have worked in South Korea, as his main customer group. This young generation of Korean Chinese enjoyed South Korean culture and mass media—music, movies, soap operas, clothing, and cosmetics— and accepted (and intensively consumed) Koreanness as a familiar part of everyday life. Most of all, these Korean Chinese youngsters were dedicated customers, supplied with money sent from their parents in South Korea.

Mr. Cho and two South Korean friends started with a pizza restaurant in downtown Yanji in 2005, decorating it themselves. He sold the idea of "modern" and "healthy" South Korean food, bringing an aesthetic of "South Korean culture" into the restaurant business. With a backdrop of South Korean songs and South Korean styles of decoration, the restaurant became known for its friendly service and pleasant environment. The restaurant was distinguished by its no-smoking policy, in contrast to most Chinese restaurants in Yanbian, and represented itself as "the South Korean place," providing South Korean food culture and a South Korean atmosphere. Whenever I went to the restaurant, it was always packed with young Korean Chinese—as well as a few young Han Chinese. As the restaurant gained popularity in Yanbian, Mr. Cho expanded his business to include a coffee shop, a "South Korean–style" Italian restaurant, and a fried-rice restaurant (fried rice was once a popular item in South Korea). By the time I left Yanbian at the end of 2009, the restaurant occupied three stories of a four-story building.

Despite his business success, Mr. Cho worried that his employees would quit as soon as they obtained an alternative job or spare money to rely on. "The most difficult thing about running a business in Yanbian is to find hardworking Korean Chinese waiters and waitresses (*fuwuyuan* in Chinese) who will work for the long term." Given that most customers were young Korean Chinese and that the three owners of the business were South Korean, he considered having Korean Chinese staff essential for good customer service. The young Korean Chinese in their early twenties who worked at the restaurant did not stay long. Nor did they work hard, in Mr. Cho's opinion:

> Young Korean Chinese are not desperate to work hard because their parents send more money than they can make in Yanbian. We pay around 2,000 yuan a month for *fuwuyuan*. This amount does not attract their interest at all. In general, parents working in South Korea feel sorry about being separated from their kids in the name of making money. These Korean Chinese kids just get used to easy money from a young age. A wage of 2,000 yuan a month is not bad by Yanbian standards, but they think it is too trivial to exhaust themselves for. Korean Chinese *fuwuyuan* quit all the time, making excuses about going to South Korea or going to larger Chinese cities. So we just have to hire Han Chinese *fuwuyuan*. They will stay here and work for years. It is truly difficult for us to communicate with Han Chinese, due to the language barrier. But they are much harder

working and sincerer. We do not have any other choice except to hire Han Chinese *fuwuyuan* right now.

Mr. Cho added that it was also hard to find middle-aged Korean Chinese to hire, particularly women cooks. Most Korean Chinese working in the restaurant considered their job temporary before they headed off to South Korea. As soon as they got their work visas, these Korean Chinese *fuwuyuan* left Yanbian right away, according to Mr. Cho.

Yanbian Korean Chinese were often criticized for their lack of a work ethic—for not taking their jobs in China seriously. "They keep thinking, if they go to South Korea, they can make several times more than what they're getting here," Mr. Cho told me. "That is why they just cannot bear another moment of being here in Yanbian." As a result, an employer like Mr. Cho was always in the position of searching for new employees. "I think half of my time is spent sorting out new job applicants and interviewing them," he said. "Once the new hire stops working, I start searching again." I met several other employers (Korean Chinese, as well as South Koreans) who, like Mr. Cho, were discouraged about being unable to find long-term Korean Chinese workers.

Although the Korean employers I met would sometimes try to resist the ethnic stereotypes shaped by differentiated mobility, such as lazy Korean Chinese versus diligent Han Chinese, they often reinforced them. For example, I heard that Korean Chinese think of nothing but quitting to move to better paying jobs, that they are dishonest when they manage company money, and that they are disorganized in their time and money management—in contrast to Han Chinese, who were considered more hardworking and dependable. These problems were traced back to one source: Korean Chinese have been spoiled by "easy money" sent by their parents or other family members, and this sudden material affluence has had a negative effect on their work ethic. As Mr. Cho told me, "There are so many Korean Chinese youngsters. But there are few who want to work." There was, paradoxically, a lack of labor when there otherwise might have been a flood of surplus labor.[20]

Practically speaking, however, these "not working" Korean Chinese are neither simply lazy nor lacking in a work ethic. In most cases, "not working" accompanies the special period of waiting to go to South Korea. These supposedly "idle" Korean Chinese believe that not working was a better choice, because they needed to be prepared to leave as soon as a visa was ready. This was not a matter of the work ethic of individual Korean

Chinese; rather it was a consequence of the fact that Korean Chinese futures are structured on the basis of an unpredictable visa regime and the constant, relentless waiting that accompanies it (see chapters 3 and 4).

I discovered when I visited farming towns that the "not working" symptom was also common in the countryside. Both rice and dry-field farming are too labor intensive for one person to manage an entire field, and if either a husband or wife goes to South Korea, the spouse who remains behind cannot run the farm on their own. The land is then usually rented to Korean Chinese neighbors or to incoming Han Chinese farmers. After this disposal of farming land, the remaining partner has to wait for their spouse to return to China, while living on the remittances sent from the partner in South Korea. Or the waiting person must also prepare to leave for South Korea to reunite with their spouse. Given that farming has a seasonal cycle, the farmland needs to be rented when the right person comes along to take over at the right moment.[21] Although the people "waiting" in this fashion throughout Yanbian tended to be thought of as "not working," they were, in fact, suspended in a liminal time and space between living and leaving.

Korean Chinese transnational migration has thrown Yanbian into flux, redefining many of its cultural and economic characteristics. Han Chinese have moved into Yanbian in search of new jobs as a "floating population," "ethnic others," or "ethnic minorities." These newcomers have caused ethnic discomfort to Korean Chinese, who have long been accustomed to Yanbian as a place of ethnic comfort. On the other hand, these ethnic others (Han Chinese) have emerged as an essential labor pool to serve the Korean Chinese customers who are enjoying the growing service sector in Yanbian, such as the three industries mentioned in Mr. Wang's joke.

Korean Chinese Customers versus Han Chinese *Dagong* (Workers)

As discussed in chapter 3, Yanbian does not feel like home to many Korean Chinese returnees, in part due to the dramatic increase of the Han Chinese population in the intervening years. It is typical to see Korean Chinese customers served by Han Chinese *fuwuyuan* (service people). Within the entertainment and service sector, massage parlors need special attention because they have attracted Han Chinese *dagong* (workers) from all over China. In Yanbian, a massage parlor is a common spot for people to visit with friends after gathering or drinking. Some massage businesses are known to provide sexual services "under the table," but most officially do not; they are public and open for twenty-four hours a day, with multiple customers getting massages at the same time in the same room, often with friends. The customers—young and old, women and men—stream in constantly, day and night.

Hearing about the high demand for massage services in Yanbian, many Han Chinese massage workers have moved to Yanbian—a kind of dream place for them, where they can make even more money than in larger Chinese cities, and with a lower cost of living. In practice, however, working conditions are not ideal. They usually have to work for twelve hours a day, with only two official days off a month. The income is unpredictable because it depends on the number of customers they serve. While waiting for customers, massage workers often sleep curled up at work, sharing a large room with dozens of co-workers. Night customers who visit after drinking and karaoke at 2 or 3 A.M. interrupt their sleep. Popular massage workers are frequently called by regular customers and make more money than those who are not often called. But they are always tired from lack of sleep, with their *qi* (energy) and health suffering as a result. They are pressured to disregard their fatigue, as the key in this business is to convert new customers into returning regulars (*tan'gol* in Korean) in order to maximize income.

I was able to interview several male massage workers from different regions of China. Many were from the Dongbei area in northeast China, especially from Jilin and Heilongjiang, but there were also some from Anhui, Shandong, and Sichuan. A Han Chinese man whom I knew only as Number 5 was in his early twenties and came from a small rural town in Heilongjiang (in the northern part of northeast China). After he graduated from middle school, he had been unsure of what to do. He did not want to be a farmer like his parents, and he had heard that massage could be a good way to make money and that Yanbian was a good place to go to if he developed his skills:

> I heard that I could make decent money if I went to Yanbian. It is because people in Yanbian, in particular Korean Chinese, like to spend money they earned in South Korea. I do not have much education or any special skills. So I decided to learn to do massage in order to go to Yanbian. I can make decent money, but it is a tiring job. Most of my customers are Korean Chinese. But most massage workers here are Han Chinese. Korean Chinese would not want to do tiring work like this because they think they can

go to South Korea to make better money. But Han Chinese do not expect this. Also, Han Chinese customers do not come to get massages because they are very stingy. Only one out of ten customers is Han Chinese. The rest are Korean Chinese.

Yanbian might not be the only "dream place" among massage workers, but Number 5's testimony helps us understand how Yanbian is imagined elsewhere: as a hotbed of consumption driven by Korean money and Korean Chinese extravagance. In addition, Number 5's comments demonstrate the ethnic distinctions often made between Han Chinese and Korean Chinese. He, along with other massage workers I talked to, assumed that Korean Chinese make money in South Korea and spend it quickly, relying on a continuing stream of remittances.

Number 5 told me that he had a difficult time when the financial crisis hit the South Korean economy in 2008. Remittances dropped off sharply, and some migrant workers and their families tried not to change Korean won into Chinese yuan, preferring to wait until the exchange rate became more favorable.[22] As a result, the economy of Yanbian stalled, suddenly lacking the generous cash flows that had been a major driving force of its service-centered economy. Number 5 reiterated the significance of remittances (Korean money) for his own earnings. "The more remittances get sent, the more money gets made in South Korea, the more Korean Chinese customers come to get my massages." It is undeniable that remittances have generated these entertainment industries and sustained a large part of the Yanbian economy, with its focus on spending rather than making, consuming rather than working.

Number 5's story underscores the Han Chinese migrant worker's connection to and dependency on the remittance-driven economy made by the Korean Wind. His story brings to the fore the intimately intertwined consequences of Korean money not only for Korean Chinese migrants and their families but also for Han Chinese businesspeople and *dagong* who rely on the influx of remittances for their incomes. When remittances decline, the whole economy of Yanbian, sensitive to such fluctuations, becomes vulnerable. Despite their differentiated mobility, both Korean Chinese and Han Chinese are swept up in the turbulence of the Korean Wind, which has actively altered the conditions of everyday life and reshaped the urban landscape of Yanji.

At the same time, Number 5's story pushes us to rethink the impact of turbulent and unstable flows of Korean money in conjunction with the global economic crisis. The South Korean economic crisis was instigated mainly by the weakened US economy. In 2008, South Korean financial markets, closely tied to the US market, tumbled when the US market collapsed due to the subprime mortgage crisis. Many South Korean companies went bankrupt, and the unemployment rate was at a record high. The service sectors, which were occupied mostly by Korean Chinese, shrank, while the sharp depreciation of the South Korean currency slowed down the export of goods. In this economic turbulence, the devalued South Korean currency especially affected Korean Chinese migrant workers, as they became victims of the instability of the currency rate; the size of remittances varies according to the currency rate of the day. Since the currency rate was disadvantageous to Korean Chinese migrants in 2008 and 2009, their income was cut in half as the South Korean won showed constant weakness against the US dollar.

On the other hand, the Chinese economy stayed relatively strong in the midst of the crisis, buoyed by state support of economic growth and protection of the currency exchange rate. Korean Chinese migrant workers began to return to Yanbian because their relative earning power was dwindling in South Korea. These returnees tried to seek the Chinese dream instead, starting new businesses in order to join the booming economy of China. At the same time, they were constantly frustrated by their inability to catch up with the rapid social changes that had occurred while they were away (I describe the returnees in chapter 6). When I lived in Yanbian in 2008 and 2009, I met many returnees who were suffering from deep anxiety and frustration, uncertain of the best path for their future, unsure of where to settle down. After much contemplation and hesitation, the majority of Korean Chinese ended up going back to South Korea, their once and future "dream place." The income gap between China and South Korea was not as vast as before, and the economic benefits from transnational migration were not quite as promising. Some migrants told me that they were too old or that it was too late to join the Chinese economic boom. Others said that they had just gotten used to working in South Korea as physical laborers and enjoyed the regular income. The Korean dream was gradually waning while the Chinese dream was still emerging. It may be that the fifth wind to sweep over Yanbian will be the Chinese Wind.

Conclusion

Focusing on differentiated mobility by ethnicity and the turbulent effects of the Korean Wind, I have examined the intersection of internal migration, transnational migration, and the remittance-fueled development occurring in Yanbian. Ethnic groups have developed different ranges and routes of mobility and, consequently, different life choices. Mobility brings interconnection between ethnic groups and mutual dependency on the remittance economy under the influence of Korean money. The particular hesitation between leaving and living, "jumping scales," disturbs the existing *hukou* system and enables the construction of complex selves that combine cosmopolitan, urban, and farming identities.

I wrap up this chapter with an anecdote of an encounter with a Han Chinese taxi driver who showed great pride in the global economic rise of China. As soon as he noticed that I was South Korean, he made the following confident declaration: "I am sure that China will be the greatest and strongest country in the world in ten years. We will exceed America, too. Let me predict, South Koreans will come to China as *dagong* (physical workers) to make money in ten years just as we Chinese have gone to South Korea as *dagong* to make money. Things will reverse as soon as China rises." Time and again, I have encountered this version of confidence in China's future that Han Chinese are proud of. This sort of preening became stronger and more common after the global financial crisis ruined the promise of the Korean dream. I increasingly came to believe that Yanbian has entered a phase of transition to the Chinese Wind, despite the vibrant remittance economy still generated by South Korean money.

Break the Cycle!

After my initial research in 2008/9, I revisited Yanbian for follow-up work in July 2011, with further visits in 2013 and 2016. When I returned in 2011, I could see that the capital, Yanji, had undergone remarkable changes in the year and a half since I had last been there. The city looked cleaner and had more high-rise buildings. As I traveled by taxi from the airport, which is on the outskirts of Yanji, to the downtown area, I saw many ongoing construction projects: the paving of new roads, extensions of major thoroughfares, and renovations of the main bridge (called *Henanqiao*) that connects the southern and northern parts of the city. The ubiquitous construction works, along with an obvious increase in private car ownership, prevented the smooth flow of traffic. Moreover, Yanji station had become part of the high-speed train network connected to Changchun and Beijing (the railroad was completed in 2019). The construction, renovation, and extension of infrastructure has dramatically reshaped both the urban and rural landscape. The high-speed train has dramatically shortened travel time from Yanji to Changchun, from seven-and-a-half to two hours, and from Yanji to Beijing, from twenty-three to nine hours. Many Korean Chinese migrants have told me during the years of my research about their confusion over the dramatic changes to Yanbian.

This chapter documents some of the hopes, frustrations, anxieties, and regrets of the post–Korean Wind moment, focusing on widely circulating reevaluations of the Korean Wind, in the wake of China's global rise. Some migrants believe that they have achieved the Korean dream, while others do not. Some are still pursuing the dream, while others are done with it. Some miss their time in South Korea, while others loathe the memory, as captured in the popular saying, "I would not even pee in the direction of South Korea." Korean Chinese migrants do not celebrate the Korean dream as they did a decade ago; they have started critically reevaluating and reflecting on what they have done, what they should (or should not) have done, and what they will do—now and in the future.

6.1 The new and the old together in Yanji, Yanbian, China, 2009. Photo by the author.

6.2 A sidewalk under construction in Yanji, 2011. Photo by the author.

6.3 Yanji apartment complexes, 2016. Photo by the author.

6.4 Reconstruction in Yanji, 2016. Photo by the author.

A common narrative has emerged from these reevaluations: that those who did not go to South Korea—such as government officers, university intellectuals, or entrepreneurs who took advantage of Yanbian's Korean Wind–driven boom economy without actually going to South Korea—are better off than those who did. This narrative implies a type of mobility that signifies a lack, whereas non-mobility (staying put in Yanbian) has become a marker of economic affluence and social stability. The emerging discourse contains a cautionary element: it discourages Korean Chinese from going abroad and encourages them to settle in China.[1] Local newspapers and Korean Chinese blogs celebrate the stories of those who have achieved business success without going to South Korea, and these "stay-at-home" entrepreneurs offer public lectures and attend social meetings to share their success stories and know-how. There is also an entrepreneur program affiliated with a local university, which helps students and alumni connect with social and professional networks. Particularly popular are stories of those who have made dramatic life changes: people who left rural farming and own restaurants, karaoke bars, massage parlors, or clothing stores. The media also celebrates the use of skills acquired in South Korea by returning migrants, who have been able to transform themselves from *dagong* (physical laborers) into *laoban* (owners). And South Korean consulting companies have entered the Yanbian market, providing coaching, tips, plans, and strategies for aspiring entrepreneurs in Yanbian's highly competitive business environment. The take-home message is that Korean Chinese should stop working under South Korean capital as *dagong* and should instead become entrepreneurs and bosses, managing their own money, businesses, and futures. Through numerous classes and social gatherings, Yanbian's new discourse of entrepreneurship channels ideas and methods of self-improvement into a comprehensive program, a kind of entrepreneurship of the self, for ambitious individuals like Meihua, discussed in chapter 5.

I see this social urge for an entrepreneurship of the self as one of the main characteristics of the current phase, which I call the post–Korean Wind. I treat the post–Korean Wind not as a linear phase clearly separated from the era of the Korean Wind but as a liminal social landscape. I explore the time and space of the post–Korean Wind in two ways. First, I shed light on the shifting meaning of mobility in Yanbian. Constant mobility has been an inevitable condition of life for the majority of Korean Chinese—nationally and transnationally—in the wake of China's economic reform, as discussed in the previous chapters. And yet, as China has gained status as a global economic power, non-mobility has increasingly come to symbolize affluence and stability—although it can still partially signify the condition of being stuck or left behind. There is an emerging contention about the concept of mobility, unlike when the Korean Wind began sweeping Yanbian. Second, alongside the increasing celebration of non-mobility, most Korean Chinese who have been migrants still have to move back and forth; they are not easily able to disengage from the circuit of transnational migration between China and South Korea, as seen in the story of Sunha and Taebong in the introduction. In addition, the migrants, who have become transnational working-class subjects over the last three decades by working in South Korea, tend to believe that physical labor, based on the body as the only means of production (see chapter 3), is more highly valued in South Korea than in China.

Looking behind the scenes of development in Yanbian (driven both by Korean money and China's economic boom) and the new Yanbian discourse of celebratory entrepreneurship, I argue that the post–Korean Wind is a critical moment in which tensions are escalating between the Korean dream and the Chinese dream. For the last decade, Korean Chinese have enjoyed freedom of mobility as a result of changes in the South Korean migration regime (see chapter 3), while at the same time they have expressed a desire to be free from South Korean capital and liberated from working under South Koreans. The Korean Wind is being rapidly recharacterized as an outdated fashion in the wake of the strong global influence of the Chinese economy. This chapter captures the futurity arising from this new juncture of Korean Chinese everyday life and borderland dreams in Yanbian. I also try not to dismiss the depression and dejection that some Korean Chinese migrants and returnees have experienced as a result of the tensions between these two dreams.

Be Entrepreneurs (*Laoban*), Not Workers (*Dagong*)!

In the social landscape based on remittances, returnees who had become wealthy working in South Korea often received positive attention, at least initially. The media celebrated their expertise, as well as their frontier spirit, characterizing them as ethnic heroes. But criticism of the returnees gradually increased as the Chinese economy began to pick up around the late 2000s. In these later accounts, most Korean Chinese returnees spent their time in South Korea as physical laborers without developing the sorts of marketable skills that could help them create their own businesses upon their return to China. After returning to Yanbian, many were viewed as unemployable, unable to compete in the new Chinese job market. And since the returnees usually did not belong to a work unit (*danwei*) in China, they were not eligible for pensions offered by the state. When the money earned in South Korea ran out, many had to repeatedly return to South Korea as *dagong* (physical laborers); these repetitive return trips became not a backup plan but a way of life. Well-off Korean Chinese started to look down on this transnational "floating population," whose work in South Korea stigmatized them as a lower or transnational working class.

Moreover, newspapers and Korean Chinese intellectuals began to warn that a trip to South Korea was a shortsighted decision. Once these migrants become *dagong* in South Korea, they would have to keep going back and face losing their social networks (*guanxi*) and social status in China.[2] While working as manual laborers in South Korea, these migrants became stuck in low-income positions. The creation of a permanent Korean Chinese ethnic working class in South Korea has also aggravated Korean Chinese subordination to South Korea.[3] Korean Chinese mass media and opinion leaders have encouraged migrants to cut off their dependence on South Korean capital, urging them to follow a new direction: "Be entrepreneurs (*laoban*), stop being manual workers (*dagong*)!" This discourse challenges Korean Chinese migrants to take advantage of the new skills and knowledge of technologies they have learned in South Korea and to enhance their *suzhi*, or civilized manners and "human quality" (Anagnost 2004; H. Yan 2008).[4] Korean Chinese migrants are urged to stop allowing themselves to be exploited by South Korean capital and instead create their own businesses and increase their marketability in an up-and-coming China.[5]

The government of the self has been contextualized by China scholars who analyze self-responsible post-socialist subjects.[6] Their studies show that the governing process is concrete but gradual, and aims to inscribe new attitudes of market logic onto bodies long habituated to what is represented as a rigid, state-centered socialism, eventually creating a new person altered by contact with ongoing dramatic changes in world capitalism (Dunn 2004; Hoffman 2010). Ethnographies of China, in particular, investigate a sort of neoliberal governmentality closely tied to a party-state-market complex, or "neoliberalism with Chinese characteristics" (Harvey 2005; H. Wang 2006; see also Rofel 2007). The party-state-market complex produces a self-governing subject not only by the application of external power but also by self-management. *Suzhi* especially emerges as a key discussion point in looking at the new working bodies fashioned to serve China in its role as the world's factory. Market requirements "individuate the body" to fit the requirements of machinery, thus facilitating efficient production in the factory (Ngai 2005); bodies must internalize work habits and a new sense of time, institutionalizing everyday life. The controlling logic modifies unruly peasants, remakes deficient and lazy bodies into cheap and docile ones, and generally requires the improvement of workers' *suzhi* (H. Yan 2008). The government of the self embraces the idea of self-improvement and economic betterment as an ethical project that market subjects should internalize and be habituated to.

In the midst of the celebration of entrepreneurship, the concept of *suzhi* frequently comes up in conversations with Korean Chinese. Within the context of Yanbian's entrepreneurship of the self, "entrepreneur" serves not only as a collection of essential attributes for a marketable subject but also as a repository of ethical aspiration: a status to be attained by improving one's self-knowledge and acquiring sophisticated social manners to become a "civil" and "cultured" subject. Here, my focus is on how the Korean Wind has played a role in shaping or reshaping the concept of *suzhi* in response to the emerging discourse of entrepreneurship of the self. Two groups—those who have gone to South Korea and those who have not—tend to develop different understandings of what it means to have good *suzhi*, or "human quality." The first group emphasizes transnational labor migration as a distinctive cosmopolitan or metropolitan urban experience, resulting in sophisticated manners acquired from South Korea, whereas the second group focuses on transnational migration as a life choice that reinforces lower-class manners and status. Exploring the competing social imperative for self-improvement and celebration of entrepreneurship in Yanbian, I suggest that a new interpretation of the Korean dream is emerging, one that emphasizes freedom—freedom of mobility and freedom from South Korean capital—and encourages Korean Chinese migrants to become owners of the self who can break the cycle of migration

After the Korean Dream

Long Journey

In August 2008, on a hot sunny day in Yanji, I stopped by a used bookstore packed with books published not only in Yanbian but also in North Korea. When I walked in, Mr. Guo, the owner, in his mid-thirties at the time, was following the stock exchange in one window on his computer, chatting with a girl through a webcam on another, and watching for shop-lifters on his surveillance camera. When he realized I was a South Korean customer (*hanguksonnim* in Korean) to whom he could sell rare books at a higher price than usual, he started bringing books out from the back. As we looked at the books, Mr. Guo told me he had returned from South Korea a few months ago, after having worked there with his parents for the previous ten years. During his ten-year absence, economic conditions had improved dramatically in China, and he found himself having a hard time "catching up" economically with other Chinese after he was back. But he was upbeat about his growing business. "You should know that these books are very rare and precious in Yanbian. I invested a lot of money that I earned in South Korea to buy these old books. I also travel to wherever I can to find them." As he gave me his business card, he asked me to tell others, especially other South Koreans, about his bookstore. He also handed me the business card of his mother's fortune-telling business, which was next door. "My mom is very good at fortune-telling. Would you like your fortune told?" I answered, "Why not?"

Guo's family had moved to Yanji from a remote farming town in Heilongjiang in the early 1990s. Guo's mother (I will call her Aunt Kim) and his father, who grew up in a Korean Chinese ethnic town and had an elementary school education, did not speak Chinese fluently. They left their hometown, a "Han world," for Yanbian because they wanted to feel at home surrounded by more Korean Chinese. But Yanbian differed from their expectations. In spite of the Korean Chinese ethnicity that they shared with the people of Yanji, Aunt Kim felt lonely there because she was treated as a stranger or outsider (*waidiren* in Chinese). They did not have any networks of friends or relatives in their new home. In Heilongjiang, the Korean Chinese community had been supportive and warmhearted, because Korean Chinese were a small ethnic group in a Han Chinese world. In Yanbian, Korean Chinese were everywhere, competing with each other. Aunt Kim felt that Yanbian people were too savvy and selfish, and thus hard to befriend. However, Aunt Kim knew that Yanbian was a better place for her to start her hair salon business with her skills.

As Aunt Kim's business in Yanbian was getting off the ground in the early 1990s, she began to hear rumors of Korean Chinese who went to South Korea for family visits and took Chinese medicine with them to sell, earning a decent amount of money in a short period of time. The thought of going to South Korea caught her interest. As the Korean dream peaked in the late 1990s, many Korean Chinese began moving to bigger cities in

6.5 Mr. Guo's used bookstore, Yanji, 2009. Photo by the author.

China, as well as to South Korea. The resulting wave of emigration caused a sharp decrease in the Korean Chinese population that made up most of Aunt Kim's clientele. One day a broker who arranged trips to South Korea visited her salon, and Aunt Kim was caught up in the desire to go there.

> Of course, it was all illegal, I knew. He asked me if I wanted to join his business or not. Since I had many customers coming and going, I could introduce them to the broker. That was his idea. By doing that, in fact, I made a fair amount of money. On the one hand, I ran my beauty salon. On the other hand, I was working with the broker. I was a so-called baby broker [*saekki* broker, who mediates the trafficking between different levels]. But one night I asked myself, why don't I go myself? First, I prepared a trip for my husband and my son. The broker helped us, and thus it happened easily. After they successfully got to South Korea through the broker, I closed my business and followed them within a year. Since I knew the broker personally, I did not have to pay as much money as others did. I thought meeting him was the luckiest thing that had happened in my life. I was so bold and brave, when I think about it.

For the first few years in South Korea, she worked as a waitress, like many other middle-aged Korean Chinese women. The labor was demanding, but she was making much more money than she had made running her beauty salon in Yanbian. Her husband was a skilled laborer and had no difficulty finding a job in South Korea, and her son was so popular with his South Korean bosses that they rewarded him with a higher wage than other Korean Chinese workers. The Korean dream was coming true for her family. According to Aunt Kim, South Korea was a very competitive and tiring place to be, and yet there was always the promise of earning more money through hard work. In fact, Aunt Kim felt more at home in South Korea than in China. She adapted to South Korean lifestyles and enjoyed being free to speak Korean with everyone around her. She viewed South Korea, and in particular Seoul, as cleaner, more organized, and more convenient than China. She thought that South Koreans were better mannered and more civilized than the Chinese. She was so satisfied with her life in South Korea that she was able to forgive the hard labor and exhausting lifestyle. Most of all, her growing material prosperity made her want to stay in South Korea, despite her family being undocumented.

Everything seemed to be going well until Aunt Kim injured her back. Unable to perform physical labor, she took classes to learn how to tell fortunes on the basis of one's date and time of birth. She was excited about her new career prospects.

> I started telling fortunes in the street in front of a subway station when I was in Seoul. Many random people came to ask me about their life issues. Also, many South Korean youngsters dropped by just to have fun, hearing about their futures and luck. The business was going great, and I was really enjoying making good money. But when the global financial crisis affected the South Korean economy in 2008, business slowed down. And the value of South Korean money was going down too. The South Korean currency was devalued by half against the Chinese yuan. That is why we suddenly decided to leave South Korea. We were afraid. We thought, if we stayed longer in South Korea, we would lose more money. As soon as we decided to leave, we packed and came back to China.

It was her son, Guo, who most strongly insisted that they should go back to China. He had become tired of doing physical work for South Korean bosses and was concerned that he would have a difficult time marrying if he stayed in South Korea; he thought that South Korean women would not marry Korean Chinese men and that it would be hard for him to find a Korean Chinese woman in South Korea. He wanted to start a new life in China by opening his own business and finding a young Korean Chinese bride in Yanbian. In the end, Aunt Kim, her husband, and her son were satisfied with their ten years in South Korea. They believed that they had achieved the Korean dream. Upon leaving South Korea they received "black stamps" on their passports because of their undocumented overstay in the country. This meant they might not be able to visit South Korea for the next several years. But they wanted to go back to China in order to catch up on the Chinese dream.

Settled: Be Laoban (Entrepreneurs)!

Aunt Kim and Mr. Guo invited me to their newly renovated apartment to celebrate the Chinese New Year of 2009. We made dumplings for her family while we chatted about different topics, and Aunt Kim reflected on her return:

> I really did not want to come back to China. But if I had stayed in South Korea, I would have worked as a waitress in restaurants or as a cleaning lady in motels until I died. I cannot work like that. In addition, the money we made in South Korea would not have been enough to support me into my old age there. With that money, however, we could start our business in China and secure the basic means of livelihood here. We can be *laoban* [business owners] and don't have to work under South Koreans. After returning from South Korea, we bought three houses and decorated all of them. My son and I also started our businesses. My life has been tough, with poverty and constant moving around in the past several decades. But, after all I have been through, I finally feel happy. This small office of mine is heaven for me.

Aunt Kim believed that "we should do something *for* ourselves and *by* ourselves, if we want to make real money." Her family followed the new ideas that celebrated entrepreneurship, spending much of the money they had earned in South Korea. They searched for the right location for a bookstore and bought new apartments to live in. Aunt Kim and her husband were excited about their new housing. They had never lived in a clean, modern apartment, and thanks to their newfound affluence, they were able to furnish their home with a wide-screen Samsung TV, new furniture, a computer, and a washing machine. Despite their rural *hukou*, Aunt Kim's family came to enjoy material prosperity in the city of Yanji—and it was the fruit of ten years' hard labor in South Korea.

Her roundabout journey appeared to have ended here, with a new apartment and a modern lifestyle; nearly everything they owned had

6.6 Aunt Kim's newly decorated home, Yanji, 2009. Photo by the author.

been purchased since her family had restarted their lives in Yanbian. Aunt Kim's warm, friendly, and welcoming personality had already enabled her to secure a number of regular customers for her fortune-telling business. "Because China is rising, Yanbian is rising, too," she told me.

> So, a lot of people are trying to open new businesses. When they do, these *laoban* come to ask me what their fortunes will be. Also, they ask me to come to perform a good luck ritual on the day they open their business. Those who are wealthy call me "*sŏnsaengnim, sŏnsaengnim*" [a Korean term that indicates "teacher" in a respectful form]. I am just an elementary school graduate from the countryside. I never imagined that the day would come when I am called *sŏnsaengnim* in my life.

Aunt Kim told me time and time again, "These are the happiest days in my life, given how much I have been through." Her "happy talk" seemed to have two sources. One was relief from not having to move any more, the fact that her family was permanently settled. The other was that she was proud of being *laoban*, owner of her own fortune-telling business and having earned the title *sŏnsaengnim*. Both her business and personal life have fulfilled the social imperative to become *laoban*. She has successfully engineered a completely new life in the aftermath of the Korean dream.

Her son, Mr. Guo, also worked hard to adjust to the new China after he returned. He filled his bookstore with a large number of Chinese, North Korean, South Korean, and Yanbian books. His savings from his decade in South Korea allowed him to build this extensive collection in just a few months. He was helped by his previous experience as a street vendor of used books before he went to South Korea.

> Whenever I have extra money, I go book hunting from individual sellers, early morning markets, and other street vendors. Even before going to South Korea, I already knew the value of old and rare books. All old things—old books, old pictures, old money—will come to have great historical value. I believe I can make a lot of money by selling these rare and old things. I have a good eye for the price and value of books. And I know who will be interested in buying them. Can you guess? South Koreans like you, who collect rare books from North Korea and Yanbian. They will buy my books, no matter how expensive. You know what my dream is? I will eat up all used bookstores in Yanbian in three years. My store will be *the* used bookstore in Yanbian.

To fulfill this aggressive plan to expand his business, Guo worked seven days a week. His mind was preoccupied with business: what used books to buy and how to sell more of them. In addition, while running the bookstore from 9 a.m. to 4 p.m., Guo would anxiously sit at his computer, trading stocks. The extra income from the stock exchange would enable him to buy more books, he believed, and thus he could arrive at his financial goals sooner. He was also developing an online used bookstore to target South Korean customers interested in books from North Korea and Yanbian. Since these books were mostly not available in South Korea, he knew he could sell them at higher prices.

Guo's family story shows us how the Korean dream has enabled a poor farming family to seek new lives as entrepreneurs in the pursuit of self-reinvention and *suzhi* improvement. Aunt Kim's long journey of escape from poverty—from poor farmer to hair stylist to migrant broker to fortune teller—has finally come to fruition. She has transformed herself not only by telling fortunes for her customers but also by making her own fortune. As she told it, she was born into a tough life and yet never stopped working to improve her situation. At the end of all her travels, Aunt Kim lives in a modern apartment surrounded by new possessions. Whenever I visited her workplace, she always said, "This small, humble office is next to heaven for me." Mr. Guo was also on the way to his dream. Whenever we had drinks or a meal, he would repeat his ambition to "eat up all used bookstores in Yanbian in three years."

After ten years of working in South Korea, a place believed to be a source of modernity and economic betterment for most Korean Chinese, Aunt Kim and Guo internalized and practiced the idea of entrepreneurship that Yanbian social media and intellectuals promoted for returnees, newly locating themselves within the rising Chinese economy. On the one hand, these returnees still embraced South Korean lifestyles; they watched South Korean soap operas and used South Korean products. On the other hand, they developed new entrepreneurial skills and new styles of networking in China. In this way, returnees' everyday lives are filled with different, and competing, symbols of modernity. I have come to understand the constant striving for entrepreneurship and improved *suzhi* as a series of gestures by former farmers and transnational workers who lack a real social safety net to protect their vulnerable futures. In the era of the post–Korean Wind, remaining in China—and *not* going to South Korea—has increasingly come to signify the adoption of a more modern and stable life.

Mark of Lack: "Going to South Korea"

The trajectories of the stories of returnees vary. Like Aunt Kim and Guo, some returnees were once farmers who would never have dreamed of living in the city if they had not gone to South Korea. The stories of Sunhua and Taebong that opened this book (see the introduction) exemplified the narratives of many other returnees from South Korea in Yanbian—those who become *laoban* but remained insecure about the unpredictable business situation and therefore still moved back and forth between Yanbian and South Korea. Taebong's friend Jungil, who had been a cook in South Korea for ten years, capitalized on his talent and successfully expanded his business after he returned to Yanbian. He opened new branches, one after another, and when I revisited Yanbian in 2016, he was the owner of five restaurants across the city. Some returnees lived on the rent they collected from apartments purchased with money earned in South Korea. Despite the economic achievements of these returnees, however, the position of Korean Chinese returnees had noticeably shifted over the years, as when Mr. Guo admitted his frustration at having a hard time "catching up" upon his return. But not everybody is as happy or satisfied as Guo or Aunt Kim after pursuing the Korean dream.

Criticism, even disrespect, of those who have pursued the Korean dream can be found among those Korean Chinese who are especially proud of China and Chinese economic success, including high-ranking Communist Party members. The Chinese boom has improved the standard of living not only for government officials but also intellectuals, entrepreneurs, and farmers. Government officials and university professors are enjoying higher incomes, and the latter are receiving increased research support from the government. Entrepreneurs have been busy expanding their businesses not only within Yanbian but across China and beyond. Farmers are receiving government support to fix their roofs and build indoor toilets (which used to be outside the house in rural areas), and they have been exempted from paying the agricultural tax since 2005. When I visited the Yanbian countryside, I often encountered a growing satisfaction with the Communist Party's favorable policies toward farmers and rural districts, and pride and confidence in the accomplishments of the Communist Party were prevalent, even though gaps between rural and urban areas remained visible.

In the midst of China's visible rise, Yanbian intellectuals and government officials often argue that it is unnecessary to go to South Korea. They believe South Korea to be a place controlled by "work-work" time (see chapter 3), and they argue that Korean Chinese migrants belong to a lower social class in South Korea, working *under* South Koreans. Mr. Long, one of the government officials with whom I had dinner one day at a North Korean restaurant in downtown Yanji, intrigued me with his critique of what he viewed as the "epidemic" of Korean Chinese going to South Korea. He insisted that "only those who have nothing special to do or no ability to break through in China have gone to South Korea." He explained why he did not need to consider going to South Korea, using his housing purchase history:

> My wife and I were offered a new apartment at an incredibly low price by our work unit [the Yanbian Zhou government] in the late 1980s when housing privatization had just started in Yanbian. We bought the first house assigned to me. Then we bought a second house, the one assigned to my wife. We did not pay much out of pocket. Also, I receive gifts and bonuses for the New Year or special occasions. Unlike us, those who have gone to South Korea have to pay for everything out of pocket. They have to

buy their houses at full price. They get no benefits since they do not belong to a work unit, let alone have access to "back-door money" [*twitdon* in Korean]. My life is far better than theirs, although I might have less cash flow. I have been able to make ends meet in China. So I have never thought of going to South Korea. Why should I?

When I met him, Mr. Long was in his late fifties and the father of a son in high school; his wife also worked for the government. After college graduation (he was in the first group of Chinese who took the college examination in 1978), he was assigned to a government job. Eventually he was promoted to a high-ranking position in the Yanbian Zhou government. As a prestigious official, he showed disdain toward those who became migrant laborers to South Korea:

> Fifteen out of twenty of my close high school friends have worked in South Korea. When there is an alumnus gathering, there are more people coming from Seoul than here—that's where the majority is. They seem to have a better life with financial stability, buying apartments and cars, and wearing clothes like South Koreans. But when you look at them more closely, their lives are full of problems and troubles. A lot of them are divorced. Their kids have gone astray. They have gotten sick or injured from the heavy labor in South Korea. Also, doing simple physical work for more than a decade under the bad treatment of South Korean bosses has made them fools [*mŏjŏri* in Korean]. They are incapable of starting a business and a new life back in China. They have made money, perhaps. But there is not much left over after buying an apartment out of pocket. Then they have to go back to South Korea over and over. They've got nothing but a South Korean accent, which is useless [said in a contemptuous tone]. Can we say that it is a good life, losing everything but a useless South Korean accent?

As we can see from this quote, speaking with a South Korean accent appears to be a criterion in evaluating the extent to which returnees have embodied the South Korean way of life—referred to as "South Korean water" (*Han'guk mul* in Korean). For instance, Yanbian people often make fun of Korean Chinese migrants who imitate the Seoul accent, "awkwardly" mixing it with the Yanbian accent. I heard many Korean Chinese in Yanbian say they were disgusted by bragging returnees who spoke with a Seoul accent and wore South Korean-style clothes. A Korean Chinese woman in her early forties named Okran, who returned to Yanbian to run her own grocery store, told me, "I have tried to use a much stronger Yan-bian accent since I came back from South Korea. People talk a lot behind my back. If I even slightly mix in the Seoul accent, they point a finger at me. People are sensitive to the accent. Having been to South Korea is not a proud thing to say, unlike before. Everybody has drunk the 'Korean water' and made money there. Going to South Korea is not a special thing anymore." Going to South Korea and speaking like a South Korean are no longer markers of high social status in Yanbian, even though South Korea retains a strong pull as a source of remittances, new lifestyles, fashions, and modern culture. Increasingly, having a South Korean accent or wearing South Korean-style clothing is instead interpreted as a marker of lack—a sign of being unable to make it in the new market economy of China.

By contrast, the perspective expressed by Mr. Long indicates confidence that his status in China is established precisely by distinguishing himself from those who went to South Korea only to make money.[7] At the same time, those who have been away from China for long periods might have a difficult time adjusting to the vast, recent changes, as Mr. Guo (the owner of the bookstore) indicated earlier. Returnees testify that they are under pressure from those who belong to privileged work units and those who have gained economically in their absence. The most successful among the Yanbian "stay at homes" tend to express their pride with a bombastic attitude. A social split is becoming clearly demarcated, as many Yanbian people bluntly say, "Those who did not go to South Korea ended up being much better off." Going to South Korea has lost the cultural currency and material potential that led to decades of rapid economic achievement.

Born to Be an Entrepreneur

During 2008/9, I witnessed the impasse of returnees faced with a slug-gish Yanbian economy as I met with a number of returning migrants from South Korea who were suffering from deep anxiety and frustration, about both their inability to land stable jobs in South Korea and the unfavorable currency exchange rate.[8] At the same time, however, the crisis brought op-portunities for those who followed the Chinese dream. Taking advantage of the strength of the Chinese yuan against the South Korean won, some Korean Chinese merchants bought products in bulk from South Korea cheaply and sold them in China at a great profit. The profit margins were much bigger than when the South Korean currency was stronger, before

6.7 Advertisements for South Korean satellite dishes, Yanji, 2016. It is illegal to own these, but Korean Chinese keep buying and installing them to watch South Korean TV programs. Photo by the author.

2008. Moreover, the strong yuan enabled Korean Chinese (but not migrants) to enjoy greater spending power when traveling in South Korea. There gradually arose a different flow of Korean Chinese to South Korea, one that included business and tourism.

In recent years Chinese tourists have become known as the main customers for imported, pricy products in luxurious South Korean department stores—the "big players" are all Chinese.[9] South Korean newspapers occasionally report that after Chinese customers visit stores, the shelves are left empty. Even though the stories about Chinese big spenders are not specific to Korean Chinese, I met several Korean Chinese merchants in Yanbian who were enthusiastic about the relatively cheap prices of quality goods in the Lotte luxury department store in downtown Seoul, a magnet for tourists. I met a businesswoman in her late forties, whom I call here Dang Laoban, who ran a well-known drug store in Yanbian, and she shared her experiences of traveling to Seoul:

> I went to Seoul with several friends of mine who have their own businesses in Yanbian. For a week, all we did in Seoul was shopping and

eating, shopping and eating. The seafood in South Korea was a lot cheaper and much better quality than in China. We ate until we could not eat anymore. I felt things were very cheap compared with Yanbian, and even to Beijing, because we exchanged Chinese yuan for South Korean won. Three of us spent more than 3,000 man won [30,000,000 won or about US$30,000] in the fur coat section of the Lotte department store. We kept trying on different coats. The clerks knew that we were Korean Chinese and assumed that we were not able to buy the expensive stuff. I could tell that they were not as kind to us as they were to other South Koreans or Japanese customers. But they had luxurious, good-quality items, and the price was comparatively low. We could not help buying the stuff. It was a great deal.

Dang Laoban's consumer power was unusual in Yanbian, although she was not the only one who could spend as much money as she wanted. The encounter with Dang Laoban, in fact, complicated my understanding of Yanbian as I had mostly experienced the region's deep dependency on the outflow of population and the influx of remittances. Additionally, she helped me rethink the spatial split that I discussed in chapter 3, with South Korea as work-filled, stress-inducing, and exhausting, and China as a place of relaxation, consumption, and recharging. That is certainly how the two countries appear from the migrant perspective. But from the point of view of newly rising, wealthy Korean Chinese merchants, the split turns out to be the opposite: South Korea is a place of consumption and fun, whereas Yanbian is a space for work and profit-making.

I was introduced to Dang Laoban by Professor Lan at Yanbian University, who had been friends with her since high school. According to Professor Lan, Dang Laoban was one of the wealthiest people in Yanbian and also one of the most successful female entrepreneurs. When we met for a couple of hours in her office in downtown Yanji, I was able to discern the natural-born merchant behind her calm and friendly manner. Her biography offers some distinctive points. Dang Laoban was from a small rural town in Yanbian and grew up going to Han Chinese schools, from elementary school to university. As a result, she was more fluent in the Chinese language than in Korean and felt more at ease with Han Chinese people than with Korean Chinese—which is quite uncommon among Korean Chinese of her generation in Yanbian. Dang Laoban explained that ever since she was young, she had tried to think of ways to make more money. She went to college in Sichuan. It took her a couple of days to get there from Yanbian by train. Whenever she came back home for breaks, she would bring goods from Sichuan and sell them in Yanbian. When she returned to school in Sichuan, she would take goods from Yanbian and sell them in Sichuan. Despite the stress and fatigue of carrying her luggage full of goods to sell back and forth, she enjoyed trading and gaining margins. She did not make large profits, but they were enough to get her through college on her own.

After she graduated, she was assigned by the government to work in a chemical factory located in Jilin City. It was a decent job, but she did not make as much money as she wanted to. In addition, after she got married, she wanted to buy the apartment assigned to her work unit, but she could not afford to buy it on her own and had to borrow money. She thought that this was a good deal at the time but did not like being in debt. So Dang Laoban decided to quit her job to find a better way to make money. She "took the plunge" (*xiahai* in Chinese), leaving behind job security in search of a new life opportunity, and she started her own business. Although she had quit her work unit, she could still rely on the network of contacts she had built there, and she began selling Chinese medicine in the early 1990s. Dang Laoban put a great deal of effort into gaining a better sense of her new business: she worked during the day and studied at night with medical books belonging to her husband, who was a doctor.

By the early 1990s, Dang Laoban's business began to gain momentum. Chinese medicine was in high demand in Yanbian, because Korean Chinese liked to take it as an authentic, special gift from China when they visited families and relatives in South Korea. Since there were few business dealings between China and South Korea at the time, Chinese medicine was rare and highly prized in South Korea in the 1990s. As more and more Korean Chinese came to realize its value in South Korea, Chinese medicine was transformed from a gift into a commodity. However, as waves of Chinese medicine began to flood the South Korean medicine market, the South Korean government tightened regulations, instituting a regimen to weed out counterfeit products. Large amounts of "inauthentic" Chinese medicine became unsellable and were disposed of, and as a result, many Korean Chinese who had bought Chinese medicine in bulk went into sudden bankruptcy. Their investment turned out to be a total loss.

However, even after the severe drop in its value in the mid-1990s, Chinese medicine remained popular because it was believed to be an essential item for Korean Chinese to carry to South Korea for their own use—for routine body care and for medical emergencies. Korean Chinese were accustomed to using Chinese medicine rather than Western medicine, and additionally the cost of drugs and remedies was thought to be too high in South Korea. As more people traveled to South Korea, the demand for Chinese medicine rose again. Although Dang Laoban never migrated to work in South Korea herself, her business expanded along with the Korean Wind. Dang Laoban, who stayed in Yanbian, depended on Korean Chinese migration for her material affluence just as much as the massage therapist Number 5 relied on the influx of remittances for his income (see chapter 5). Remittances have provided a critical thread that connects disparate subjects who contribute to and benefit from Yanbian's economy of transnational migration.

Dang Laoban also successfully diversified into a new business—a hot pot (*huoguo* in Chinese) restaurant. I asked her what the method of her success was.

> I just like to make money. Also, I like to spend money. And I like to give away money to the poor and sometimes my employees. I thought of going to South Korea. But then I would have to do some simple job like waitress or nanny. I don't want to do that—and I don't want to work under South Korean bosses. Those who go to South Korea cannot use their brains; they are only using their *bodies*. You know what? I cannot communicate with my friends who come back from South Korea. They have all become fools (*mŏjŏri* in Korean) after working in South Korea for a decade, while here I keep thinking of how to expand my business.

Dang Laoban summed up the main aspect of the waning Korean dream: Yanbian people were literally saying (as did Mr. Long in a previous section) that labor migrants who go to South Korea to do simple and tedious work become "fools" (*mŏjŏri* or *pabo* in Korean). In this view, Korean Chinese migrants are lacking in *suzhi*. My encounter with Dang Laoban highlights the rapid economic and social differentiation occurring in Yanbian, as a rising, newly wealthy class makes migrants/returnees feel left behind.

Proudly Staying at Home

The testimonies of Mr. Long and Dang Laoban demonstrate a new understanding of mobility in Yanbian—namely, that moving freely across borders is no longer celebrated but is instead seen as a sign of lack, of

6.8 A wine bar owner (*laoban*) who broke the cycle of migration, Yanji, 2016. Photo by the author.

inability to compete. The ways in which Dang Laoban and other well-off Korean Chinese in Yanbian understand mobility seems to be quite distinct from what has been observed in other transnational migration studies. For example, along with the rise of globalization in the 1990s, Aihwa Ong (1999) argues that flexible citizenship is a part of the cultural logic of capitalism that enables transnational subjects to have a more fluid means of accumulating capital and acquiring social prestige. In an accelerated transnational setting, wealthy diasporic Chinese collect multiple passports and challenge the static relationship between the state and citizen. Ong does not mean here that state control has abated but rather that nation-states and mobile subjects develop new methods of articulation with capitalism in the late modernity. In this era, mobility serves as a symbol of economic power and political potential to allow mobile subjects to negotiate with the state and market in search of capital accumulation. On the other hand, in a study focused on a later period of Chinese migration in the 2000s, Julie Chu (2010) discusses the experiences of Longyan Chinese who pay to be smuggled into the United States in pursuit of a better life, and she provides an account of their earnest desperation, often maintained through multiple unsuccessful attempts. According to Chu, "Immobility in all senses of the word—physical, social, and economic—had become the ultimate form of displacement in a post-Mao world boasting of forward momentum and global openings" (Chu 2010, 259). Chu sees mobility as a normative choice, in the sense that a majority of Longyan Chinese have pursued or hoped for it, and also as a necessary condition of modernity that enables marginalized subjects to overcome the stagnant and delimiting positioning of them as "peasants" in a "peasant village."

Even though these two books explore Chinese emigration in the different economic context of China in the global economy, the experience of Korean Chinese migrants might be analogous to that of the overseas Chinese or Longyan's peasants in that all three have pursued their dreams by becoming flexible and mobile subjects. However, focusing on the testimony of Dang Laoban and Mr. Long, we can also see a new set of narratives surrounding mobility, one in which some Korean Chinese have begun to mock the kind of mobility that evinces economic insecurity. This group of Korean Chinese believe that "non-mobility"—staying in Yanbian and expanding their businesses—is a symbol of economic stability and prestigious status rooted in local politics and economics. Mobility has become a less celebrated life choice because it causes migrants and returnees to lack sufficient social networking and thereby fall out of step in the lively, emerging Chinese economy. In the discourse generated by the current global rise of China, "non-mobility"—in contrast to Chu's Longyan research, in which she speaks of immobility as a form of displacement (Chu 2010, 11)—is understood as an effective means by which non-migrating Korean Chinese have achieved economic gains as they have embedded themselves within the booming Chinese economy.

Out of Their League

While I was studying the implicit but embedded social split between those who went to South Korea and those who did not, one lingering question concerned the actual dynamics and feelings between the two groups. One returnee named Sungchul Park, in his late thirties in 2009 and still migrating back and forth between China and South Korea, highlighted his anxiety by describing the widened social split in Yanbian in a tone of frustrated confession—how he felt about being back at home and the meaning attached to his work in South Korea.

> Now I feel ashamed of working in South Korea. If I say to my friends that I am going back to South Korea to work, then, they say, "You're *still* going there? What for?" They look down on me, I think. That's why I often just

say that I have a business in southern China—Shenzhen or Guangdong. I don't want to say what exactly I am doing in South Korea. I'm kind of secretively moving back and forth without telling the truth. I have no education, no special skills. All I have is my body [*momttungari* in Korean; the word actually connotes something more like "flesh"]. Thus, what I, as a Korean Chinese, can do in South Korea is nothing more than simple, low-end physical labor, by using my body. I have been working hard as well as spending hard. To be honest with you, I don't have much savings since I tend to spend money as soon as I make it. I just assume that I can keep earning as long as I work in South Korea. That is true for all Korean Chinese. But the job is boring, same old, same old. When it gets really bad, I think I can't live like this forever. But once my money runs out in Yanbian, there is no way for me to make it up except by going back to South Korea. I have a son and a wife to support, and there is a limit to the money I can make in Yanbian. I don't know what to do to make money here. I don't have enough of a social network to start up a new business. Here people spend a lot of money eating and drinking. If I kept pace with them, I'd go broke quickly. I have no idea where their money is coming from. When I meet these wealthy friends, who used to be poorer than me, I can't talk to them. There's something in common among them, but I don't know what it is. I feel like there is *something* that I am missing. I can't cut into their conversation. I feel out of their league, lagging behind what's going on in Yanbian and in China.

Mr. Long and Dang Laoban's denigration of transnational migrants as "fools" dovetails with Sungchul's feelings of loss and inferiority. Sungchul expressed feelings of embarrassment about staying in Yanbian and believes he can never be as well integrated into Yanbian as he was before. This new feeling of being uncomfortable at home has made him start reevaluating the gains and losses of his pursuit of the Korean dream.

His Korean dream began in the late 1990s when the mania for migrating swept through Yanbian. Sungchul made up his mind to go to South Korea and found a broker to give him fake documents. He recalled he was full of dreams and believed the saying, "If you go to South Korea, your back will ache from gathering the dollars." Of course, the rumor turned out to be an exaggeration, but his work in South Korea was fairly rewarding. He enjoyed the metropolitan style of life—the convenient subways and public transportation, clean streets, and well-mannered citizens. Sungchul witnessed the power of remittances, expressed in his capacity to purchase new apartments and fancy clothes. Sungchul, one of the earlier seekers of the Korean dream in his rural hometown, diligently followed it, determined not to live like his parents, who had been poor farmers.

Yet the limits of the Korean dream have been gradually revealed over the past couple of years. Many returnees that I met, including Sungchul, Sunhua, Taebong, and Mr. Guo, have accumulated anxieties, concerns, and frustrations pertaining to their life of transnational migration. The frustrations seem to be multilayered. First, the relative value of remittances has sharply diminished, because the income gap between China and South Korea has become much smaller than it was a few years ago and the exchange rate has come to work against Korean Chinese migrants since the global financial crisis of 2008. Second, remittances cannot be accumulated or expanded if the families of migrants merely spend it on the day-to-day cost of living without making investments. Remittances cannot work properly as a source of wealth unless the money is carefully managed and reinvested (as Mr. Ho emphasized in chapter 4). Third, unskilled, service-centered, low-end jobs do not promise a better tomorrow but instead the endless repetition of the same simple work patterns. Transnational migrants who have moved between two countries seem to be free, flexible, and mobile, but at the same time they are trapped within the transnational migration circuit as a cheap source of labor (see chapter 3). Taebong, Mr. Guo, and the owner of the wine bar in figure 6.8 all told me that they had gotten sick of going back into the cycle of migration. The Korean Wind is now a less attractive option to Korean Chinese than it was in the early 1990s. Most importantly, long absences from Yanbian have caused migrants to lose the social networks that are essential for doing business in China. The feeling of displacement and loss was actual and material, as well as emotional. According to Sungchul, he is missing something he should have known. This "something"—the unspoken but embodied behavior code for economic and social success—might be key to overcoming his situation, but the gap between the already successful and the recent returnees becomes wider and more visible all the time.

Despite the drawbacks, Sungchul had tried to stay positive: he wanted to end his construction career in South Korea and start a new business in China. At the end of 2009, he traveled to several cities in China, making plans to open a restaurant business. He did some market research, but the results were not promising. Yanji was already packed with restaurants and other service industries, and cities in Shandong where South Koreans and Korean Chinese are concentrated, such as Qingdao, Yantai, and Weihai, were too expensive. One day when I joined a gathering of Sungchul and his friends over drinks at a bar in Yanji, he was filled with regrets. "I should have come back a few years earlier, before the boom," he said. "I'm afraid I'm too late. My friend who came several years earlier than me already made a lot of money." Two of his friends disagreed. One of them said: "We did the right thing at the time. I made a lot and spent a lot. No regrets. I miss the time in South Korea so much: working, drinking, eating, traveling around in the clean and developed cities. I also have learned etiquette, to speak softly and pay attention to streetlights, which I could not have learned if I had not gone to South Korea." And another friend spoke with some nostalgia: "I feel so excited and happy when landing at the Incheon airport [in Seoul]. Work is tiring in South Korea. But there are many diverse programs in the local cultural center, such as computers, dancing, healthy activities. The quality of life in Seoul is much better and more active than in Yanbian."[10] I called Sungchul two weeks later to ask how his market research had gone. His phone was off. One of his friends told me that he had left for South Korea two days ago and that his wife had decided to stay in Yanbian to take care of their teenaged son. Sungchul had rejoined the "one-three-two" circuit, pursuing a temporary future, caught between two dreams.

Conclusion

In the wake of economic reform, many Chinese have gone through dramatic self-modifications and transformations by jumping between different occupations, becoming the other to the self, as Xin Liu powerfully illustrates in his study of the new landscape of rapid development in southern China (Liu 2002). This chapter has shown how the Korean Wind—an ethnically specific fashion for transnational migration that is also a reflection of the shifting East Asian political economy—has converged with and diverged from the overall pattern of Chinese development and self-transformation, reinventing Korean Chinese as self-responsible subjects in a rapidly privatizing China. My field research was primarily conducted during the financial crisis of 2008/9, and allowed me to observe the emergence of the liminal social landscape of the post–Korean Wind. This particular moment exhibits a new intensity and contentiousness surrounding the concepts of mobility, modernity, and futurity, as Korean Chinese find themselves situated between the Chinese dream and Korean dream. My ethnography analyzes the ongoing hope and frustrations of transnational migrants and the growing Korean Chinese reevaluation of the Korean Wind, with a focus on the widely circulated social imperative for entrepreneurship and the transformation of the self.

Despite the social split documented in this chapter, I do not mean to suggest that the Chinese dream has fully replaced the Korean dream in Yanbian. Rather, I highlight how the afterlife of Korean dreams has led to a new interpretation of transnational mobility and how the idea of modern subjectivity—having good *suzhi*—is not fixed but instead open to debate. This depends on the extent to which personal transnational, cosmopolitan, or metropolitan experiences and social capital are integrated into the idea of what it means to be a "more modern" subject. The thriving, yet oddly dejected, borderland of Yanbian, a place where nobody is truly immune to the Korean Wind, showcases the intersection between socialism and capitalism, and the flux and transition between two dreams. The three-decade-long desire that defined the region—leaving to live and living to leave—is being rethought and reevaluated. The Korean dream is in crisis, as the call goes out to "break the cycle": stop being a migrant worker, become an owner!

The Afterlife of the Korean Dream

What began as the Korean dream has become increasingly diversified, gradually losing its status as the dominant dream for Korean Chinese in Yanbian, especially as it has competed with the rise of the Chinese dream. All of these borderland dreams have deep roots, which have helped shape the forms they take. Since the late nineteenth century, border-crossing Koreans dreamed of escaping poverty by reclaiming barren lands for the purpose of farming in an area where sovereignty over different borders was frequently contested—as China, Korea, Russia, and later Japan (which encroached into Manchuria) competed for control. During the 1940s, many of these Korean migrant farmers actively participated in the Communist Revolution in northeast China and, as a result, gained official recognition from the Chinese Communist Party as a Chinese ethnic minority group—Korean Chinese—that would enjoy ethnic autonomy over its own government, education, language, and media. The Communist Revolution enabled these Koreans to gain farmland but also isolated them within the borderland area. After the Chinese economic reforms that started in the 1980s, these Korean Chinese experienced several winds of migration, as they began to reconnect to the external world, first to the large Chinese cities (*waidi* in Chinese), and later to North Korea, the Soviet Union, South Korea, Japan, and the United States. The dream of "better living through leaving" and "more development through migration" could only be realized by a constant negotiation between bordered geographical locations (China, Russia, Korea), bordered ethnic identities (Chinese, Korean), and bordered ideological conditions (socialism, capitalism). While these dreams have indeed led to a better life for many Korean Chinese, many members of this community ultimately feel betrayed by the fragile nexus between migration and development, love and money, home, and work—a nexus never fully solidified or confirmed.

Through more than a decade-long ethnographic engagement, I was able to observe the multiple dimensions and vulnerable forms of the Korean dream, as it was altered by legal changes, labor market conditions,

China–South Korean relationships, and the global economy. At the intersection between a privatized, post-socialist China and the post–Cold War neoliberal politics of South Korea, Korean Chinese bodies have become highly ethnicized—marked and distinguished by their cultural proximity and linguistic similarity to South Koreans, in contrast to other foreign workers. At the same time, this very similarity-with-a-difference of ethnicized bodies has served as a foundation for disrespect, discrimination, and exploitation, resulting in a unique form of Korean Chinese vulnerability within South Korea.

In this un/welcoming homeland, Korean Chinese migrants have been shaped by the transformative power of remittances—Korean money—which has created a fraught connection between money senders and money receivers, wives and husbands, parents and children. These remittances have also generated a new ethnic interdependence between Han Chinese and Korean Chinese in Yanbian, as Han Chinese began renting newly empty lands and as both ethnic groups began feeding each other's businesses. These interdependencies complicate any simplistic bifurcation between mobility and immobility, emplacement and displacement, living and leaving. These two seemingly contradictory modes of being reinforce the liminal condition of many Korean Chinese, as they travel between two worlds and live in "divided homes" (Zavella 2011). Korean Chinese liminality is especially exacerbated by South Korean visa regulations, which force migrants into a split life under a rhythm of multiple temporalities: working and making money in South Korea, resting and spending in Yanbian. Transnational temporality ends up weaving two different worlds into a common everyday life and requiring that bodies switch between two different modes of time. The Korean dream has thus been propped up by ethnicized Korean Chinese bodies, an influx of South Korean remittances, and the effects of transnational time. Meanwhile, the afterlife of this dream is being reshaped by a new material reality and new transnational subjectivity, one that is very much still in the making.

Dream Evolutions

The waxing of the Chinese dream and the waning of the Korean dream were juxtaposed throughout my main field research (in 2009) and follow-up research (until 2016). On the one hand, the pursuit of the Korean dream was considered an inevitable life phase that enabled Korean

Chinese migrants to quickly move up the economic ladder to survive economic privatization in China. On the other, the Chinese dream was believed to be a promising gateway to rapid economic success, preferable to the wage-based income earned in South Korea. A prediction that a Han Chinese taxi driver shared with me that "South Koreans will come to China as *dagong* [workers], and in ten years we Chinese will exceed America" seemed to be quickly becoming a reality. I repeatedly heard stories of personal economic betterment combined with strong national pride, accompanied by concrete examples of national development.

Even though I have used the term "Chinese dream" in the previous chapters as a periodization that captures the post–Korean Wind or the post–Korean dream, the term did not come up often in public or vernacular use until I revisited Yanbian in 2013. In fact, the notion of the Chinese dream (中国梦) was officially used and promoted as a "mission statement" and "political manifesto" for the Communist Party and the development of "socialism with Chinese characteristics" when Xi Jinping took office in 2012 (Peters 2017; Mahoney 2014; Z. Wang 2014). Until then, the widespread aspirations and elevated excitement sparked by China's global rise had not been captured by a specific term. But from daily encounters as well as growing journalistic attention, I felt an intangible but obvious energy animating expressions of pride and confidence in the Chinese Communist Party's economic accomplishments and favorable policies toward Yanbian. In addition, scholarly works began to pay attention to the concept of the Chinese dream, including the *Journal of Chinese Political Science*, which compiled a special issue on the Chinese dream in 2014. Zheng Wang (2014), one of the contributors, introduced the concept and context of the Chinese dream, with a focus on the idea of rejuvenation of the Chinese nation. According to Wang, the rejuvenation narrative is a response to humiliation discourses based on defeats by Western forces in the past, and it has been used to boost group identity and national unity. Chinese leaders have emphasized this rejuvenation as a political platform, with President Xi Jinping mobilizing globalism as a path to unprecedented wealth and power, giving the Chinese dream a global character.[1]

I would like to reconsider my use of the term "Chinese dream" in the context of the post–Korean dream era in this conclusion. When I refer to a nationalized form of dream, such as the Korean dream (*koriandeurim* in Korean) or Chinese dream, it primarily indicates the place where dreams come true (South Korea or China) or the group of people who pursue a particular dream in response to the shifting political economy of East

Asia. However, as I write this conclusion in the midst of a pandemic that originated in China in early 2020, Chinese influence has become much deeper and wider across the world, challenging US global hegemony.[2] The Chinese dream, which initially appeared as an imaginary and nebulous political platform in Xi's statement on the great rejuvenation of the Chinese nation, has become aggressively materialized through the Belt and Road Initiative, which aims to build infrastructure such as roads and dams and develop energy sources on a global scale. The Chinese dream is not only a political slogan that unifies the diverse national members of China but also an economic engine that is enabling China to become a global leader by engaging in economic investment and infrastructure development across the world. In contrast to my use of the term "Chinese dream" to express a vernacular excitement about the sudden global rise of China before 2012, the Chinese dream promoted as Xi's political mission has gone beyond the territory of China—framing Chinese influence through globalized nationalism as well as nationalized globalism.

Within the context of the Chinese dream that is still evolving, this book offers a critical analysis of the Korean dream that has been going through its own life cycle of birth, aging, sickness, death—and also rebirth. As I have tried to untangle the affective, material, and visceral dimension of the Korean dream throughout this book, I have discovered that dreams have their own forms of temporality; they move and change, and sometimes hit an impasse. Borderland dreams—embracing aspiration and frustration, joy and devastation, connection and disconnection, movement and stuckness—undergo their own metamorphoses.

Channeling New Dreams

Celebration of the Chinese dream was increasingly common across Yanbian when I revisited the prefecture in 2011, 2013, and 2016. A meeting in 2013 with members of the Association of Korean Chinese Writers can serve as a telling example. The writers gave me a warm welcome, informing me of all the news I had missed while I had been away. Our conversation mainly covered the economic boom and the increasing budget assigned to the association—money that enabled some of the writers to travel to South Korea. This financial support made the writers feel more like the equals of South Korean writers, who (they felt) used to disrespect them on the basis of their assumed lack of cultural and economic capital. One of the writers,

Mr. Chin, told me, "We do not have to be daunted by South Koreans anymore. I felt thrilled about my fat wallet [*jigabi dudukada* in Korean]. It wasn't like the last time when we were always in an inferior position, always asking South Koreans for more money."

In this sense, the Korean Chinese of Yanbian have clearly transitioned to a different stage of economic development, enabling a different kind of relationship with South Koreans. And like these Korean Chinese writers, the professors, journalists, and entrepreneurs I met during my later visits are recharacterizing what it means to be Korean Chinese, highlighting the strong potential of the Chinese dream. But a story told by Mr. Chin in the midst of the writers' dinner also conveyed the emotional complexity and economic/political entanglement that Korean Chinese still face by living in a complex borderland.

Mr. Chin is a renowned, award-winning Korean Chinese novelist. He is originally from a small border town, as is his wife. Their hometown, like so many towns on the border, has suffered from steep population decline. Beginning in the early 1990s, many Korean Chinese women, in particular, left Yanbian with the Korean Wind, going to work for South Korean companies that needed low-wage workers who spoke both Korean and Chinese, and these women often ended up marrying South Korean men. The growing shortage of Korean Chinese women is popularly blamed for the low birth rate in the community, and has also been condemned as a moral crisis because the women are seen as having left in pursuit of money instead of maintaining a family life back home (Noh 2011). In the midst of this perceived crisis (which unfairly stigmatizes women for pursuing economic opportunities), North Korean women who defected during the food crises in North Korea in the mid-1990s and the mid-2000s have gradually filled the roles that Korean Chinese women left behind. The exact numbers are unknown, but many of these North Korean women settled in Yanbian border towns and entered informal (common law) marriages with Korean Chinese (and sometimes Han Chinese) men.

During my field research trip, I heard stories about North Korean brides who had crossed the Tumen River, yet their whereabouts were considered secret because the brides could be deported if their identities were revealed. Moreover, the children born to relationships between (Korean) Chinese and North Koreans could not be registered in the Chinese household system since they were born to mothers without official legal status in China. Due to these legal complexities and security concerns, the brides' lives remain concealed, although the social impact of these "North

Korean ladies" was obvious within the borderland communities. In general, the North Korean women seemed to be well integrated with Korean Chinese and Han Chinese. However, I also heard stories about North Korean women who had suffered from physical and sexual abuse by Chinese husbands and labor exploitation by their families; some of these women had fled, eventually making it to South Korea as refugees.

Mr. Chin's brother-in-law (his wife's younger brother), like many other aging Korean Chinese male farmers, had been unable to find a Korean Chinese woman to marry and had ended up in a common-law marriage with a North Korean woman. Since their marriage was not officially recognized, the twins born to the couple could not be registered. In order to help, Mr. Chin and his wife registered the twins with their own household, as if they were the parents. The story became more complex, though, as the North Korean common-law wife eventually moved to South Korea, claiming refugee status, and settling there. After three years, she attained South Korean citizenship and invited her Korean Chinese husband to join her, but when he arrived, he found out that she was having an affair with another Korean Chinese man. Mr. Chin told me that she cut off all contact with his brother-in-law, but the brother-in-law wanted to stay in South Korea because he could not support the twins by himself in China if he returned. "Whenever I see the twins, my heart is broken," Mr. Chin said, with tears in his eyes. "I am worried about whether we can raise them properly—as if we were their real parents."

Mr. Chin's story provided an important counterpoint to otherwise rosy talk about Yanbian's thriving economy and China's rise to becoming a global power. It was a melancholy note after all the bravado from the writers about how well off they were. At the same time, the story exemplified the precariousness of the border location of Yanbian, where so many overlapping crossings continue to take place. In this narrative, we can see how some North Koreans secretively cross the river and settle in Yanbian because of its relative affluence and geographical adjacency, before eventually continuing to South Korea as refugees.

Some North Koreans also come to Yanbian in order to work in the restaurant business, under a contract between the Yanbian and North Korean governments. Often, these workers (again, mostly women) are treated as exotic others, wearing North Korean attire (reformed Korean traditional clothing), singing North Korean songs, and playing instruments, while at the same time, they are Korean-speaking workers who could take over roles that Korean Chinese had previously played before they left for South

Korea. Han Chinese also have been flocking to Yanbian in pursuit of new economic opportunities generated by Korean money, as discussed in previous chapters. They have rapidly filled many former Korean Chinese farming towns, taking over rice fields that Korean Chinese left behind or serving as migrant construction workers. In addition, South Koreans and other international agents have taken advantage of the border location of Yanbian as a connecting node to North Korea for economic, political, or religious reasons (J. Han 2013; J. Jung 2015).[3] And some South Koreans are moving to Yanbian in order to further their children's education in a rising China. In these ways, Yanbian has continued to evolve as a passage channeling people, goods, and money: an ethnic borderland intersected by different groups of people attempting to realize a variety of compelling and sometimes conflicting dreams.

Diversified Dreams

My follow-up visits to Yanbian after my initial research also made me realize that the afterlife of the Korean dream has led to diversified life strategies and living locations. The destinations of Korean Chinese migration have multiplied—to include not only South Korea and Chinese metropolitan cities, but also Tokyo, New York City (mainly Flushing, Queens), Los Angeles, London, Sydney, and more. The couple discussed in the book's introduction—Sunhua and Taebong—diversified their life opportunities and minimized risk by pursuing both the Chinese dream and the Korean dream simultaneously in Yanbian and Seoul. My friend Jielan, whose story appears in chapter 2, quit her stable government job in order to focus on her own trading business mediating between China, South Korea, and the United States. Her parents also moved from a rural town (Tumen) in Yanbian to Seoul when her father secured a stable income in the construction field. Jielan's house in her rural hometown, like other houses there, has remained empty.

I encountered many other cases of Korean Chinese maintaining multiple households across the world. For example, when I did my follow-up research in 2016, I rented an empty apartment whose owner, in her mid-thirties, has been working in the Dominican Republic running a textile factory with her parents. She owned three apartments in Yanbian, so that she could rent them out to gain extra income and so that she and her parents could stay there on their visits to Yanbian. These empty houses play a key role in shaping the remittance landscape; their vacancy maintains a bond between Yanbian and those migrants who plan to return eventually but do not know exactly when. Even though the vacancies have sometimes been construed as evidence of an ethnic crisis, with Yanbian's population lost to the Korean Wind, the relative emptiness of some regions can be understood as an active material fact that has reshaped the prefecture's ethnic composition (bringing in new Han Chinese migrants) and redirected the flow of migration across and beyond Yanbian. The absences—the empty houses—materialize the diversified dreams of Yanbian's people but also confirm that those dreams are constantly evolving.[4]

Although this book interprets the Korean dream in its past and current configurations, my follow-up research in Yanbian and South Korea is ultimately not sufficient to capture every aspect of the region's rapidly evolving dreams. The last three decades have borne witness to a starkly contrasting intergenerational difference in the economic achievement, social status, and political engagement of migrants in South Korea. Younger Korean Chinese have dramatically changed their material reality by diversifying the kinds of professions they can occupy—from physical labor to white-collar professional jobs to entrepreneurship. Even though media portrayals have channeled, reinforced, and perpetuated the stereotype of Korean Chinese as not-well-off and working-class (and often criminal), these stereotypes have increasingly been challenged. In contrast to the generation of Korean Chinese I have primarily focused on here, a new generation is coming to South Korea as international students or as nonphysical workers in order to pursue master's or doctoral degrees or dreams of entrepreneurship.[5] This new generation has established roots in South Korea, taking positions as university professors, lawyers, consultants, or other professionals, and leading lives quite different from those of their parents. They have been vocal in criticizing the ongoing discrimination against Korean Chinese and the outdated image of them as working-class people with Yanbian accents. Moreover, as more and more Korean Chinese can receive green cards or South Korean citizenship, Korean Chinese have ended up living in South Korea for longer periods of time.[6] They are doing this not as temporary migrant workers but as permanent residents, enjoying both political citizenship and the economic agency of entrepreneurship.[7] It is impossible for us to think of the Korean dream without considering the generation of Korean Chinese who founded a transnational ethnic working class, but this newest iteration of the Korean dream is fundamentally transforming what it means to be Korean Chinese; this version of the Korean dream forms a remarkable contrast with the previous generation's experiences discussed throughout this book.

By engaging with the journey of this ethnography, which has chronicled my fieldwork over the course of several important "winds" of migration, we can come to see that Yanbian has been recharacterized through the reproduction of new interrelationships and the possibilities of multiplicity. Yanbian is a place where ethnicized and gendered bodies and the flow of Korean money have intersected with transnational time, a place that both transforms and is transformed by border crossings. In a borderland in flux and transition, the long predominant Korean dream has itself been transformed. In this afterlife of the Korean dream, there are new actions to take and new plans to make, as the next generation of Korean Chinese begins to shape a new form of borderland dreams.

Introduction: Winds of Migration

1   All translations from Chinese and Korean are mine, unless otherwise noted.

2   In another work, I use the term "forbidden homeland" (J. Kwon 2019a). Any connection to South Korea, a capitalist enemy, was forbidden to Korean Chinese during the Cold War. My earlier work analyzes the fear and hesitancy toward South Korea—feelings that older Korean Chinese Communist Party members developed—mainly during the era of the Cultural Revolution.

3   Manchuria is a borderland area that had long been the subject of territorial disputes between China, Japan, Korea (Chosŏn dynasty), and Russia. Andre Schmid (1997) illuminates the complex territorial desire for Koreans to regain Manchuria as a "lost land" by focusing on the discourse introduced by Sin Ch'aeho. Manchuria was also subject to territorial disputes during the first Sino-Japanese War, the Russo-Japanese War, and the First World War (see N. Song 2018). It was also a sphere for Russia to try sovereignty experiments, along with China and Japan (see A. Park 2019).

4   Chinese ethnic minority policy is based on the notion of "plural singularity" (Mullaney 2011), which recognizes diversity while emphasizing the central control of the government.

5   In Yanbian, old Communist Party members recalled their memories of the Cold War and descriptions of capitalism as a "devil" or "enemy" of communism. Conversations with the author.

6   The rise of the market in the post-socialist context has been discussed by former-Soviet studies scholars; see Mandel and Humphry 2002; Rivkin-Fish 2009.

7   In fact, the merchants I happened to meet were predominantly women. And when we went to the Yanji West Market (*Sŏsijang* in Korean), most owners (*laoban*) were female. In Yanbian, a common saying has it that "there is no place where Korean Chinese do not go," along with a more gender-specific saying that "the first business travelers were those who went to sell kimchi in Han caves [Han Chinese–populated areas, meaning most Chinese cities, with a bit of a derogatory meaning]." In many cases, these female merchants did not speak Chinese at all or very little when they started doing business with Han Chinese. All business was a learning process—involving not only the Chinese language but also the Chinese way of doing business. Gowoon Noh (2011) discusses female entrepreneurs in the Yanji West Market.

8   Various Korean Chinese informants testified how the "advanced" culture of North Korea was influenced by Korean Japanese who returned to North Korea from Japan. As I mention in a note below, Tessa Morris-Suzuki (2007) discusses how Koreans were repatriated from Japan to North Korea. This repatriation program was intended to tighten the relationship between North Korea and Koreans in Japan, who might serve as a conduit to transfer "advanced" and modernized culture from Japan to North Korea. Japanese products were sold and exported to China through Korean Chinese merchants. As a result, Yanbian was one of the first places in China to enjoy color TVs, audio recorders, and video players imported from Japan, according to informants in Yanbian.

9   In Yanbian, people frequently alternate between "Russia" and "Soviet Union" and use the terms interchangeably. Here, I use "Russia" because the area where Korean Chinese did business is mostly in current Russian territory. Yet when Korean Chinese refer to the "wind," only the term "Soviet Wind" (*Ssoryŏn param*) is used.

10   It is common to see Russian merchants or tourists shopping in Yanbian, particularly in Hunchun, a city that borders China, North Korea, and the far eastern part of Russia.

11   As South Korean companies and businesspeople came to China starting in 1992 in search of new business opportunities, especially in the Shandong area, young Korean Chinese who could fluently speak both Chinese and Korean moved to larger Chinese cities to serve as translators or mediators in South Korean businesses. See Jaesok Kim's *Chinese Labor in a Korean Factory* (2013).

12   The majority of Korean Chinese living outside Yanbian (in Jilin, Heilongjiang, and Liaoning) are descended from migrants from the southern part of Korea—current South Korea—who came during the Japanese occupation. Consequently, they could easily demonstrate family ties to South Korea and were, as a group, able to enter the South Korean labor market earlier than the Yanbian Korean Chinese.

13   Korean Chinese victims of the fraudulent brokers organized the Association for the Fraud Victim in 1996, giving voice to the tragic situation and requesting that the South Korean government accept the victims into South Korea to pay off the debt (*Donga Ilbo* [East Asia Daily], November 30, 1996). I interviewed the president of the association, Youngsook Lee, and heard about the victims' situations, their desperate need, and the association's activities that helped them recover from their endebtedness.

14   Jaeeun Kim (2016) describes Korean border-crossing during the colonial era as a form of "transborder membership." Hyun Gwi Park (2018) discusses Koreans in Russia and their complex identities under Soviet ethnic politics by showing the rise in importance of kin networks rather than ethnic networks. Alyssa Park (2019) discusses the diverse jurisdiction practices

applied to Koreans by China, Russia, Japan, and Chosŏn (the last Korean dynasty, which fell to Japanese imperialism in 1910), which she calls "sovereignty experiments."

15 Hongkoo Han (2013) has elaborated on the struggles of Korean members of the Communist Party in China as a minority group under the "one country, one party policy" promulgated by Stalin, focusing on the Minsaengdan incident. Zainichi Korean scholar Keun-Cha Yoon (2016) illustrates the close connections between members of the Chosŏn Communist Party and members of the Japanese Communist Party, connections that offered great support for Koreans in Japan as an ethnic minority that was exploited not only by the Japanese but also by capitalism—even though it exacerbated ethnic tensions within the Japanese party. Sonia Ryang (1997) has written about Koreans in Japan who have supported, and been supported by, North Korea, particularly the Chongryon association, and the complexity of diasporic identities in Japan, North Korea, and South Korea.

16 Tessa Morris-Suzuki (2007) elaborates on the choice of approximately 90,000 Koreans in Japan to move to North Korea beginning in 1959 as part of a humanitarian gesture by the Red Cross—in collaboration with North Korea, Japan, the Soviet Union, and the United States. Yet those Koreans who were willing to "return" to North Korea to avoid extreme discrimination and exploitation in Japan faced different realities than they had imagined, including poverty and political constraints.

17 Korean Chinese who lived through the Cultural Revolution developed a habit of silence about their ethnic and national identity, especially in relation to South Korea, which was considered a forbidden homeland (Kwon 2019a). In addition, according to interviews I conducted with older Korean Chinese people, when a political split between North Korea and China developed in the 1960s, Korean Chinese were not allowed contact with their North Korean relatives, and some were accused of being "North Korean special spies," especially during the Cultural Revolution. However, Korean Chinese who were trained for and contributed to the Chinese Communist Revolution participated in the Korean War, fighting on the side of North Korea, China's communist ally (Cumings 2010; Kissinger 2011).

18 Because Koreans in Japan supported an ethnic organization with strong ties to North Korea, they were often accused of spying for North Korea (Hong 2020). Du-yul Song, a renowned professor based in Germany, was subjected to legal punishment that prevented him from entering South Korea due to his visits and possible political ties to North Korea (see D. Song 2017).

19 There have been many lawsuits against the state's false accusations of overseas Koreans as North Korean spies. After several decades, the victims finally established their innocence. See Hong (2020) for multiple cases of such accusations against overseas Koreans by the authoritarian regimes, including against Koreans in Japan, Germany, and the United States.

20 A Truth and Reconciliation Commission was created in 2005 to investigate the South Korean state's violence, reveal truths long concealed by the authoritarian regimes, and compensate victims for the state's wrongdoing.

21 According to the *Encyclopedia of Korean Culture*, Korean Chinese have been able to visit relatives in South Korea since the Chinese government allowed travel to South Korea in 1982. Korean Chinese travel and migration were expedited after the Seoul Olympic Games in 1988 for the purposes of hometown visits, labor migration, and study abroad. See http://encykorea.aks.ac .kr/Contents/Index?contents_id=E0068435.

22 Andrew Kipnis (2007) has raised critical concerns about how the concept of neoliberalism has been reified and overused in a holistic way to encompass diverse political, economic, and cultural phenomena across the world, described variously as the "neoliberal system," the "neoliberal world order," and "neoliberal capitalism." He introduces different approaches to neoliberalism: (1) Marxist approaches to neoliberal global capitalism; (2) free market individualism based on the policies of Reagan and Thatcher; (3) neoliberalism as ideology and policy; (4) neoliberalism that links economic policies and cultural effects, producing a population with the health, housing, education, and employment necessary to act as autonomous individuals. Kipnis suggests that instead of taking a broad, holistic approach, "neoliberalism should be particularized to show exactly which policies, or traditions of thoughts, or discursive actions the author is defining as neoliberal" (Kipnis 2007, 388). I use Kipnis's criticisms to think through the ways in which Korean Chinese migrants have been juggling two different neoliberalisms—South Korean and Chinese.

23 Minwoo Jung (2017) discusses urban inequality, introducing three precarious housing styles: *Oktapbang* (rooftop), *Banjiha* (half underground), *Gosiwon* (a tiny cubicle). In the midst of precarious housing inequality, Korean Chinese and other migrant workers have occupied these types of housing due to their low price and easier accessibility, but this has left them vulnerable to fires, hygiene issues, and security problems.

24 In the process of "migration," migrants experience abjection and precariousness, as many migration scholars have documented and described through different lenses: out-of-placeness (Ameeriar 2017; Constable 2014; Mathews 2011), vulnerability and deportation (Cabot 2014; De Genova 2010), transnational intimacy (Brennan 2004, 2014; Cheng 2013; Faier 2009; Freeman 2011), state violence and displacement (Coutin 2016), life-and-death danger (Andersson 2014; De León 2015; Lucht 2011), extreme labor exploitation (Holmes 2013), and deep liminality/ long waiting to claim a desired status (Fassin 2011; Ticktin 2011).

25 In addition to previous migration studies that questioned cultural adaptation, identity formation, and capital accumulation (Basch, Schiller, and Blanc 1993; Clifford 1997; Gilroy 1993; Hall 1966; Ong 1999; Ong and

Nonini 1996), current scholarship has focused on the emerging extreme marginalization of migrants who are fleeing war-ravaged or impoverished home countries—places they had to leave in order to live (Andersson 2014; De León 2015; Fassin 2011; Lucht 2011; Ticktin 2011).

26 In *Post-Soviet Social: Neoliberalism, Social Modernity, Biopolitics*, Stephen Collier points out one of characteristics of economic reforms in the Post-Soviet era is the aim to "responsibilize" citizens, "not just as subjects of need but as sovereign consumers making calculative choices based on individual preferences" (2011, 8). This gradual inscription of the sense of responsibility is parallel to "neoliberalism with Chinese characteristics."

27 I build on conversations about ethnicity as a site of "value production" (Comaroff and Comaroff 2009, 4) and "cultural currency" (Cattelino 2008). Recent studies have started conceptualizing "Ethnicity Inc." (Co-maroff and Comaroff 2009), "ethno-enterprisez" (Cattelino 2008), "natural economic groups" (Dirlik 2000, 129), and "ethnic entrepreneurs" (DeHart 2007, 2010), offering various perspectives on how ethnic difference is integrated and interpolated into the domain of the market. The economic currency that ethnic culture creates can also help to secure the political sovereignty of ethnic groups, as seen in the case of Native Americans in the United States (Cattelino 2008).

28 Bhabha describes "mimicry," borrowed from Lacan, as one of the illusive and effective strategies of colonial power and knowledge, and he asserts that it is "the desire for a recognizable Other as a subject of a difference that is *almost the same but not quite*" (Bhabha 1994, 122). However, colonial mimicry is not a simple narcissistic identification with the Other, or a desire for the impossibility of the Other. Rather, while not having an obvious desiring object, colonial mimicry has "strategic objectives," producing an anomalous representation of the colonized. Even though I am aware that Korean Chinese transnational migration differs greatly from colonial India, and Korean Chinese are not actually "mimicking" or trying to "become" exactly like South Koreans, the concept of mimicry—"almost the same, but not quite"—is essential for me to develop my discussion of the particular way in which Korean Chinese have created and promoted their ethnic niche and relationality and become integrated into the transnational labor market. "Al-most Korean" was the name of a panel (in which I participated) organized at the annual meeting of American Anthropological Association in 2007.

29 Here I borrow the concept of "performativity" that Judith Butler developed in *Gender Trouble* (1990) and *Bodies That Matter* (1993) in order to overcome dichotomous, fixed understandings of gender identity constructed between nature and culture, biology and sociology, determinism and voluntarism. Butler mainly argues, in *Gender Trouble*, that sex becomes a naturalized norm and that gender is the effect of the constraints of normativity, produced through forcible heterosexual normativity. Developing

this argument in *Bodies That Matter*, Butler argues that "performativity is not a singular act, for it is always a reiteration of a norm or set of norms, and the extent that it acquires an act-like status in the present, it conceals or dissimulates the conventions of which it is a repetition"(Butler 1993, xxi). The point is that gender identity is the effect of a compulsory reiteration of gender norms rather than a preexisting essence or an intractable construction (Weeks 1998, 125–34).

Chapter 1. Ethnic Borderland

1   What is on the move in this poem is not only the people of Yanbian but also the symbolic Yanbian, which has been transferred along with migrant workers to other places, such as Seoul, Beijing, Shanghai, and so forth.

2   These are districts in and near Seoul where Korean Chinese live and work in large numbers.

3   *Chosŏn* connotes multiple meanings. It can indicate the name of a dynasty that existed prior to modern Korea; it can imply the ethnic identity of Koreans—as Chosŏn ethnic people; and it can mean "North Korea."

4   For representative novels about the history of Korean Chinese migration, see Hongil Choi, *Nunmul chŏjŭn Tuman'gang* [Tearing Tumen River] (1994); Su-gil An, *Pukkando* (1995; originally published in parts, 1959–67, in the journal *Sasanggye*); Kuk-ch'ŏl Ch'oe, *Kando chŏnsŏl* [Legend of Kando] and *Kwangbok ŭi huyedŭl* [Descendants of the liberation] (1999; 2017).

5   This "unhomeliness" also takes the form of melancholia, a condition generated by the loss of a loved one who cannot be grieved properly (Butler 1997; Eng and Han 2003; Navaro-Yashin 2012; Zavella 2011). I take melancholia as a useful lens onto the dominant structure of feeling of Yanbian: anticipation and waiting, the affect expressed in the local saying, "Everybody is gone with the Korean wind." This constant and common melancholia as "unfinished process of grieving" (Butler 1997) is part and parcel of everyday life in Yanbian.

6   Relevant Korean Chinese history books include *Common Sense of Korean Chinese History* (Kim, Kang, and Kim 1998), *The Traces of Korean Chinese* (CTKCH 1991), *One Hundred Years of Korean Chinese History* (Hyun, Lee, and Huh 1982), *Jilin Korean Chinese* (JPA 1995), and multiple collections of local histories written by local historians (Yanji, Longjing, Tumen, Helong, Wangqing, Hunchun). See also CTKCH 1996. All are written in Korean and published in Yanbian.

7   The Qing government did not allow Chinese to live in what is now northeast China because it was the birthplace of their dynasty, their "holy land." During the late nineteenth century, Koreans began sneaking across the Tumen River to farm, while Russians were aggressively moving south into

Manchuria. Around 1880 the Qing government lifted the prohibition and started allowing Chinese farmers into northeast China, distributing farming land at low prices and offering tax benefits.

8   In his novel *Pukkando*, Su-gil An (2004), a Korean writer, deals with Korean farmers crossing the border and settling in Northeast China. In the novel, China is described as more prosperous than Chosŏn (Korea). Yet Koreans had to face issues of cultural assimilation and ethnic discrimination (see also H. O. Park 2005).

9   The war took place between the Chosŏn dynasty and the early Qing dynasty from 1636 to 1637. The victorious Qing took Korean hostages, including princes, officers, and related people.

10 Until the late nineteenth century, the Qing and Chosŏn governments had disputed the territory of Kando, the former name of Yanbian. As a result of the Qing's defeat in the Qing-Japan War, Japan acquired the right to build railroads in the southern part of Manchuria while yielding the territory of Kando to the Qing government. Kando's status as part of Chinese territory was formalized in the Kando Treaty of 1909 (G. Lim 2005; H. O. Park 2005; N. Song 2017).

11 When Japan occupied Chosŏn in 1910, Chosŏn was deprived of its sovereignty and diplomatic rights, and Koreans under Japanese control became Japanese citizens. However, in truth, Japan did not acknowledge Koreans as full citizens, adding the distinction of "Chosŏn" to their citizenship. During the colonial period, Koreans' citizenship status was ambiguous, especially in Manchuria, until 1945, when Chosŏn became independent from Japan. Jaeeun Kim has discussed the transborder membership of Koreans during the colonial era (J. Kim 2009, 2016).

12 The Korean Chinese historian Chunri Sun has discussed the condition of Korean Chinese society after independence from Japan, highlighting the contrasting treatment of Koreans in northeast China by the Guomindang and the Chinese Communist Party. The first planned to move Korean Chinese back to the Korean peninsula, while the latter encouraged Koreans to apply for Chinese citizenship, accepting them as an ethnic Chinese minority (Sun 2008).

13 Minsaengdan, a pro-Japanese organization that included Koreans in Manchuria, intended to weaken the ties between Chinese and Koreans in the Chinese Communist Party. Because Minsaengdan was (falsely) accused of spying for Japan, Koreans in the organization were heavily persecuted in and by the Chinese Communist Party. Hongkoo Han sees this as a form of ethnic persecution caused by conflicts among Chinese, Japanese, and Koreans (H. Han 2013).

14 Kim Il Sung, the founder of North Korea, had been an active member of the Chosŏn Communist Party and later active in the Chinese Communist Party. Yanbian was the main domain for his socialist revolutionary

activities under Japanese imperialism. When Yanbian was designated an autonomous prefecture in 1952, North Korea became an important supporter of Korean Chinese education by exchanging teachers and supplying textbooks. This socialist reciprocity continued until Kim Il Sung criticized Mao's socialism as "revisionism." His critique caused considerable trouble for Korean Chinese during the Cultural Revolution (G. Lim 2005).

15 Anthropologists have also discussed "writing against the culture"—culture as a fixed and frozen entity (Abu-Lughod 1997).

16 The Yanbian Korean Chinese Prefecture considered the Pyongyang dialect to be the standard for the Korean language until South Korean media became available on satellite television in the 2000s. The Korean language heard on Yanbian television or radio is not exactly the same as the dialects heard in Pyongyang or Seoul. In everyday life, many Yanbian Korean Chinese have a Hamgyŏng-bukto accent, although there are minor variations and differences in speaking.

17 Ethnic education has been considered a default choice among Korean Chinese in order to maintain their ethnic identity. And yet there is a new fashion for Korean Chinese parents to send their children to Han Chinese schools in order for their children to be able to speak fluent Chinese (unlike previous generations) and gain Chinese education to live in China.

18 There is an unofficial "policy" that in order to maintain the status of ethnic autonomous zone, the ethnic minority population should amount to more than 30 percent of the region. Yanbian is experiencing a sharp decrease in its Korean Chinese population due to the Korean Wind.

19 These stereotypes are commonly circulated in Yanbian: Korean Chinese men are supposed to be patriarchal, refusing to help with housework and lacking respect for women, while Korean Chinese women are considered to be very domestic, devoted to housework and serving their husbands and family. Han Chinese are generally thought to be more frugal and diligent than Korean Chinese. Han Chinese men are family-centered and respect women, while Han Chinese women are believed to be strong and dominating, unlike Korean Chinese women. Belief in these ethnic stereotypes has helped to structure networking patterns, social relationships, and marriages.

20 It is true that Korean Chinese living outside the prefecture of Yanbian have to frequently interact with Chinese-speaking Han people, whereas Yanbian Korean Chinese do not necessarily need to speak Chinese or develop networks with Han Chinese. This is because non-fluency in Chinese is still acceptable in Yanbian, and Korean culture and language enjoy official status. In fact, despite the view of Yanbian as a "small pond," Yanbian actively interacted with North Korea and Russia. In particular, North Korea, better off than China and South Korea especially in the 1960s, was Yanbian's channel for "Western" materials coming from Japan because Koreans who

moved from Japan to North Korea after 1959 received materials from their families in Japan (see Morris-Suzuki 2007).

21 Chari and Verdery discuss the intersection of different "post" situations, including postcolonialism (2009).

22 Hyun Ok Park states that "Korean Chinese juxtapose the capitalist present with the era of the Cultural Revolution" (H. O. Park 2015, 148), highlighting how the Cultural Revolution was construed as the antithesis of capitalism as currently experienced by Korean Chinese.

Chapter 2. The Un/Welcoming Homeland

1   A 2010 movie directed by Zhang Liu and known variously as *Tumen River*, *Dooman River*, and *La Rivière Tumen*, was shot in a Yanbian border town and dramatizes the ambivalent relationship between Korean Chinese and North Koreans as co-ethnic groups. On the one hand, North Koreans are seen as impoverished neighbors in desperate need, and the movie portrays the friendship that develops between a Korean Chinese boy and a North Korean boy who crosses the river in search of food. On the other hand, North Korean defectors are also seen as criminal outsiders. The movie also contains a scene in which a North Korean man rapes a Korean Chinese girl who has fed him.

2   At the beginning stage of the post–Cold War migration, Korean Chinese tended to express excitement about the reunion by using the metaphor of "blood tie." Schneider, referencing the saying "blood is thicker than water," also sees "relatives" as defined by blood relationships in biogenetic terms, as symbols for biogenetic substance (Schneider 1980; see also Carsten 2004). But as the cases show, the Korean Chinese kinship ties with South Koreans rapidly grew thin.

3   Since 2007, one of the most common types of visas has been the H-2, which guarantees free entry for five years in order to work in designated fields (mostly physical labor and the service sector). In order to acquire the H-2, applicants have to take a qualifying exam that tests their fluency in Korean and knowledge of Korean law and society. If participants score 60 percent or better, they qualify for a lottery, and if they are chosen in the lottery they are allowed to go to South Korea. Jielan's mother and Jielan herself both passed the exam and won a place in the lottery.

4   Regarding "paper kinship," the concept of the "paper son" also appeared in the United States as part of the Chinese Exclusion Act. See, e.g., the documentary *The Chinese Exclusion Act*, broadcast by PBS IN 2018.

5   Sahlins argues that "unlike kinship by procreation alone, an extended temporality is a condition of the relatedness at issue, since it requires a cumulative process of parental care—a condition more or less true of many

forms of performative kinship" (Sahlins 2012, 8). Carsten and Weston also think communal affect and sociality are built upon continuity and long-term temporality (Carsten 2000, 2004; Weston 1997). Franklin discusses a new kinship practice in the wake of new biologies (Franklin 2002). Eleana Kim raises the question of kinship in the context of transnational adoption (E. Kim 2010).

6　McKinnon discusses the economies of kinship, looking into the relationship between paternity and the emergence of private property, analyzing kinship as a cause of perpetuating patriarchal genealogy by "enterprising up" paternity (McKinnon 2001, 284) that has been reinvented and employed for economic reasons.

7　Korean Chinese have been able to apply for permanent residence since 2013, once they are "qualified" and can demonstrate economic potential and no criminal background.

8　Some social critics and NGO workers noted that the disparate treatment of overseas Koreans threatened Korean ethnic nationalism and its sense of the "oneness" and the homogeneity of Korean ethnicity (e.g., Shin 2006). In the Act, Korean ethnicity is expressed as a bridge of emotional belonging to and political association with the homeland, as an "imagined community" conceived as a horizontal comradeship "regardless of the actual inequality and exploitation that may prevail" (Anderson 2006, 7). Ethnic membership facilitates group formation as part of global Korea through ethnic imagination—a "political artificiality" and "ethnic fiction" in Weber's term (Sollors 1995, 55; Weber 1997)—with something like quasi-citizenship granted to overseas Koreans in the form of the F-4 visa.

9　The Korean government did begin to recognize the descendants of people who had participated in the independence movement against Japanese imperialism. Once they had proved their status as descendants, they were eligible for monetary compensation from the South Korean government and were given the right to South Korean citizenship. In order to prove their eligibility for this recognition, applicants had to testify about their personal and family history and were sometimes required to provide DNA evidence.

10　The role of Korean churches in giving a voice to undocumented Korean Chinese workers should not be overlooked. Ministers from the 1980s democracy movement, such as Minister Lim, turned their attention to human rights and have emerged as central figures dealing with the concerns of Korean Chinese and other migrant workers that have poured into South Korea (formerly a labor-exporting country). The ministers established centers and organizations for migrant workers that offered legal services, emotional community, and shelter, while encouraging the workers to attend Sunday services. Christianity goes hand in hand with human rights in South Korea, as some churches have pressed the government to change policies working against the human rights of migrants. Most Korean Chinese are not Christian, yet they assume that churches are the places for them to get help settling in an unfamiliar country. I became familiar with several Korean Chinese churches in and around Seoul. Minister Lim was distinctive in the sense that he led the year-long demonstrations in close collaboration with the Korean Chinese Association, a community that was formed and maintained by Korean Chinese workers themselves with his support.

11 As Giorgio Agamben writes, "Bare life remains included in politics in the form of the exception, that is, as something that is included solely through an exclusion" (Agamben 1998, 11). Bare life is included in politics through exclusion, and yet excluded if there is no exception under the liminal condition of exclusive inclusion and inclusive exclusion.

12 According to statistics published by the South Korean government, as of August 2012 the total number of foreign nationals was 1,409,577. Of these, 570,158 (40 percent) were Korean Chinese, among whom 68,012 had acquired Korean citizenship. The total number of foreign nationals working in South Korea was 588,944. Korean Chinese with H-2 visas amounted to 295,604, which was more than half the foreigners working in Korea.

13 Korean Chinese migration has become a matter of population regulation, which treats migrants as coded and numbered beings in a form of biopolitics of population (Foucault 2007; Lemke 2002) or "government is the right disposition of men things" (Foucault 1991, 93). Foucault points out that the abstract governing of a population is based on the eradication of individual subjectivity, arguing that "population is not a collection of juridical subjects in an individual or collective relationship with a sovereign will. It is a set of elements in which we can note constants and regularities even in accidents, in which we can identify the universal of desire regularly producing the benefit of all, and with regard to which we can identify a number of modifiable variables on which it depends" (Foucault 2007, 74).

14 Louis Althusser articulates the way that capitalism has been inevitably reproduced through the reproduction of state apparatuses and a certain subject formation; "all ideology hails and interpellates concrete individuals as concrete subjects, by the functioning of the category of the subject. . . . I shall suggest that ideology 'acts' or 'functions' in such a way that it 'recruits' subjects among the individuals, or 'transforms' the individuals into subjects by that very precise operation that I have called *interpellation* or *hailing,* and which can be imagined along the lines of the most commonplace everyday police hailing: 'Hey, you there!'" (2001, 117–18). The distinctive *categorization* of Korean Chinese as working-class subjects by the Korean government enables the Korean labor market to rely on a cheaper pool of labor made up of Korean Chinese. It reinforces the national/ethnic hierarchy and keeps labor costs low.

15 Robyn Magalit Rodriguez (2010) has demonstrated how the Philippine state has systematically brokered its own people to the world as migrant

workers. While the government plays a leading role in controlling and exporting migration in the case of the Philippines, the governments of China and South Korea have not actively engaged in the process of migration. Instead, labor migration between these countries has been expanded by illegal brokers who manipulate kinship, marriages, and work visas.

Chapter 3. Rhythms of "Free" Movement

This chapter is based on my article "Rhythms of 'Free' Movement: Migrants' Bodies and Time under South Korean Visa Regimes," *Journal of Ethnic and Migration Studies* 45, no. 15 (June 2018): 2953–2970.

1   Under H-2 visa regulations, Korean Chinese are allowed to legally work in thirty-eight fields, including hotel and restaurant-related sectors, construction, car repair, nursing care for the sick and old, and domestic work. The H-2 visa is also given to those who take part in an annual lottery after passing a Korean language test—a new system introduced in 2007. The lottery is based on the designated quota of migrant workers that the Korean government plans to maintain (Y. Yoon 2013).

2   Migration scholars have documented the nonexistent zone of migrants through the concept of the "border spectacle"—a law-enforcement regime that renders the undocumented visible and their exclusion only ostensible (De Genova 2013). Their status becomes "nonexistent" (Coutin 2007), a legal limbo represented by the "pink card" that confers the fragile and disposable status of the asylum seeker (Cabot 2014).

3   The anthropology of time has paid attention to repetitive religious rituals and interactions between human beings and natural cycles, understanding rhythm as a thread connecting physical, ecological, and social domains (Evans-Prichard 1969) and as a means of coordinating social events and rituals (Malinowski 2002). In this discussion, rhythm works as an essential social category of time that reasserts regularity and symbolic order in a way that synchronizes collective lives (Durkheim 1965). Rhythm provides a perception of order and recurrence that allows anticipation of, and preparation for, the future (You 1994). According to Katherine Verdery's account of the "etatization of time," the transition to a socialist state entailed the making of "socialist man," as the state aimed to break from religiously based "normal" rhythms or rituals and to impose new temporal punctuations through unpredictable and scattered schedules organized by the Communist Party (Verdery 1996).

4   In addition to highlighting rhythm as an orchestrating social principle and disruptive power within capitalism, I draw on Nancy Munn's notion of temporalization, which views time as "a symbolic process continually being produced in everyday practices" and that entails tacit knowing and bodily memories (Munn 1992, 116). Munn defines rhythm as "media of

diffuse political control exerted as power in the embodying process" (112), pointing out how time is closely tied to bodily activities and space, drawing on Bourdieu (107–8) as well as Foucault's discussions of the "temporal elaboration of the act" (111). Munn sees bodily activities and movement as making, or being made by, the space of their enactment. Here, the body is a place where cultural meaning is invested and imbued with relationships of time. It is also divided into spatio-temporal units, while at the same time these units integrate bodily motion into a preplanned rhythm. To Munn, the body is not only a critical means of tacit temporalization but also a conduit between the self and the world: the body constructs the world, and the world reconstructs the body's time (112).

5 Takeyuki Tsuda discusses how, in the case of Japanese migrants returning from Brazil, home feels like unfamiliar place (Tsuda 2003).

6 Recent anthropology tends to see mobility as normative and attachment to place as exceptional (Salazar and Smart 2011)—and yet, Korean Chinese migration shows that the bifurcation between mobility and immobility, emplacement and displacement, living and leaving is not always clear-cut.

7 Ambivalent feelings on the part of Korean Chinese toward South Korea are common in Yanbian. For example, going to South Korea to work came to be looked down upon, whereas going to South Korea for fun became something to be proud of.

8 Reciprocity matters in social life (see Y. Yan 1996).

9 The "work unit" used to be a complex place where Chinese workers lived and worked together. However, as privatization has accelerated, the work unit supported by the state lost competitive power in the market. Thus, many work units in China had to close down. However, people in Yanbian often call their workplace—whether in a governmental office or in private business—their work unit. In this context, the work unit indicates a government-related job. Government jobs are commonly thought to confer stability, not only due to secure pensions and benefits but also due to extra money given as bonuses or gifts in order to maintain political networks.

10 David Harvey suggests that consumption and production can constitute an "immediate identity" because the act of production accompanies the consumption of raw materials, instruments of labor, and labor power, while the act of consumption provides the motive for production by promoting human needs and desires. Harvey points out how "productive consumption" and "consumptive production" lead to the social process of reproduction (Harvey 1999, 80). In these terms, production and consumption are usually conceived as occurring in the same place at the same time.

11 Adorno discusses the concept of "free time" as a symptom of capitalist society: "Free time does not merely stand in opposition to labor. In a system where full employment itself has become the ideal, free time is nothing more than a shadowy continuation of labor" (Adorno 2009, 168). Since free

time is described as an extension of work, I see those who spend free time without working as not truly enjoying free time.

12   Hyun Mee Kim also shows the Korean Chinese returnee's anxiety, writing that time in Yanbian is mainly considered "time to lose money" or "time to make a workable body" (H. Kim 2008, 51). Korean Chinese labor has been discussed by South Korean scholars with a focus on domestic labor (Joo Y. Lee 2004) and ethnic identity formation (H.-E. Lee 2005; M. Lee 2008; S. Lim 2004; Noh 2001).

13   In 2009 the daily wage for electricians and carpenters ranged from the equivalent of US$100 to US$150, with a monthly income that could range from US$2,500 to US$3,500. Korean GDP per capita was equivalent to US$25,910 in 2010. Working hours are the highest in the world, at 2,255.8 hours per year.

14   A random encounter with a taxi driver indicated to me the depth of some Koreans' feelings against Korean Chinese migrants. On a summer day in 2008 in Korea, I took a taxi in Karibong-tong, a neighborhood referred to as "Korean Chinese Town" in Seoul. The taxi driver started a conversation with me, expressing his fury about the unruly and troublesome Korean Chinese who, he thought, caused social disorder. He also claimed that they were taking job opportunities from Koreans and siphoning money from South Korea to China. According to the Korean Labor Research Institute (D. Cho 2010), however, the labor markets for Korean and Korean Chinese workers do not overlap: South Koreans and Korean Chinese generally do not compete for the same jobs. Thus, the tension is heavily emotional and discursive, rather than a reflection of actual conflict in the labor market.

15   According to Korean Chinese workers in 2022, the daily wage for female restaurant workers was equivalent to about US$100 per day. The wages of construction workers—male or female—ranged from the equivalent of US$120 to US$240 dollars, depending on experience, expertise, and work ethic. Yet, since the COVID-19 situation prevented foreign workers from entering South Korea, daily wages had gone up and many employers who needed to hire foreign workers struggled with the critical labor shortage in South Korea. See, e.g., "Pinilchari 17mankae kujikchaga ŏpta" [170,000 job vacancies, no job seekers], Chosun Daily News, July 30, 2022, https://www.chosun.com/national/labor/2022/07/30/AXIPXNOOPRFDJAJFYVKCVGCERM/.

16   The pace is inscribed in the body as Foucault suggests in Discipline and Punish (1995, 152). In "Time, Work-Discipline and Industrial Capitalism," E. P. Thompson points out that time, in the industrial society, becomes abstract, homogenous, linear, and task-fragmented whereas the pre-industrial society experiences time as concrete, cyclical, and task-oriented (Thompson 1967).

17   Discussing the limits of upward mobility and the attrition of the fantasy of the "good life" in neoliberal capitalism, Lauren Berlant illustrates how a

cruel optimism, attached to compromised conditions of possibility in the midst of deep impossibilities, serves as a defense against the contingencies of the present (Berlant 2011).

18 Labor, "the living, form-giving fire," may serve as a basic causal force or principle of the historical motion of being (Weeks 1998, 122).

Chapter 4. The Work of Waiting

This chapter is based on my article "The Work of Waiting: Love and Money in Korean Chinese Transnational Migration," *Cultural Anthropology* 30, no. 3 (2015): 477–500.

1 Regarding affective labor, I understand affect as a communicative "action on action" of the self and others, "the capacity to be affected," and a medium through which intersubjective relations circulate (Deleuze 1988; Richard and Rudnuckyj 2009; Spinoza 1994). Affective labor includes an intimate (Boris and Prennas 2010) and immaterial (Lazzarato 1996) labor, one that at times trades in communication and information. Affective labor often aims to create a feeling of ease and well-being, as in personal and caring services (Hardt and Negri 2000).

2 The *danwei* system is the basis of the livelihood and employment security of the urban working class in China (C. Lee 2007). Some have called this system "organized dependence" (Walder 1986) and "*danwei* welfare socialism" (Gu 2002).

3 *Xiagang* (stepping down from one's post) is the state of no longer being employed while still maintaining a contractual relationship with one's enterprise (work unit) and retaining enterprise based-benefits for two to three years (Hung and Chiu 2003, 205).

4 The number of undocumented Korean Chinese is hard to gather from government statistics, given that most Korean Chinese workers remained undocumented until the amnesty granted in 2004.

5 Entire families can also migrate permanently to South Korea, provided they can obtain a South Korean household registration and recover their South Korean nationality. According to recent research by the Overseas Koreans Foundation, about 100,000 Korean Chinese have gained South Korean citizenship this way (OKF 2016). Yet most Korean Chinese migrant workers maintain their lives in China for the sake of their children's education and for the economic opportunities increasingly to be found in the Chinese economy.

6 In December 2017, sixty-two Korean Chinese filed a lawsuit against a popular movie called *Midnight Runners* (*Ch'ŏngnyŏn kyŏngch'al*) because of the movie's malicious portrayal of Korean Chinese, which stigmatized them as a criminal ethnic group. The plaintiffs requested that the movie be withdrawn from theaters and that the equivalent of approximately US$100,000

be paid as compensation for psychological damages. The lawsuit was denied in the first round, but in the second round the court requested that the filmmakers apologize for the discomfort and marginalization caused by their representation of Korean Chinese in the film, and they were asked to contemplate not including any similarly offensive portrayals in future films (*Donga Ilbo* [East Asia Daily], June 18, 2020).

7   Unofficial statistics indicate that 33 percent of the Yanbian economy is "Korean money." See "Chosŏnjok 1% sidae 5. Hŭndŭllinŭn Yŏnbyŏn chach'iju" [The era of 1% Korean Chinese, the Korean Chinese Autonomous Prefecture of Yanbian in crisis], *Yanhap News*, July 8, 2010, https://www.yna .co.kr/view/AKR20110630119600097.

8   I have witnessed numerous cases of "fake" marriages by middle-aged Korean Chinese women. They divorce their current husbands and marry fake husbands on paper. In 2009, I wrote about Korean Chinese migration stories I encountered while staying in Seoul and Yanbian in a series called "Kwon June Hee's Yanbian Diary," published in the *Chungguk tongp'o sinmun* [Korean Chinese newspaper]. The widespread and commonly observed moral and sexual anxiety—*love in crisis*—among Korean Chinese is closely overlapped with discussions about the commodification of love and care as "the new gold" (Constable 2009; Parrenas 2001, 2004; Sassen 2000, 2004; Hochschild 2004). The commodification of love has thrived on the development of international "marriage markets" (Constable 2003, 2005; Freeman 2005, 2011) and Internet dating sites (Constable 2007; Tyner 2009) in a transnational setting. Love is not simply a force for creating interpersonal ties (Fromm 2006) but also a means of producing value that is then circulated on the market. Nicole Constable examines the "commodification" of love on a global stage, describing the ways in which intimacy or intimate relations can be treated as if they have entered the market, and be bought or sold as part of the global capitalist flow of goods (Constable 2009).

9   The won is the currency of South Korea. A 10-won coin represents a small amount of money.

10 In *Crises of the Republic*, Arendt argues that promises are the unique human way of ordering the future, making it predictable and reliable to the extent that this is possible (1972, 102; citation from Ahmed 2010, 29).

11 Until the H-2 visa issuance was stabilized in a way that Korean Chinese could rely on, visas to enter South Korea were difficult for Korean Chinese to access.

12 When Bokja's husband disappeared from her life around 2005, entrance to South Korea was still limited. According to Jielan (a niece of Bokja), whom I have been in touch with on a regular basis, after the H-2 visa became widely available to Korean Chinese, Bokja was able to obtain a work-visit visa around 2012 and was eventually reunited with her husband in South Korea.

13   Karl Marx suggests the potential of money is not always creative or binding. It possesses destructive power as in the following: "If money is the bond binding me to human life, binding society to me, binding me and nature and man, is not money the bond of all bonds? Can it not dissolve and bind all ties? Is it not, therefore, the universal agent of divorce? It is the true agent of divorce as well as the true binding agent—the universal galvano-chemical power of society" (Marx 1988, 138). To George Simmel, money is a medium circulating between the subjective desire and desirable objects in the realm of exchange, without paying much attention to production and human labor. As a mere medium of exchangeability (2004, 130), money enables an impersonal bond between subject and thing.

14   Sarah Lynn Lopez's work explores the remittance space shaped by the flow of migration between rural Mexico and the urban United States (Lopez 2015). Here, remittances enabled the construction boom in rural Mexico and served as a structural link between migrants and their hometowns, creating alliances between "here" and "there." But the empty houses and the absence of the actual remittance senders is also a critical part of the remittance landscape, which shows how "remitting is [both] an action and a postponement" (Lopez 2015, 253). The empty houses are evidence of the material and historical continuity that the migrants wish to maintain, yet they cannot be part of the present while they are gone. Dace Dzenovska (2018) discusses the emptiness of Latvian post-Soviet capitalism, with the loss of population and collapse of infrastructure in the pursuit of the new reality, discussing emptying both as a transition state and as an enduring state of affairs with its own internal and temporal dynamics.

15   Giovanni Gasparini (1995) describes manifestations of waiting: waiting as interstitial time; waiting as blockage of action; and waiting as an experience field with substitute meanings. In addition, commenting on dictionary definitions of waiting as "the action of remaining stationary or quiescent in expectation of something" or "remaining in a state of repose or inaction, until something expected happens," he highlights how waiting embraces expectation, and how it is a future-oriented action that attempts to control uncertainty (Gasparini 1995, 30). Waiting is a special "crossroads" between the present and the future, between certainty and uncertainty. And waiting is the "present of the future" (St. Augustine, cited in Gasparini 1995, 30). In a liminal temporality, waiting can be a passive activity producing feelings of powerlessness, helplessness, and vulnerability (Crapanzano 1986). On the other hand, waiting can be a rigorous activity, since it may require a constant state of alertness and preparation.

16   To Marcel Mauss, the gift is not a mere thing attached to a person, but rather assumes a wholeness deeply connected with "souls"—"souls mixed with things, things mixed with souls" (Mauss 1990, 20)—"the spirit of the gift." Jacques Derrida develops the significance of reciprocation within a

time limit in his book, *Given Time*, focusing on the time boundary and temporality that conditions the gift exchange. "The gift is not a gift; the gift only gives to the extent it gives time. The difference between a gift and every other operation of pure and simple exchange is that the gift gives time. There where there is gift, there is time. What it gives, the gift is time, but this gift of time is also a demand of time. The thing must not be restituted immediately and right away. There must be time, it must last, there must be waiting—without forgetting" (Derrida 1992, 41).

17   In India, the educated young who experience "timepass" end up "being left behind" (Jeffrey 2010). Romanians mired in lengthy periods of underemployment have suffered from "a brutal kind of boredom" without any social security net (O'Neil 2014, 9). Ethiopian youngsters with too much unstructured time struggle with an inability to progress in life (Mains 2007).

18   Relevant here are Barbara Adam's remarks: "The essential temporality of everyday life means that humans experience not only the passing of time, but also the necessity to wait until one temporal process has run its course in order for another to begin. All humans wait, and in the fullest sense of the term, only humans wait. Waiting is an experience based on the interpretation and understanding of the temporal structures of events and human desires" (Adam 1991, 121).

19   As Arjun Appadurai (1986), Christopher Gregory (1982) and Daniel Miller (2002) discuss, gift and commodity cannot be clear-cut distinctive categories.

20   Regarding "not-yet-consciousness," Ernest Bloch writes of "the preconscious of what is to come, the psychological birth place of the new" (Bloch 1995, 116). The not-yet-conscious and the not-yet-become exist in a space of concrete anticipation—that is, a space in which something new may come into being. Potential futures live in the present moment without revealing their real appearance. Meanwhile, the essential temporality of everyday life means that humans experience not only the passing of time but also the necessity to wait. An anticipatory regime emerges as follows: it is formed through seeing the future as palpable in the present; it has epistemic value for knowledge production and ethnicized value for the subject; it is formed through modes of prediction and instrumentality; and it has an affective dimension, binding subjects in affective economies of fear, hope, salvation, and precariousness as they aspire to futures already made real in the present (Adams, Murphy, and Clarke 2009). Here, anticipation is an activity that imagines the future as a more knowable present form and also as an affective state that generates a certain knowledge value in order to manage future uncertainty and maintain the present.

Chapter 5. The Leaving and the Living

1   The close relationship between remittance and development has been pointed out in a UNDP report that highlights the positive agency of migrants in development (UNDP 2009; Schiller and Faist 2010). Remittance is conceived as a "livelihood strategy" by which migrants spread risk and create insurance, thereby improving well-being, reducing poverty, and stimulating economic growth (de Hass 2007). By means of remittances, transnational migration can become a resource for the production of capital and a dynamic force that promotes entrepreneurial activity and economic expansion (Messy and Parado 1998). Most of all, migrants facilitate not only the transfer of money but also "social remittances," such as new perceptions of human rights, gender equity, and democracy (Faist 2010; Levitt 2001; Levitt and Lamba-Nieves 2011). Although the negative effects—brain drain, reduced economic activity, productive disarticulation, and increasing local disparities in sending countries—have been highlighted (Schiller and Faist 2010; Wise and Covarrubias 2010), the migration-development nexus is affirmed by the force of remittances, the money transfers vital to social transformation and economic development in both sending and receiving countries. The body of literature on development views development as a purportedly self-evident modern standard (Ferguson 1990, 1999), and as a set of relations among institutions, practices, and systematization for a whole (Escobar 1995).

2   Changes in the exchange rate of the South Korean won against the Chinese yuan were a notable feature of the economic climate during the period of my research. In 2008, 10,000 won was worth 40 yuan, while in 2011 10,000 won was worth 58.90 yuan. This increase in the value of the won drove consumption up again in Yanbian. (*Yŏnhap News* [Seoul], April 2, 2011, https://www.yna.co.kr/view/AKR20110402040900097). In 2021, 10,000 won was worth 59.24 yuan.

3   Yanji plays a double role in Korean Chinese identity: as an ethnic hub that has protected Korean identity and as an ethnic enclave that has kept Korean Chinese isolated in an ethnically bounded and geographically remote region.

4   Doreen Massey critiques the concept "time-space compression," coined by David Harvey, as too broad and undifferentiated. Instead, she introduces the notion of the "power-geometry of time-space compression," showing how mobility can be differentiated: "different social groups and different individuals are placed in very distinctive ways in relation to these flows and interconnections. . . . Different social groups have distinct relationships to this anyway differentiated mobility; some are more in charge of it than others; some initiate flows and movement, others don't; some are more on the receiving end of it than others; some are effectively imprisoned by it" (Massey 1993, 61).

5   Rey Chow describes this concept, drawing on Fredric Jameson's discussion of the stereotype: stereotypes brushing against each other are "an encounter between surfaces rather than interiors—[they] cannot really be foreclosed again by the liberalist suggestion that everyone is entitled to her own stereotypes of herself, which others should simply adopt for general use" (Chow 2002, 57).

6   Sarah Lynn Lopez introduces the term "remittance landscape" to describe "the amalgam of migrant's life stories and the macro political, social, economic, and historical forces that shape migration" (Lopez 2015, 8).

7   According to the employment agencies where I did fieldwork, Han Chinese migration to South Korea has increased over the last few years. As of January 6, 2021, the South Korean government statistics are as follows: Korean Chinese female, 334,066; Korean Chinese male, 367,032; Chinese female (non-Korean Chinese), 228,460; Chinese male (non-Korean Chinese), 172,224. See https://kosis.kr/statHtml/statHtml.do?orgId=111&tblId=DT_1B040A6.

8   Ayşe Çağlar and Nina Glick Schiller (2011) attempt to relocate the relationship between migrants and cities by looking at the city not as a self-evident spatial unit in the global economy but rather as "city scale"—that is, a domain of restructuring and rescaling in relationship to its mutual constitution of other sites of organized power. Their discussion helps me think of Yanji not as a simple spatial unit but as an intersection of multiple dynamics and traffics: urban and rural, national and transnational, ethnic enclave and emerging consumer space. Biao Xiang discuss multi-scalar ethnography to study migration (Xiang 2013).

9   Julie Chu (2009) discusses the term *nongmin*, "peasant" in English, as a state identification that reeks of social and economic limitations. *Nongmin* conveys the stigmatic meaning attached to the "backward," "superstitious," and unproductive rural masses who are considered the major obstacle to national development and salvation (Chu 2009, 63).

10 In addition to this "exclusive inclusion," Cho elaborates on how poor rural migrants' desire to settle in either urban or rural areas is troubled and frustrated by conflicts over land rights in rural areas and policies that benefit urban household registration holders over rural people (M. Cho 2009, 53).

11 According to Ann Anagnost (2004), *suzhi* involves the appraisal of the biological individual's embodied capacities, looking at the body as a site of investment through entrepreneurialization of the self. The yearning for self-development is attained by transformation of consciousness and capitalization of subjectivity (H. Yan 2003). From the Marxist sense, Pierre Bourdieu defines *habitus* as "embodied history, internalized as second nature, and so forgotten as history . . . the active presence of the whole past of which it is the product" (Bourdieu 1990, 56).

12   As urban migration has rapidly increased in China, *hukou* has become
       flexible and problematic in that it reveals migrants' unequal access to city
       resources and state benefits such as education and health care. To resolve
       the predicament that *hukou* imposes on migrants, cities such as Shanghai
       partially allow the issue of urban *hukou* to migrants, under limited condi-
       tions: migrants are required to purchase a house or invest a certain amount
       of money (Mackenzie 2002). Since the permit is based on economic poten-
       tial, the urban *hukou* is still not easy for migrants to attain. The urban/rural
       distinction still remains.

13   By "structure of feeling," Raymond Williams means the affective elements
       of consciousness and relationships that are "not feeling against thought but
       thought as felt and feeling as thought." That is a practical consciousness of
       a present kind in a living and inter-relating continuity as a living process
       (Williams 1977, 132–33).

14   This income comparison is based on 2009 figures, the year when I inter-
       viewed Ms. Ran. The current monthly wage of Korean Chinese in South
       Korea equates to about US$2,000 to US$2,500, but the cost of living in
       China has increased as well.

15   I use a pseudonym because the cadres in the local government did not want
       the town's identity to be known, although they welcomed me and willingly
       discussed the town's history and situation.

16   The government office includes its own restaurant, and they have their own
       cook for the office staff.

17   Eva Hung and Stephen Chiu (2003) discuss the predicament of *xiagang*
       workers in Beijing, calling them "the lost generation." Given the histori-
       cal turmoil of modern Chinese history, which ranges from being "sent
       down to the village" (where education was poor or nonexistent) during
       the Cultural Revolution to the rampant privatization and loss of jobs in the
       contemporary era, Chinese of a particular age are considered by some to be
       a "lost" generation, so "culturally malnourished" that they are more vulner-
       able than other age groups to economic dislocations and crises (Hung and
       Chiu 2003).

18   The *danwei* system is the basis of the livelihood and employment security
       of the urban working class in China (C. Lee 2007). The flow of people is
       carefully monitored, and rights of access strictly controlled, like a "gated
       community" (Anagnost 2004). Job security, housing, childcare, and pen-
       sions are supplied through state-owned enterprises (Hung and Chiu 2003).
       Parents' work positions are frequently inherited by children, a situation
       which functions as another form of job security.

19   Fitzgerald (2009) discusses the "cultural price" of Mexican emigration
       to the United States by looking at cultural dissimilation, such as losing
       the Spanish language and converting from Catholicism to Protestant-
       ism. At the same time, Mexican emigration is considered a way to acquire

"culture" and modern labor discipline, forces seen as helping to modern-
ize local Mexican culture. He calls migration "a threatening conduit of
cultural change" (Fitzgerald 2009, 135). I agree with this perspective—yet
I must point out that the case of Korean Chinese emigration has less to do
with state culture than with ethnic culture, unlike Mexican emigration as
Fitzgerald discusses it.

20   Karl Marx describes the contrast between necessary labor and surplus labor
      as follows: "I call the portion of the working day during which this repro-
      duction takes necessary labor time, and the labor expended during that time
      necessary labor . . . During the second period of the labor process, that in
      which his labor is no longer necessary labor, the worker does indeed expend
      labor power, he does work but his labor is no longer necessary labor, and he
      creates no value for himself. He creates surplus value, which, for the capital-
      ist, has all the charms of something created out of nothing. This part of the
      working day I call surplus labor time, and to the labor expended during that
      time I give the name of *surplus labor*" (Marx 1992, 324–25). Marx's concept
      of surplus labor helps me in two respects. First, I use the term "surplus
      labor" to denote the excess flood of laborers who do not want to take an
      active part in the labor market of Yanbian, as Mr. Cho described them.
      Second, I view nonworking Korean Chinese who are willing to participate
      in the South Korean labor market as a sort of "reserve army," a cheap source
      of labor, which continues to produce surplus value. In fact, it is the excess
      of Korean Chinese who badly want to go to South Korea that keeps Korean
      Chinese wages there low (equal to about US$1,500 to US$2,000 per month
      around 2010), leading to constant labor exploitation.

21   In China, farmers have a land-use right for thirty years. During this period,
      the right can be rented out or passed over to other farmers, depending
      on the contract. But the property continues to belong to the local govern-
      ment, not to individuals (Oi 1991).

22   See note 1 above.

Chapter 6. Break the Cycle!

1   Li Zhang looks into the emerging middle class and their housing/consum-
      ing practice in Kunming, China; homeownership and spatial reordering
      have risen as a contentious domain of class tension (Zhang 2010).

2   Mayfair Mei-hui Yang (1994) introduced the term *guanxi* to describe a
      relationship between objects, forces, or persons. Once *guanxi* is established
      between two people, each can ask a favor of the other with the expectation
      that the debt incurred will be repaid sometime in the future.

3   Many Korean Chinese migrants have testified to the harsh discrimination
      of Koreans toward Korean Chinese. One Korean Chinese waitress asked,
      "Why do they treat fellow Koreans in this bad way? But what can I do

besides put up with this treatment? Making money is not easy." Discrimination has been internalized and naturalized as an inevitable part of the Korean dream.

4   Andrew Kipnis (2006) unravels the term *suzhi* by tracing its genealogy. *Suzhi* literally means the "innate nature" of human beings. The term began to be used when modern eugenics was introduced in the late nineteenth century, and its use rose in the Mao era, when the population began to be seen as an object to be regulated or controlled in a socialist manner. Over time, the term's meaning of "innate nature" grew to encompass an element of nurture. In particular, as the post-Mao era imposed the one-child policy on the Chinese people, the term was applied to competition in the education system and job market. It is also used mostly in a nationalist context (Kipnis 2006). Kipnis has also discussed the rise of *suzhi* discourse in the context of neoliberalism, arguing that it connotes human hierarchy and (economic) class without using the actual term *class*, by allowing a certain distance from Mao-era discourse (Kipnis 2007).

5   A South Korean scholar, Dong-Jin Seo, discusses neoliberal selves in relation to flexible capitalism in South Korea (Seo 2009). He analyzes the publication boom of self-development documents in South Korea since the rapid neoliberal economic restructuring of the late 1990s. Seo identifies a predominant concept that appeared during the boom, the "entrepreneurial individual endowed with freedom and autonomy"—the entrepreneur as an active citizen "in the pursuit of personal fulfillment and the incessant calculation to achieve it" (Seo 2009, 85). Seo's analysis of the entrepreneurial self highlights the social imperative for self-modification in South Korea. But I employ his idea to understand the emerging social imperative of entrepreneurship in Yanbian, given that the discourse also focuses on the necessity of freedom and autonomy to achieve "human quality" (*suzhi*)—rather than physical labor under the management of South Koreans.

6   The emerging subjectivity of *laoban* (entrepreneurs) reveals the strong encouragement to become an "entrepreneur of the self" in the post–Korean Wind period; the idea emphasizes the model of those who endlessly pursue their own interest. Foucault articulated it as responding systematically to modifications in the environment and symbolizing an entrepreneurship of self-realization through an interface between government and the individual (Foucault 2008, 252–53). The term *government* here concerns not only practices of government of the other but also practices of the self, the practices that try to shape and mobilize the choices, desires, aspirations, needs, wants, and lifestyles of individuals and groups (Dean 1999, 12). "Governing people is not a way to force people to do what the governor wants," Foucault argues. "It is always a versatile equilibrium, with complementarity and conflicts between techniques which assure coercion and processes through which *the self is constructed or modified by himself*" (Foucault 1993, 203–4, emphasis added). Foucault characterizes the production of an autonomous

and self-regulating subjectivity as a key to government of the self—that is, an action of the "self on self" (Dean 1999; Miller and Rose 1990, 26–28). Yet Foucault sees the government of the self as more than a simple investment for economic gain or reward, and furthers an ethical issue: the government of the self is a practice that is explicitly self-conscious of its status as forging the self in relation to existing rules of conduct or styles of existence.

7 Other Korean Chinese Communist Party members expressed little interest in going to South Korea due to their stable political and economic status. Yet while they did not go themselves, their wives went to South Korea in order to enable the purchase of apartments or to support their children's education and marriages (J. Kwon 2019a).

8 In 2008, in the wake of the global financial crisis, there was a sharp depreciation of the South Korean won. See chapter 5.

9 In 2011, the Korean Chamber of Commerce and Industries and Hana Tour conducted a survey of three hundred shopping tourists from China and Japan. The result demonstrates the rising consumer power of Chinese tourists: 32.3 percent of the Chinese surveyed spent the equivalent of more than US$1,000 in South Korea, compared to only 4.2 percent of Japanese tourists. Meanwhile, 37.79 percent of Chinese and 81.5 percent of Japanese visitors spent less than US$500. See *Money Today* (Seoul), September 7, 2011.

10 In *The Problem with Work*, Kathi Weeks analyzes work not as a simple economic practice, but as the primary means by which individuals are integrated into social, political, and familial modes of cooperation—as the experiences reported here demonstrate. Weeks also views work as an essential part of life that transforms subjects into the independent individuals of the liberal imaginary; it is construed as a basic obligation of citizenship (2011, 7–8). But she remains critical of work's domination of life in the modern world.

Conclusion: The Afterlife of the Korean Dream

1 Guided by a vision of "two upcoming centenaries," Xi pursues a well-off society by 2021 (the centennial of the Chinese Communist Party) and a fully developed nation by 2049 (the centennial of the foundation of the People's Republic of China) (Peters 2017; Z. Wang 2014).

2 According to Korean Chinese migrant workers in Seoul whom I met in the summer of 2022, the COVID-19 situation has dramatically changed the nature of the Chinese dream and their plans to go back to China. The way that the Chinese state has controlled the COVID crisis has been too oppressive and

the media surveillance has been too intrusive for them to handle after living for many years in South Korea.

3   Jin Heon Jung (2015) examines evangelical missionary work related to humanitarian aid for North Korean refugees in the Sino-North Korean border area by looking into the role of South Korean churches. Jung focuses on North Korean refugees' religious conversion as a complex cultural project, as religious freedom and salvation become contested in the very logic of "saving," in both humanitarian and biblical terms. Judy Han (2013) also explores how decentralized underground Christian networks in China have assisted countless undocumented North Korean migrants in desperate need. Han describes a Christian missionary safe house in China that practices a political theology of custody through its employment of care and control of vulnerable populations.

4   I was introduced to the concept of absence as an important feature of the remittance landscape and emptiness as a transition to a new future through the work of Sarah Lynn Lopez (2015) and Dace Dzenovska (2020) respectively.

5   For a collection written by members of this third generation, who have gotten educations and jobs in South Korea as lawyers, professors, scientists, consultants, and entrepreneurs, and are pursuing a new Korean dream, see *Chosŏnjok 3-Sedŭl Ŭi Sŏul Iyagi* [The Seoul stories of the third generation of Korean Chinese] (Ye 2011). The South Korean news agency Yanhap News published a special series on "the age of Korean Chinese success" in 2017; see, for example, https://www.yna.co.kr/view/AKR20170113128600371. Even though the term "third generation" is common, it is hard to define generations, since every family has a different migration history.

6   According to a report on Korean Chinese published by the Overseas Korean Foundation in 2016, some 87,258 Korean Chinese gained South Korean citizenship from 2001 to 2015. Since the South Korean government initiated the permanent residence right (the F-5 visa) in 2018, Korean Chinese have applied for it, but statistics are not yet available.

7   Woo Park (2020) explores the emerging Korean Chinese entrepreneurs who run businesses such as restaurants, travel agencies, and trading companies. He discusses how Korean Chinese champion equal rights while facing discrimination and stigmatization in South Korea.

Abu-Lughod, Lila. 1991. "Writing against Culture." In *Recapturing Anthropology: Working in the Present*, edited by Richard Fox, 137–62. Santa Fe, NM: School of American Research Press.

Adam, Barbara. 1991. *Time and Social Theory*. Philadelphia: Temple University Press.

Adams, Vincanne, Michelle Murphy, and Adele E. Clarke. 2009. "Anticipation: Technoscience, Life, Affect, Temporality." *Subjectivity* 28: 246–65.

Adorno, Teodor. 2009 [1991]. *The Culture Industry: Selected Essays on Mass Culture*. Edited by J. M. Bernstein. London: Routledge.

Agamben, Giorgio. 1998. *Homo Sacer: Sovereign Power and Bare Life*. Stanford, CA: Stanford University Press.

Ahmed, Sara. 2010. *The Promise of Happiness*. Durham, NC: Duke University Press.

Allison, Anne. 2015. *Precarious Japan*. Durham, NC: Duke University Press.

Althusser, Louis. 2001 [1971]. "Ideology and Ideological State Apparatuses." In *Lenin and Philosophy, and Other Essays*, translated by Ben Brewster, 85–126. New York: Monthly Review Press.

Ameeriar, Lalaie. 2017. *Downwardly Global: Women, Work, and Citizenship in the Pakistan Diaspora*. Durham, NC: Duke University Press.

An, Su-gil. 1995 [1959–67]. *Pukkando*. Seoul: Donga Publisher.

Anagnost, Ann. 2004. "The Corporeal Politics of Quality (*Suzhi*)." *Public Culture* 16, no. 2: 189–208.

Anderson, Benedict. 1992. *Imagined Communities: Reflections on the Origin and Spread of Nationalism*. London: Verso.

Andersson, Ruben. 2014. *Illegality, Inc.: Clandestine Migration and the Business of Bordering Europe*. Oakland: University of California Press.

Anzaldúa, Gloria. 1987. *Borderlands/La Frontera: The New Mestiza*. San Francisco: Spinsters/Aunt Lute.

Appadurai, Arjun. 1986. "Introduction: Commodities and the Politics of Value." In *The Social Life of Things: Commodities in Cultural Perspective*, edited by Arjun Appadurai, 3–63. Cambridge: Cambridge University Press.

Appadurai, Arjun. 1996. *Modernity at Large: Cultural Dimensions of Globalization*. Minneapolis: University of Minnesota Press.

Arendt, Hannah. 1972. *Crises of the Republic: Lying in Politics; Civil Disobedience; On Violence; Thoughts on Politics and Revolution*. New York: Harcourt Brace

Athukorala, Prema-Chandra, and Chris Manning. 1999. *Structural Change and International Migration in East Asia: Adjusting to Labour Scarcity.* Oxford: Oxford University Press.

Axel, Brian. 2004. "The Context of Diaspora." *Cultural Anthropology* 19, no. 1: 26–60.

Baldassar, Loretta, and Laura Merla. 2013. "Locating Transnational Care Circulation in Migration and Family Studies." In *Transnational Families, Migration, and the Circulation of Care: Understanding Mobility and Absence in Family Life,* edited by Loretta Baldassar and Laura Merla, 25–58. London: Routledge.

Baoliang, Chen. 1998. "To Be Defined *Liumang.*" In *Streetlife China,* edited by Michael Dutton, 63–65. Cambridge: Cambridge University Press.

Barry, Andrew, Thomas Osborne, and Nicholas Rose. 1996. "Introduction." In *Foucault and Political Reason: Liberalism, Neo-liberalism, and Rationalities of Government,* edited by Andrew Barry, Thomas Osborne, and Niklas Rose, 1–17. Chicago: University of Chicago Press.

Barth, Fredrick. 1969. *Ethnic Groups and Boundaries: The Social Organization of Culture Difference.* Long Grove, IL: Waveland Press.

Basch, Linda, Nina Glick Schiller, and Cristina Szanton Blanc. 1993. *Nations Unbound: Transnational Projects, Postcolonial Predicaments, and Deterritorialized Nation States.* London: Routledge.

Berlant, Lauren. 2011. *Cruel Optimism.* Durham, NC: Duke University Press.

Bhabha, Homi. 1994. *The Location of Culture.* London: Routledge.

Binkley, Sam. 2009. "The Work of Neoliberal Governmentality: Temporality and Ethical Substance in the Tale of Two Dads." *Foucault Studies* 6: 60–78.

Bloch, Ernest. 1995 [1959]. *The Principle of Hope,* vol. I. Translated by Neville Plaice, Stephen Plaice, and Paul Knight. Cambridge, MA: MIT Press.

Boris, Eileen, and Rachel Prennas. 2010. *Intimate Labors: Culture, Technologies, and the Politics of Care.* Stanford, CA: Stanford University Press.

Bourdieu, Pierre. 1990. *The Logic of Practice.* Stanford, CA: Stanford University Press.

Bourdieu, Pierre. 2000. *The Weight of the World: Social Suffering in Contemporary Society.* Stanford, CA: Stanford University Press.

Brennan, Denise. 2004. *What's Love Got to Do with It: Transnational Desires and Sex Tourism in the Dominican Republic.* Durham, NC: Duke University Press.

Brennan, Denise. 2014. *Life Interrupted: Trafficking into Forced Labor in the United States.* Durham, NC: Duke University Press.

Brown, Wendy. 2015. *Undoing the Demos: Neoliberalism's Stealth Revolution.* New York: Zone Books.

Brubaker, Rogers. 2004. *Ethnicity without Groups*. Cambridge, MA: Harvard University Press.

Butler, Judith. 1990. *Gender Trouble: Feminism and the Subversion of Identity*. New York: Routledge.

Butler, Judith. 1993. *Bodies that Matter: On the Discursive Limits of "Sex."* New York: Routledge.

Butler, Judith. 1997. *The Psychic Life of Power: Theories in Subjection*. Stanford, CA: Stanford University Press.

Butler, Judith. 2010. *Frames of War: When Is Life Grievable?* London: Verso.

Cabot, Heath. 2014. *On the Doorstep of Europe: Asylum and Citizenship in Greece*. Philadelphia: University of Pennsylvania Press.

Çağlar, Ayşe, and Nina Glick Schiller. 2011. "Introduction: Migrants and Cities." In *Locating Migration: Rescaling Cities and Migrants*, edited by Nina Glick Schiller and Ayşe Çağlar, 1–19. Ithaca, NY: Cornell University Press.

Carsten, Janet. 2004. *After Kinship*. Cambridge: Cambridge University Press.

Carsten, Janet, ed. 2000. *Cultures of Relatedness: New Approaches to the Study of Kinship*. Cambridge: Cambridge University Press.

Castree, Noel. 2009. "The Spatio-Temporality of Capitalism." *Time and Society* 18, no. 1: 26–61.

Cattelino, Jessica. 2008. *High Stakes: Florida Seminole Gaming and Sovereignty*. Durham, NC: Duke University Press.

Chari, Shard, and Katherine Verdery. 2009. "Thinking between the Posts: Postcolonialism, Postsocialism, and Ethnography after the Cold War." *Comparative Studies in Society and History* 51, no. 1: 6–34.

Cheng, Sealing. 2013. *On the Move for Love: Migrant Entertainers and the U.S. Military in South Korea*. Philadelphia: University of Pennsylvania Press.

Cho, Donghoon. 2010. "Analysis of Wage Differentials between Domestic and Foreign Workers in Korea." *Journal of Labor Policy* 10, no. 3: 65–86.

Cho, Munyoung. 2009. "Forced Flexibility: A Migrant Woman's Struggle for Settlement." *China Journal* 61: 51–76.

Ch'oe, Kuk-ch'ŏl. 1999. *Kando chŏnsŏl* [Legend of Kando]. Mudanjiang, China: Hŭngnyonggang Chosŏn Minjok Ch'ulp'ansa.

Ch'oe, Kuk-ch'ŏl. 2017. *Kwangbok ŭi huyedŭl* [Descendants of the liberation]. Yanji, China: Yŏnbyŏn Inmin Ch'ulp'ansa.

Choi, Hongil. 1994. *Nunmul chŏjŭn Tuman'gang* [Tearing Tumen River]. Beijing: Minjok Ch'ulp'ansa.

Chow, Rey. 2002. *The Protestant Ethnic and the Spirit of Capitalism*. New York: Columbia University Press.

Chu, Julie. 2010. *Cosmologies of Credit: Transnational Mobility and the Politics of Destination in China*. Durham, NC: Duke University Press.

Chua, Joselyin. 2011. "Making Time for Children: Self-Temporalization and the Cultivation of Anti-Suicidal Subjects in South India." *Cultural Anthropology* 26, no. 1: 112–37.

Clifford, James. 1994. "Diasporas." *Cultural Anthropology* 9, no. 3: 302–38.

Clifford, James. 1997. *Routes: Travel and Translation in the Late Twentieth Century*. Cambridge, MA: Harvard University Press.

Collier, Stephen. 2011. *Post-Soviet Social: Neoliberalism, Social Modernity, Biopolitics*. Princeton, NJ: Princeton University Press.

Comaroff, John, and Jean Comaroff. 1996. *Ethnography and the Historical Imagination*. Boulder, CO: Westview Press.

Comaroff, John, and Jean Comaroff. 2009. *Ethnicity, Inc*. Chicago: University of Chicago Press.

Constable, Nicole. 2003. *Romance on a Global Stage: Pen Pals, Virtual Ethnography, and "Mail Order Marriages."* Berkeley: University of California Press.

Constable, Nicole. 2005. *Cross-Border Marriages: Gender and Mobility in Transnational Asia*. Philadelphia: University of Pennsylvania Press.

Constable, Nicole. 2007. *Maid to Order in Hong Kong: Stories of Migrant Workers*. Ithaca, NY: Cornell University Press.

Constable, Nicole. 2009. "The Commodification of Intimacy: Marriage, Sex, and Reproductive Labor." *Annual Review of Anthropology* 38: 49–64.

Constable, Nicole. 2014. *Born out of Place: Migrant Mothers and the Politics of International Labor*. Berkeley: University of California Press.

Coutin, Susan B. 2007. *Nation of Emigrants: Shifting Boundaries of Citizenship in El Salvador and the United States*. Ithaca, NY: Cornell University Press

Coutin, Susan B. 2016. *Exiled Home: Salvadoran Transnational Youth in the Aftermath of Violence*. Durham, NC: Duke University Press.

Crapanzano, Vincent. 1986. *Waiting: The Whites of South Africa*. New York: Random House.

CTKCH (Committee of Traces of Korean Chinese History / Chungguk Chosŏn Minjok Palchach'wi" Ch'ongsŏ P'yŏnjip Wiwŏnhoe). 1991. *Chosŏnjok baljachwi ch'ongsŏ* [The traces of Korean Chinese]. Beijing: Ethnicity.

CTKCH. 1996. *Kaech'ŏk* [Dawn]. Beijing: Minjok Ch'ulp'ansa.

Cumings, Bruce. 2010. *The Korean War: A History*. New York: Modern Library.

Dautcher, Jay. 2009. *Down a Narrow Road: Identity and Masculinity in a Uyghur Community in Xinjiang, China*. Cambridge, MA: Harvard University Asia Center.

Dean, Mitchelle. 1999. *Governmentality: Power and Rule in Modern Society.* London: Sage Publications.

De Genova, Nicholas. 2010. "Introduction." In *Deportation Regime: Sovereignty, Space and Freedom of Movement*, edited by Nicholas De Genova, 1–29. Durham, NC: Duke University Press.

De Genova, Nicholas. 2013. "Spectacles of Migrant 'Illegality': The Scene of Exclusion, the Obscene of Inclusion." *Ethnic and Racial Studies* 36, no. 7: 1–19.

De Haas, Hein. 2007. "Remittances, Migration and Social Development: A Conceptual Review of the Literature." Social Policy and Development Program Paper No. 34. United Nations Research Institute for Social Development. https://www.files.ethz.ch/isn/102848/34.pdf.

DeHart, Monica. 2010. *Ethnic Entrepreneurs: Identity and Development Politics in Latin America.* Stanford, CA: Stanford University Press.

De León, Jason. 2015. *The Land of Open Graves: Living and Dying on the Migrant Trail.* Berkeley: University of California Press.

Deleuze, Gilles. 1988. *Spinoza: Practical Philosophy.* San Francisco: City Lights.

Derrida, Jacques. 1992. *Given Time: I, Counterfeit Money.* Chicago: University of Chicago Press.

Dilts, Andrew. 2011. "From 'Entrepreneur of the Self' to 'Care of the Self': Neo-Liberal Governmentality and Foucault's Ethics." *Foucault Studies* 12: 130–46.

Dirlik, Arif. 2000. "Reversals, Ironies, Hegemonies: Notes on the Contemporary Historiography of Modern China." In *History after the Three Worlds: Post-Eurocentric Historiographies*, edited by Arif Dirlik, Vinay Bahl, and Peter Gran, 125–156. Lanham, MD: Rowman and Littlefield.

Donnan, Hastings, and Thomas M. Wilson, eds. 1999. *Borders: Frontiers of Identity, Nation, and State.* Oxford: Berg.

Dunn, Elizabeth. 2004. *Privatizing Poland: Baby Food, Big Business, and the Remaking of Labor.* Ithaca, NY: Cornell University Press.

Durkheim, Émile. 1965. *The Elementary Forms of the Religious Life.* New York: Free Press.

Dutton, Michael, ed. 1998. *Streetlife in China.* Cambridge: Cambridge University Press.

Dzenovska, Dace. 2018. *School of Europeanness: Tolerance and Other Lessons in Political Liberalism in Latvia.* Ithaca, NY: Cornell University Press.

Dzenovska, Dace. 2020. "Emptiness: Capitalism without People in the Latvian Countryside." *American Ethnologist* 47, no. 1: 19–26.

Edensor, Tim. 2012. "Introduction: Thinking about Rhythm and Space." In *Geographies of Rhythm: Nature, Places, Mobilities, and Bodies*, edited by Tim Edensor, 1–20. Andover, UK: Ashgate.

Ehrenreich, Barbara, and Arlie Russell Hochschild, eds. 2004. *Global Woman: Nannies, Maids, and Sex Workers in the New Economy*. New York: Henry Holt.

Eng, David L., and Shinhee Han. 2002. "A Dialogue on Racial Melancholia." In *Loss: The Politics of Mourning*, edited by David L. Eng and David Kazanjian, 343–71. Berkeley: University of California Press.

Escobar, Arturo. 1995. *Encountering Development: The Making and Unmaking of the Third World*. Princeton, NJ: Princeton University Press.

Evans Prichard, E. E. 1969. *The Nuer: A Description of the Modes of Livelihood and Political Institutions of a Nilotic People*. Oxford: Oxford University Press.

Faier, Lieba. 2007. "Filipina Migrants in Rural Japan and Their Professions of Love." *American Ethnologist* 34, no. 1: 148–62.

Faier, Lieba. 2009. *Intimate Encounters: Filipina Women and the Remaking of Rural Japan*. Berkeley: University of California Press.

Faist, Thomas. 2010. "Transnationalization and Development: Toward an Alternative Agenda." In *Migration, Development, and Transnationalization: A Critical Stance*, edited by Nina Glick Shiller and Thomas Faist, 63–99. New York: Berghahn Books.

Fassin, Didier. 2011. *Humanitarian Reason: A Moral History of the Present*. Berkeley: University of California Press.

Felski, Rita. 2000. *Doing Time: Feminist Theory and Postmodern Culture*. New York: NYU Press.

Ferguson, James. 1990. *The Anti-Politics Machine: "Development," Depoliticization, and Bureaucratic Power in Lesotho*. Cambridge: Cambridge University Press.

Ferguson, James. 1999. *Expectations of Modernity: Myths and Meanings of Urban Life on the Zambian Copperbelt*. Berkeley: University of California Press.

Fitzgerald, David. 2009. *A Nation of Emigrants: How Mexico Manages Its Migration*. Berkeley: University of California Press.

Foucault, Michel. 1991. "Governmentality." In *The Foucault Effect: Studies in Governmentality*, edited by Graham Burchell, Colin Gordon, and Peter Miller, 87–104. Chicago: University of Chicago Press.

Foucault, Michel. 1993. "About the Beginning of the Hermeneutics of the Self." *Political Theory* 21, no. 2: 198–227.

Foucault, Michel. 1995 [1975]. *Discipline and Punish: The Birth of the Prison*. New York: Vintage.

Foucault, Michel. 2007. *Security, Territory, Population*. Basingstoke, UK: Palgrave Macmillan.

Foucault, Michel. 2008. *The Birth of Biopolitics: Lectures at the Collège de France, 1978–1979*. New York: Picador.

Franklin, Sarah. 2002. "Biologization Revisited: Kinship Theory in the Context of New Biologies." In *Relative Values: Reconfiguring Kinship Studies*, edited by Sarah Franklin and Susan McKinnon, 302–325. Durham, NC: Duke University Press.

Freeman, Caren. 2005. "Marrying Up and Marrying Down: The Paradoxes of Marital Mobility for Chosunjok Brides in South Korea." In *Cross-Border Marriages: Gender and Mobility in Transnational Asia*, edited by Nicole Constable, 80–100. Philadelphia: University of Pennsylvania Press.

Freeman, Caren. 2011. *Making and Faking Kinships: Marriage and Labor Migration between China and South Korea*. Ithaca, NY: Cornell University Press.

Friedman, Sara. 2006. *Intimate Politics: Marriage, the Market, and State Power in Southeastern China*. Cambridge, MA: Harvard University Press.

Fromm, Erich. 2006 [1956]. *The Art of Loving*. New York: Harper Perennial.

Gasparini, Giovanni. 1995. "On Waiting." *Time and Society* 4, no. 1: 29–45.

Gilroy, Paul. 1991. "'It Ain't Where You're From, It's Where You're At . . . : The Dialectics of Diasporic Identification." *Third Text* 13: 3–16.

Gilroy, Paul. 1993. *The Black Atlantic: Modernity and Double Consciousness*. Cambridge, MA: Harvard University Press.

Greenhalgh, Susan, and Edwin A. Winckler. 2005. *Governing China's Population: From Leninist to Neoliberal Biopolitics*. Stanford, CA: Stanford University Press.

Gregory, Christopher. 1982. *Gifts and Commodities*. London: Academic Press.

Gu, Edward. 2002. "The State Socialist Welfare System and the Political Economy of Public Housing Reform in Urban China." *Review of Research Policy* 19, no. 2: 179–211.

Gupta, Akhil, and James Ferguson, eds. 1997. *Culture, Power, Place: Explorations in Critical Anthropology*. Durham, NC: Duke University Press.

Hage, Ghassan. 2009. "Waiting Out the Crisis: On Stuckness and Governmentality." In *Waiting*, edited by Ghassan Hage, 97–106. Melbourne: University of Melbourne Press.

Hall, Stuart. 1996. "Cultural Identity and Diaspora." In *Contemporary Postcolonial Theory: A Reader*, edited by Padmini Mongia, 110–121. London: Edward Arnold.

Han, Clara. 2012. *Life in Debt: Times of Care and Violence in Neoliberal Chile*. Berkeley: University of California Press.

Han, Geon-Soo. 2003. "Making 'the Other': Korean Society and the Representation of Immigrant Workers." *Comparative Cultural Studies* 9, no. 2: 157–93.

Han, Hongkoo. 2013. "Colonial Origins of Juche: The Minsaengdan Incident of the 1930s and the Birth of the North Korea-China Relationship." In *Origins of North Korea's Juche: Colonialism, War, and Development*, edited by Jae-Jung Suh, 33–62. Lanham, MD: Lexington Books.

Han, Ju Hui Judy. 2013. "Beyond Safe Haven." *Critical Asian Studies* 45, no. 4: 533–60.

Hann, Chris, Caroline Humphrey, and Katherine Verdery. 2002. "Introduction: Postsocialism as a Topic of Anthropology." In *Postsocialism: Ideals, Ideologies and Practices in Eurasia*, edited by Chris Hann, 1–28. London: Routledge.

Hannerz, Ulf. 1997. "Borders." *International Social Science Journal* 154: 537–548.

Hardt, Michael, and Antonio Negri. 2000. *Empire*. Cambridge, MA: Harvard University Press.

Harms, Erik. 2013. "Eviction Time in the New Saigon: Temporalities of Displacement in the Rubble of Development." *Cultural Anthropology* 28, no. 2: 344–68.

Harrel, Stevan. 1995. *Cultural Encounters on China's Ethnic Frontiers*. Seattle: University of Washington Press.

Harvey, David. 1989. *The Condition of Postmodernity: An Inquiry into the Origin of Cultural Change*. Oxford: Blackwell.

Harvey, David. 1999. *The Limit of Capital*. London: Verso.

Harvey, David. 2005. *A Brief History of Neoliberalism*. Oxford: Oxford University Press.

Hochschild, Arlie Russel. 2004. "Love and Gold." In *Global Woman: Nannies, Maids, and Sex Workers in the New Economy*, edited by Barbara Ehrenreich and Arlie Russell Hochschild, 15–30. New York: Henry Holt.

Hoffman, Lisa. 2010. *Patriotic Professionalism in Urban China: Fostering Talent*. Philadelphia: Temple University Press.

Holmes, Seth M. 2013. *Fresh Fruit, Broken Bodies: Migrant Farmworkers in the United States*. Berkeley: University of California Press.

Hong, Jongwook. 2020. "Who were made as spies?: Koreans in Japan" [Nugureul gancheobeuro mandeureonna: Jaeilhanin]. In *Kanch'ŏp Sidae: Han'guk Hyŏndaesa Wa Chojak Kanch'ŏp*, edited by Chŏng-in Kim and Pyŏng-ju Hwang, 229–62. Seoul: Ch'aek Kwa Hamkke.

Huang, Yu Fu. 2009. *We Are 100% Korean Chinese*. Jilin, China: Overseas Korean Forum.

Hung, Eva. P. W., and Stephen W. K. Chiu. 2003. "The Lost Generation: Life Course Dynamics and *Xiagang* in China." *Modern China* 29, no. 2: 204–36.

Hyun, Ryongsoon, Jungmoon Lee, and Ryongguo Huh. 1982. *Chosŏnjok paengnyŏn sahwa* [One hundred years of Korean-Chinese history]. Yanji, China: Yonbyŏn Inmin Ch'ulp'ansa.

Jeffrey, Craig. 2010. "Timepass: Youth, Class, and Time among Unemployed Young Men in India." *American Ethnologist* 37, no. 3: 465–81.

Jonas, Andrew. 1994. "The Scale Politics of Spatiality." *Environment and Planning D: Society and Space* 12: 257–64.

Jones, Kate. 1998. "Scale as Epistemology." *Political Geography* 17: 25–8.

JPA (Jilin Political Association, Historical Archive Committee/Jilin Sheng zheng xie, Wen shi zi liao wei yuan hui). 1995. *Killim Chosŏnjok* [Jilin Korean Chinese]. Yanbian, China: Yŏnbyŏn Inmin Ch'ulp'ansa; Yŏnbyŏn Sinhwa Sŏjŏm parhaeng.

Jung, Jin-Heon. 2015. *Migration and Religion in East Asia: North Korean Migrants' Evangelical Encounters*. Basingstoke, UK: Palgrave Macmillan.

Jung, Minwoo. 2017. "Precarious Seoul: Urban Inequality and Belonging of Young Adults in South Korea." *Positions* 25, no. 4: 745–67.

Kawashima, Ken. 2009. *The Proletarian Gamble: Korean Workers in Interwar Japan*. Durham, NC: Duke University Press

Kim, Chulsu, Ryungbum Kang, and Chulhwan Kim. 1998. *Chungguk Chosŏnjok Yŏksa Sansik* [Common sense of Korean Chinese history]. Yanji, China: Yŏnbyŏn Inmin Ch'ulp'ansa.

Kim, Eleana. 2010. *Adopted Territory: Transnational Korean Adoptees and the Politics of Belonging*. Durham, NC: Duke University Press.

Kim, Hyun Mee. 2008. "The Korean Chinese Migration Experience in England: The Case of Residents in Korea Town." *Korean Anthropology* 41, no. 2: 39–77.

Kim, Jaeeun. 2009. "The Making and Unmaking of a 'Transborder Nation': South Korea During and After the Cold War." *Theory and Society* 38, no. 2: 133–64.

Kim, Jaeeun. 2016. *Contested Embrace: Transborder Membership Politics in Twentieth-Century Korea*. Stanford, CA; Stanford University Press.

Kim, Jaesok. 2013. *Chinese Labor in a Korean Factory: Class, Ethnicity, and Productivity on the Shop Floor in Globalizing China*. Stanford, CA: Stanford University Press.

Kim, Samuel. 2000. *Korea's Globalization*. Cambridge: Cambridge University Press.

Kipnis, Andrew. 2006. "*Suzhi*: A Key Word Approach." *China Quarterly*, no. 186: 295–313.

Kipnis, Andrew. 2007. "Neoliberalism Reified: *Suzhi* Discourse and Tropes of Neoliberalism in the People's Republic of China." *Journal of the Royal Anthropological Institute* 13, no. 2: 383–400.

Kissinger, Henry. 2011. *On China*. New York: Penguin Press.

Kwon, Heonik. 2008. *Ghosts of War in Vietnam*. Cambridge: Cambridge University Press.

Kwon, Heonik. 2010. *The Other Cold War*. New York: Columbia University Press.

Kwon, June Hee. 2015. "The Work of Waiting: Love and Money in Korean Chinese Transnational Migration." *Cultural Anthropology* 30, no. 3: 477–500.

Kwon, June Hee. 2019a. "Forbidden Homeland: Divided Belonging on the China-Korea Border." *Critique of Anthropology* 39, no. 1: 74–94

Kwon, June Hee. 2019b. "Rhythms of 'Free' Movement: Migrants' Bodies and Time under South Korean Visa Regimes." *Journal of Ethnic and Migration Studies* 45, no. 15: 2953–70.

Laclau, Ernesto, and Chantal Mouffe. 1985. *Hegemony and Socialist Strategy: Toward a Radical Democratic Politics*. London: Verso.

Lazzarato, Maurizio. 1996. "Immaterial Labor." In *Radical Thought In Italy: A Potential Politics*, edited by Paolo Virno and Michael Hardt, 133–150. Minneapolis: University of Minnesota Press.

Lee, Ching-Kwan. 2007. *Against the Law: Labor Protests in China's Rustbelt and Sunbelt*. Berkeley: University of California Press.

Lee, Hae-Eung. 2005. "The Transformation of Subjectivity of Korean Chinese Married Women through the Migration Experience." MA thesis, Ewha Women's University, Seoul.

Lee, Helene K. 2018. *Between Foreign and Family: Return Migration and Identity Construction among Korean Americans and Korean Chinese*. New Brunswick, NJ: Rutgers University Press.

Lee, Jin Young. 2002. "Chosunineso Chosunjokero: Yanbianjiyeok jangakgwa Jeonchesong byunhwa (1945–1949)" [From Korean ethnic to Korean Chinese: The occupation of Yanbian and identity shift (1945–1949)]. *Chinese Studies* 95: 90–116.

Lee, Jinyoung, Lee Hyekyung, and Hyunmee Kim. 2008. *The Effect of Satisfaction of the Visit and Employment System*. Seoul: Korean Immigration Service.

Lee, Joo Young. 2004. "Domestic Work Experience of Female Korean Chinese Working in Korea." MA thesis, Yonsei University, Seoul.

Lee, Min Joo. 2008. "The Commercial Activity and Identity Formation of Korean Chinese." MA thesis, Yonsei University, Seoul.

Lefebvre, Henri. 2004. *Rhythmanalysis: Space, Time, and Everyday Life*. New York: Continuum.

Lemke, Thomas. 2002. "Foucault, Governmentality, and Critique." *Rethinking Marxism* 14, no. 3: 49–64.

Levin, Caroline. 2015. *Forms: Whole, Rhythm, Hierarch, Network*. Princeton, NJ: Princeton University Press.

Levitt, Peggy. 2001. *The Transnational Villagers*. Berkeley: University of California Press.

Levitt, Peggy, and Deepak Lamba-Nieves. 2011. "Social Remittances Revisited." *Journal of Ethnic and Migration Studies* 37, no. 1: 1–22.

Lim, Gesoon. 2005. *Uriegedagaon Chosunjokeun nuguinga* [Who are the Korean Chinese Coming to Us]. Seoul: Hyunamsa.

Lim, Sung Sook. 2004. "The Process of Formation of Korean Chinese Ethnic Identity." MA thesis, Hanyang University, Seoul.

Lim, Yun-Chin, and Suk-Man Hwang. 2002. "The Political Economy of South Korean Structural Adjustment: Reality and Façade." *African and Asian Studies* 1, no. 2: 87–112.

Litzinger, Ralph. 1998. "Memory Work: Reconstituting the Ethnic in Post-Mao China." *Cultural Anthropology* 13, no. 2: 224–55.

Litzinger, Ralph. 2000. *Other Chinas: The Yao and the Politics of National Belonging*. Durham, NC: Duke University Press.

Liu, Xin. 2002. *The Otherness of Self: A Genealogy of the Self in Contemporary China*. Ann Arbor: University of Michigan Press.

Lopez, Sarah Lynn. 2015. *The Remittance Landscape: Spaces of Migration in Rural Mexico and Urban USA*. Chicago: University of Chicago Press.

Lucht, Hans. 2011. *Darkness before Daybreak: African Migrants Living on the Margin in Southern Italy Today*. Berkeley: University of California Press.

Mackenzie, Peter. 2002. "Strangers in the City: The *Hukou* and Urban Citizenship in China." *Journal of International Affairs* 56, no. 1: 305–19.

Mahoney, Josef Gregory. 2014. "Interpreting the Chinese Dream: An Exercise of Political Hermeneutics." *Journal of Chinese Political Science* 19, no. 1: 15–34.

Mains, Daniel. 2007. "Neoliberal Times: Progress, Boredom, and Shame among Young Men in Urban Ethiopia." *American Ethnologist* 34, no. 4: 659–73.

Malinowski, Bronislaw. 2002 [1922]. *Argonauts of the Western Pacific: An Account of Native Enterprise and Adventure in the Archipelagoes of Melanesian New Guinea*. London: Routledge.

Mandel, Ruth, and Caroline Humphrey. 2002. "The Market in Everyday Life: Ethnographies of Postsocialism." In *Markets and Moralities: Ethnographies of Postsocialism*, edited by Ruth Mandel and Caroline Humphrey, 1–16. Oxford: Berg.

Marx, Karl. 1988. *The Economic and Philosophic Manuscripts of 1844*. Amherst, NY: Prometheus Books.

Marx, Karl. 1992 [1867]. *Capital, Volume 1*. London: Penguin Books.

Masquelier, Adeline, and Deborah Durham. 2023. "Introduction: Minding the Gap in the Meantime." In *In the Meantime: Toward an Anthropol-*

ogy of the Possible, edited by Adeline Masquelier and Deborah Durham, 1–25. New York: Berghahn Books.

Massey, Doreen. 1993. "Power-Geometry and a Progressive Sense of Place." In *Mapping the Futures: Local Cultures, Global Change*, edited by Jon Bird, Barry Curtis, Tim Putnam, George Robertson, and Lisa Tickner, 60–70. New York: Routledge.

Massey, Douglass, and Emilio Parrado. 1998. "International Migration and Business Formation in Mexico." *Social Science Quarterly* 1, no. 79: 1–34.

Mathews, Gordon. 2011. *Ghetto at the Center of the World: Chungking Mansions, Hong Kong*. Chicago: University of Chicago Press.

Mauss, Marcel. 2000 [1925]. *The Gift: The Form and Reason of Exchange in Archaic Societies*. Translated by W. D. Halls. New York: Norton.

Mezzadra, Sandro, and Brett Neilson. 2013. *Border as Method, or, the Multiplication of Labor*. Durham, NC: Duke University Press.

McKinnon, Susan. 2002. "The Economies of Kinship and the Paternity of Culture: Origin Stories in Kinship Theory." In *Relative Values: Reconfiguring Kinship Studies*, edited by Sarah Franklin and Susan McKinnon, 277–301. Durham, NC: Duke University Press.

Meisner, Maurice J. 1999. *Mao's China and After: A History of the People's Republic*. 3rd ed. New York: Free Press.

Miller, Daniel. 2002. "Alienable Gifts and Inalienable Commodities." In *The Empire of Things: Regimes of Value and Material Culture*, edited by Fred R. Myers, 91–115. Santa Fe, NM: School of American Research Press.

Miller, Peter, and Nicholas Rose. 1990. "Governing Economic Life." *Economy and Society* 19, no. 1: 1–31.

Mineggal, Monica. 2009. "The Time Is Right: Waiting, Reciprocity, and Sociality." In *Waiting*, edited by Ghassan Hage, 89–92. Melbourne: Melbourne University Publishing.

Moon, Katharine. 2000. "Strangers in the Midst: Foreign Workers and Korean Nationalism." In *Korea's Globalization*, edited by Samuel S. Kim, 147–69. Cambridge: Cambridge University Press.

Morris-Suzuki, Tessa. 2007. *Exodus to North Korea: Shadows from Japan's Cold War*. Lanham, MD: Rowman and Littlefield.

Mueggler, Erik. 2001. *The Age of Wild Ghosts: Memory, Violence, and Place in Southwest China*. Berkeley: University of California Press.

Mullaney, Thomas. 2011. *Coming to Terms with the Nation: Ethnic Classification in Modern China*. Berkeley: University of California Press.

Munn, Nancy. 1992. "The Cultural Anthropology of Time: A Critical Essay." *Annual Review of Anthropology* 21: 93–123.

Navaro-Yashin, Yael. 2012. *The Make-Believe Space: Affective Geography in a Postwar Polity*. Durham, NC: Duke University Press.

Ngai, Pun. 2005. *Made in China: Women Factory Workers in a Global Work-place*. Durham, NC: Duke University Press.

Noh, Gowoon. 2001. "Between Expectation and Reality: The Life and Adaptation Strategies of Korean Chinese." MA thesis, Seoul National University.

Noh, Gowoon. 2011. "Life on the Border: Korean Chinese Negotiating National Belonging in Transnational Space." PhD diss., University of California, Davis.

Oi, Jean. 1991. *State and Peasant in Contemporary China*. Berkeley: University of California Press.

OKF (Overseas Koreans Foundation). 2016. *Report on the Korean Chinese Living in South Korea*. Seoul: Overseas Koreans Foundation.

O'Neill, Bruce. 2014. "Cast Aside: Boredom, Downward Mobility, and Homelessness in Post-Communist Bucharest." *Cultural Anthropology* 29, no. 1: 8–31.

Ong, Aihwa. 1999. *Flexible Citizenship: The Cultural Logics of Transnationality*. Durham, NC: Duke University Press.

Ong, Aihwa. 2006. *Neoliberalism as Exception: Mutations in Citizenship and Sovereignty*. Durham, NC: Duke University Press.

Ong, Aihwa, and Donald Nonini, eds. 1996. *Ungrounded Empires: The Cultural Politics of Chinese Modern Transnationalism*. New York: Routledge.

Papastergiadis, Nikos. 2000. *The Turbulence of Migration: Globalization, Deterritorialization, and Hybridity*. Cambridge: Polity.

Park, Alyssa M. 2019. *Sovereignty Experiments: Korean Migrants and the Building of Borders in Northeast Asia, 1860–1945*. Ithaca, NY: Cornell University Press.

Park, Gwang Sung. 2006. "The Movement of Korean Chinese Labor and Social Change in the Age of Globalization." PhD diss., Seoul National University.

Park, Hyun Gwi. 2018. *The Displacement of Borders among Russian Koreans in Northeast Asia*. Amsterdam: Amsterdam University Press.

Park, Hyun Ok. 2005. *Two Dreams in One Bed: Empire, Social Life, and the Origins of the North Korean Revolution in Manchuria*. Durham, NC: Duke University Press.

Park, Hyun Ok. 2015. *The Capitalist Unconscious: From Korean Unification to Transnational Korea*. New York: Columbia University Press.

Park, Jung-Sun, and Paul Chang. 2005. "Contention in the Construction of a Global Korean Community: The Case of the Overseas Korean Act." *Journal of Korean Studies* 10, no. 1: 1–27.

Park, Woo. 2020. *Chaoxianzu Entrepreneurs in Korea: Searching for Citizenship in the Ethnic Homeland*. Abingdon, UK: Routledge.

Parrenas, Rachel Salaza. 2001. *Servants of Globalization: Migration and Domestic Work*. Stanford, CA: Stanford University Press.

Parrenas, Rachel Salaza. 2004. "The Care Crisis in the Philippines: Children and Transnational Families in the New Global Economy." In *Global Woman: Nannies, Maids, and Sex Workers in the New Economy*, edited by Barbara Ehrenreich and Arlie Russell Hochschild, 39–54. New York: Henry Holt.

Peters, Michael A. 2017. "The Chinese Dream: Xi Jinping Thought on Socialism with Chinese Characteristics for a New Era." *Educational Philosophy and Theory* 49, no. 14: 1299–1304.

Piore, Michel. 1979. *Birds of Passage: Migrant Labor and Industrial Societies*. Cambridge: Cambridge University Press.

Richard, Analiese, and Daromir Rudnyckyj. 2009. "Economies of Affect." *Journal of the Royal Anthropological Institute* 15, no. 1: 57–77.

Rivkin-Fish, Michele. 2009. "Tracing the Landscape of the Past in Class Subjectivity: Practices of Memory and Distinction in Marketizing Russia." *American Ethnologist* 36, no. 1: 79–95.

Rodriguez, Robyn Magalit. 2010. *Migrants for Export: How the Philippine State Brokers Labor to the World*. Minneapolis: University of Minnesota Press.

Rofel, Lisa. 2007. *Desiring China: Experiments in Neoliberalism, Sexuality, and Public Culture*. Durham, NC: Duke University Press.

Rofel, Lisa. 2016. "Temporal-Spatial Migration: Workers in Transnational Supply-Chain Factories." In *Ghost Protocol: Development and Displacement in Global China*, edited by Carlos Rojas and Ralph Litzinger, 167–190. Durham, NC: Duke University Press.

Rojas, Carlos. 2016. "Specters of Marx, Shades of Mao, and the Ghosts of Global Capital." In *Ghost Protocol: Development and Displacement in Global China*, edited by Carlos Rojas and Ralph Litzinger, 1–12. Durham, NC: Duke University Press.

Rose, Nicholas. 1996. "Governing 'Advanced' Liberal Democracies." In *Foucault and Political Reason: Liberalism, Neo-Liberalism, and Rationalities of Government*, edited by Andrew Barry, Thomas Osborne, and Nicholas Rose, 37–64. Chicago: University of Chicago Press.

Rundell, John. 2009. "Temporal Horizons of Modernity and Modalities of Waiting." In *Waiting*, edited by Ghassan Hage, 42–53. Melbourne: Melbourne University Publishing.

Ryang, Sonia. 1997. *North Koreans in Japan: Language, Ideology, and Identity*. Boulder, CO: Westview Press.

Safran, William. 1991. "Diasporas in Modern Societies: Myths of Homeland and Return." *Diaspora* 1, no. 1: 83–99.

Sahlins, Marshall. 2012. *What Kinship Is—And Is Not*. Chicago: University of Chicago Press.

Salazar, Noel, and Alan Smart. 2011. "Introduction: Anthropological Takes on Im/Mobility." *Identities* 18, no. 6: i–ix.

Salter, Mark B. 2006. "The Global Visa Regime and the Political Technologies of the International Self: Borders, Bodies, Biopolitics." *Alternatives: Global, Local, Political* 31, no. 2: 167–89.

Salter, Mark B. 2012. "Theory of the /: The Suture and Critical Border Studies." *Geopolitics* 17, no. 4: 734–55.

Sassen, Saskia. 2000. "Countergeographies of Globalization: The Feminization of Survival." *Journal of International Affairs* 53, no. 2: 503–24.

Sassen, Saskia. 2004. "Global Cities and Survival Circuits." In *Global Woman: Nannies, Maids, and Sex Workers in the New Economy*, edited by Barbara Ehrenreich and Arlie Russell Hochschild, 254–74. New York: Henry Holt.

Schein, Louisa. 2000. *The Minority Rules: The Miao and the Feminine in China's Cultural Politics*. Durham, NC: Duke University Press.

Schiller, Nina Glick, and Thomas Faist. 2010. "Introduction: Migration, Development, and Social Transformation." In *Migration, Development, and Transnationalization: A Critical Stance*, edited by Nina Glick Shiller and Thomas Faist, 1–21. New York: Berghahn Books.

Schmid, Andre. 1997. "Rediscovering Manchuria: Sin Ch'aeho and the Politics of Territorial History in Korea." *Journal of Asian Studies* 56, no. 1: 26–46.

Schneider, David. 1980. *American Kinship: A Cultural Account*, 2nd ed. Chicago: University of Chicago Press.

Seo, Dong-Jin. 2009. *Chayu ŭi ŭiji chagi kyebal ŭi ŭiji: sinjayujuŭi Han'guk sahoe esŏ chagi kyebal hanŭn chuch'e ŭi t'ansaeng* [The will to freedom, the will to self-improvement: The birth of the self-improving subject in neolibreal Korean society]. Paju, South Korea: Tolbegae.

Seol, Dong-Hoon. 2002. "Korean Chinese Working in Korea: Are They Overseas Koreans or Foreigners?" *Trend and Perspective* 52: 200–223.

Seol, Dong-Hoon, and John Skrentny. 2009. "Ethnic Return Migration and Hierarchical Nationhood: Korean Chinese Foreign Workers in South Korea." *Ethnicities* 9, no. 2: 147–74.

Shin, Gi-wook. 2006. *Ethnic Nationalism in Korea: Genealogy, Politics, and Legacy*. Stanford, CA: Stanford University Press.

Simmel, George. 2004 [1907]. *The Philosophy of Money*. 3rd ed. Translated by Tom Bottomore and David Frisby. London: Routledge.

Smith, Anthony. 1986. *The Ethnic Origins of Nations*. Oxford: Blackwell.

Smith, Neil. 1984. *Uneven Development: Nature, Capital, and the Production of Space*. Oxford: Blackwell.

Smith, Neil. 2003. "Remaking Scale: Competition and Cooperation in Pre-National and Post-National Europe." In *State/Space: A Reader*, edited by Neil Brenner, Bob Jessop, Martin Jones, and Gordon Macleod, 227–38. Chichester, UK: Wiley.

Solingr, Dorothy. 1999. *Contesting Citizenship in Urban China: Peasant Migrants, the State, and the Logic of the Market.* Berkeley: University of California Press.

Sollors, Werner. 1995. "Ethnicity." In *Critical Terms for Literary Study*, edited by Frank Lentricchia and Thomas McLaughlin, 288–305. Chicago: University of Chicago Press.

Song, Du-Yul. 2017. *Pul T'anŭn Ŏrŭm: Kyŏnggyein Song Tu-Yul Ŭi Chajŏnjŏk Esei* [Burning ice: Man on the border, autobiography of Song Tu-Yul]. Seoul: Humanit'asu.

Song, Jesook. 2009. *South Koreans in the Debt Crisis: The Creation of a Neoliberal Welfare Society.* Durham, NC: Duke University Press.

Song, Nianshen. 2017. "The Journey towards 'No Man's Land': Interpreting the China-Korea Borderland within Imperial and Colonial Contexts." *Journal of Asian Studies* 76, no. 4: 1035–58.

Song, Nianshen. 2018. *Making Borders in Modern East Asia: The Tumen River Demarcation, 1881–1919.* Cambridge: Cambridge University Press.

Spinoza, Benedict de. 1994 [1677]. *Ethics*, translated by Edwin Curley. London: Penguin.

Squire, Vicki. 2010. "The Contested Politics of Mobility: Politicizing Mobility, Mobilizing Politics." In *The Contested Politics of Mobility: Borderzones and Irregularity*, 1–25. New York: Routledge.

Standing, Guy. 2011. *The Precariat: The New Dangerous Class.* London: Bloomsbury Academic.

Stiglitz, Joseph E. 2003. *Globalization and Its Discontents.* New York: Norton.

Sukhwa, 2006. *Yŏnbyŏn* [Yanbian]. Yanbian, China: Yanbian People's Publishing.

Sun, Chunri. 2008. "The Problems of Koreans in Manchuria before and after the Liberation Period." *Journal of Manchurian Studies* 8, no. 8: 181–97.

Thompson, E. P. 1967. "Time, Work-Discipline and Industrial Capitalism." *Past and Present* 38, no. 1: 56–97.

Ticktin, Maria. 2011. *Casualities of Care: Immigration and the Politics of Humanitarianism in France.* Berkeley: University of California Press.

Tsuda, Takeyuki. 2003. *Strangers in the Ethnic Homeland: Japanese Brazilian Migration in Transnational Perspective.* New York: Columbia University Press.

Tyner, James A. 2009. *The Philippines: Mobilities, Identities, Globalization.* London: Routledge.

UNDP (United Nations Development Programme). 2007. *Human Develop-*
ment Report 2007: Human Development and Climate Change. United
Nations Development Programme. https://hdr.undp.org/content
/human-development-report-20078.

Verdery, Katherine. 1996. *What Was Socialism, and What Comes Next?*
Princeton, NJ: Princeton University Press.

Walder, Andrew. 1986. *Communist Neo-Traditionalism: Work and Authority*
in Chinese Industry. Berkeley: University of California Press.

Wallerstein, Immanuel. 1991. "The Construction of Peoplehood." In *Race,*
Nation, Class, edited by Immanuel Wallerstein and Étienne Balibar,
71–85. New York: Verso.

Wang, Hui. 2006. *China's New Order: Society, Politics, and Economy in Tran-*
sition. Cambridge, MA: Harvard University Press.

Wang, Zheng. 2014. "The Chinese Dream: Concept and Context." *Journal*
of Chinese Political Science 19, no. 1: 1–13.

Weber, Max. 1997. "What Is an Ethnic Group?" In *The Ethnicity Reader:*
Nationalism, Multiculturalism, and Migration, edited by Montserrat
Guibernau and John Rex, 15–26. Cambridge, UK: Polity.

Weeks, Kathi. 1998. *Constituting Feminist Subjects.* Ithaca, NY: Cornell
University Press.

Weeks, Kathi. 2011. *The Problem with Work: Feminism, Marxism, Antiwork*
Politics, and Postwork Imaginaries. Durham, NC: Duke University
Press.

Weiner, Annette. 1992. *Inalienable Possessions: The Paradox of Keeping-*
While-Giving. Berkeley: University of California Press.

Weston, Kath. 1997. *Families We Choose: Lesbians, Gays, Kinship.* New York:
Columbia University Press.

Whitfield, Stephen. 1991. *The Culture of the Cold War.* Baltimore: Johns
Hopkins University Press.

Williams, Raymond. 1977. *Marxism and Literature.* Oxford: Oxford University Press.

Wise, Raúl Delgado, and Humberto Márquez Covarrubias. 2010. "Understanding the Relationship between Migration and Development:
Toward a New Theoretical Approach." In *Migration, Development, and*
Transnationalization: A Critical Stance, edited by Nina Glick Shiller
and Thomas Faist, 142–75. Oxford: Berghahn Books.

Xiang, Biao. 2005. *Transcending Boundaries: Zhejiangcun: The Story of a Mi-*
grant Village in Beijing. Leiden: Brill.

Xiang, Biao. 2013. "Multi-Scalar Ethnography: An Approach for Critical
Engagement with Migration and Social Change." *Ethnography* 14, no. 3:
282–99.

Xiang, Biao. 2016. "'You've Got to Rely On Yourself . . . and the State!':
A Structural Chasm in the Chinese Political Moral Order." In *Ghost*

Protocol: Development and Displacement in Global China, edited by Carlos Rojas and Ralph Litzinger, 131–49. Durham, NC: Duke University Press.

Xikui, Gong. 1998. "Household Registration and the Caste-Like Quality of Peasant Life." In *Streetlife China*, edited by Michael Dutton, 81–85. Cambridge: Cambridge University Press.

Xu, Lianshun. 1996. *Paramkkot* [The windflower]. Seoul: Pŏmusa.

Yamamura, Chigusa. 2020. *Marriage and Marriageability: The Practices of Matchmaking between Men from Japan and Women from Northeast China*. Ithaca, NY: Cornell University Press

Yan, Hairong. 2003. "Neoliberal Governmentality and Neohumanism: Organizing Suzhi/Value Flow through Labor Recruitment Networks." *Cultural Anthropology* 18, no. 4: 493–523.

Yan, Hairong. 2008. *New Masters, New Servants: Migration, Development, and Women Workers in China*. Durham, NC: Duke University Press.

Yan, Yunxiang. 1996. *The Flow of Gifts: Reciprocity and Social Networks in a Chinese Village*. Stanford, CA: Stanford University Press.

Yang, Mayfair Mei-hui. 1994. *Gifts, Favors, and Banquets: The Art of Social Relationships in China*. Ithaca, NY: Cornell University Press.

Ye, Tong-gŭn. 2011. *Chosŏnjok 3-Sedŭl Ŭi Sŏul Iyagi* [Stories of the third generation of Korean Chinese]. Seoul: Paeksan Sŏdang.

Yoon, Keun-Cha. 2016. *Chainich'i Ŭi Chŏngsinsa: Nam-puk-il Segae Ŭi Kukka Sai Esŏ* [The thought history of Koreans in Japan: Between the three countries South Korea, North Korea, and Japan]. Seoul: Han'gyŏre Ch'ulp'an.

Yoon, Yongdo. 2013. "Korean Chinese and Korean Russians' Transnational Return/Migration and the State Regulation of Post-Nation." In *Kwihwan hokeun Sunhwan* [Return or circulation], edited by Shin Hyunjoon, 76–148. Seoul: Greenbi.

You, Haili. 1994. "Defining Rhythm: Aspects of an Anthropology of Rhythm." *Culture, Medicine, and Psychiatry* 18, no. 3: 361–84.

Zavella, Patricia. 2011. *I'm Neither Here nor There: Mexicans' Quotidian Struggles with Migration and Poverty*. Durham, NC: Duke University Press.

Zhang, Li. 2001. *Strangers in the City: Reconfiguration of Space, Power, and Social Networks within China's Floating Population*. Stanford, CA: Stanford University Press.

Zhang, Li. 2010. *In Search of Paradise: Middle-Class Living in a Chinese Metropolis*. Ithaca, NY: Cornell University Press.

daughter-in-law theory, of Zheng Panlong, 38–39

Deng Xiaoping, economic reforms of, 7, 40, 155, 175

deportation, of migrants from South Korea, 53, 65, 72, 82, 102; attempts to hide identity and, 68–69; female workers' experiences of, 68–71; tension and nervousness over, 68–69; undocumented threat of, 66–67

Derrida, Jacques, 203n16

deterioration, of bodies, 94–95, 99

development: Korean Chinese transition to economic, 181; remittance relationship with, 123, 149, 205n1; Xin Liu on southern China, 175; Yanbian changes from 2008–2016, 150–52

devil capitalism, South Korea as locus of, 5, 187n5

differentiated mobility: by ethnicity, 127–28, 149; ethnic stereotype as context of, 127; in Korean Wind, 125; in transnational migration, 125, 147–48; turbulence of migration and, 147–48

disdain, for migrant workers, 164–65, 173–74

displacement: Chu on mobility and, 170–71; feelings of, 174

diversified dreams, 183–85

dreams: channeling of, 180–83; diversified, 183–85; evolution of, 178–80. *See also* Chinese dream; Korean dream

economic reform: of Deng Xiaoping, 7, 40, 155, 175; Korean Wind and, 50

economy: China and North Korea disparity in, 54; China globally rising, 25, 30, 155–56, 164; China privatization and, 178–79; Korean Wind betterment of, 50, 81; remittance-dependent, 22, 147; South Korea development and remittances, 60; South Korea migrant labor and political, 3; transnational migration and Yanbian, 145; Yanbian social stability and affluence of, 153

employment agencies, in South Korea, 85–90, 206n7

entrepreneurs. *See laoban*

ethnic borderland, of Yanbian, 29, 49–51; crossing history in, 34–38; description of, 42–45; ethnic feelings and, 45–48; geopolitical space of, 32–34; Han Chinese and, 30–31; rise of ethnic talk regarding, 38–41; socialism and Korean Wind intersection in, 48–50

ethnic comfort, Yanbian and, 46–48

ethnic crisis, 53

ethnic enclave, Yanji as, 125–28, 205n3, 206n8

ethnicity, 33, 43, 70, 74; defined, 39; differentiated mobility by, 127–28, 149; ethnic education and, 47, 194n17; as form of exclusion, 39; inequality maintained using, 39–40; Korean Chinese de-emphasis of, 38; Korean Chinese as mobile, 24, 31, 127; Korean Chinese transnational border crossing, 41; Overseas Korean Act on, 59–63, 196n8; peoplehood and otherness of, 39; stereotypes in, 194n19; theories of articulation and, 21; value production and cultural currency in, 191n27

ethnicization, inequality maintained through, 39–40

ethnicized ethnic bodies, 4, 21, 178

ethnic others: Chinese Communist Party recognition of, 40; Korean Chinese perception of, 42

ethnic talk, on Korean Chinese: apple-pear graft theory and, 38–49; daughter-in-law theory and, 38–39; on "100 percent Korean Chinese" identity, 39

ethno-national groups, in China, 39–40

"Everybody Is Gone" (song), 100

evolution, of dreams, 178–80

exclusion, 63; ethnicity as form of, 39; of *mangliu*, 130

F-4 visas, for professional and business fields, 73

factory work lay-offs, Meihua experience with, 137–41

fake marriages, 202n8; South Korea and, 21, 54, 107, 109; for Soviet Wind, 14–15

family registration. *See hukou*

feelings: of displacement, 174; structure of, 125, 131, 192n5, 207n13; Yanbian ethnic, 45–48

female workers: body clock and intensive labor of, 92–95, 99; daily wages for, 200n14; deportation experiences of, 68–71; in H-2 visa rhythm, 78; remittances control by, 113–14; transnational temporality of working body and service labor, 94–95

financial crisis (2008), 25; Korean money unstable in, 147–48; remittances impacted by, 123, 147

Fitzgerald, David, 142, 207n19

flexible citizenship, Ong on, 171

floating population: in China *hukou*, 129–30; of migrant workers, 1, 7, 63, 86, 129–30, 145, 155

free time, Adorno on, 199n11

Gasparini, Giovanni, 116

gender: division of labor in Soviet Wind and, 14–15; identity, 191n29. *See also* female workers

Gender Trouble (Butler), 191n29

Given Time (Derrida), 203n16

global hypergamy, 109

global mobilization, of Xi Jinping, 179

government of self, in China, 155–56

Guo (Mr.): bookstore of, 156–58, 162; entrepreneur experience of, 156–63; parents of, 157–64; Yanbian ten-year absence of, 157, 166. *See also* Kim (Aunt) (mother of Mr. Guo)

H-2 Overseas Korean Visit-Work Visa, 106, 202n11; for designated service and physical labor sectors, 73, 77, 89–90, 195n3, 198n1; female workers and, 78; as form of amnesty, 72–73; Korean Chinese numbers of, 197n12; lottery for, 198n1; one-three-two rhythm of, 80, 175; post-amnesty, 53, 72–74; requirements of, 72, 77

Han Chinese, 30, 175; confidence in future of China of, 149; ethnic tensions with Korean Chinese, 46–48, 136; Korean Chinese ethnic distinction from, 31, 35, 46–47, 146–48;

Korean Chinese interdependency with, 124–25, 178; massage services of, 145–47; move against Russia encroachment, 34; perceived as hard working, 144–45; service industry work by, 46, 145–46; spending habits ethnic stereotype, 126–27; stigmatized identity of, 40; transnational migration difficulties for, 128; as Yanbian *dagong*, 145–49; Yanbian population increase of, 45, 145–46; Yanbian settled by, 20, 22, 79

Han'guk Param. See South Korean Wind

Harvey, David, 199n10, 205n4

Ho (Mr.), remittances experience of, 112–15, 117–18

home: Marx on, 84; rhythm 1 defined in, 79–80; Tsuda on unfamiliarity of, 199n5

homeland, un/welcoming (South Korea), 52–54, 178; currency of kin and, 55–59; Korean Chinese on edge of deportation from, 65–72, 74; Overseas Korean Act, 59–63; post-amnesty and H-2 visa, 53, 72–74; Uijuro Church camp for undocumented, 53, 63–66

Huasun Yang: H-2 visa of, 106; waiting experience of, 104–6

hukou (family registration), in China, 129, 206n12; blurred due to migration, 130–31; rural migrants in cities and, 129–30; transnational migration and, 131. *See also* *mangliu*

human quality. *See suzhi*

illegal market for migration, 17, 32, 52–53, 59–61

IMF (International Monetary Fund), 19, 61

immobility, within mobility, 101–2

income gap, between Yanbian and South Korea, 135–37, 207n14

inequality: maintenance of through ethnicization, 39–40; urban, 190n23

internal migration, in China, 123–25; of Korean Chinese, 128, 135, 149; of Han Chinese, 125, 127; scale and, 129–30

International Monetary Fund (IMF), 19, 61

Korean dream (continued)
of, 17–20; South Korea as place for making money, 24; of Sungchul Park, 173–74; transnational temporality in, 24–25; undocumented status and, 101; waning of, 148; Yanbian as place for spending money, 24

Korean money, 21; Chinese currency exchange and, 23, 98, 123, 166–67, 205n2; cost of living and consumption in Yanbian increased by, 140; ethnic stereotypes and, 126–27, 141–42; Korean Chinese dependency on, 126; rapid urbanization and, 22; remittance-dependent economy and, 22; as transnational emblem, 22; turbulent and unstable flows of, 147–48; Yanbian regional economy and, 126

Korean War (1950–1953), 18, 32, 35, 60, 189n17

Korean Wind: capitalism and, 6, 176; criticism of, 6; differentiated mobility in, 125; economic betterment in, 50, 81; economic reform and open economy in, 50; emigration and, 4–7; ethnic and remittance landscape in, 128; Han Chinese and social changes from, 22; Han Chinese reaction to, 125; Korean Chinese as transnational border-crossing ethnicity and, 41; Korean Chinese reaction to, 125; less attraction for now, 174; multidimensional mobility from, 100; remittance-driven economy of, 147; sudden affluence in, 2; waiting as part of, 104; Yanbian remake by, 125; Yanbian socialism and, 48–50. See also post-Korean Wind

labor: affective, 104, 119, 201n1; bodies and intensity of, 91–92, 94; Korean Chinese in service industries, 21, 53, 57, 61, 89–90; Marx on, 95, 208n20; migrant workers as cheap source of, 174; South Korea shortages in, 60–61; Yanbian lacking in, 141–44

labor market: Fitzgerald on options in, 142, 207n19; Korean Chinese in South Korea, 24, 60, 73–74, 197n14; Mr. Cho experience of in Yanji, 142–44

language: boundaries in migration, 135, 165–66; of Yanbian, 42, 43, 194n20

laoban (entrepreneurs), 209n6; China encouragement of, 155; Dan Laoban as successful, 167–72; Mr. Guo experience with, 156–63; post-Korean Wind and, 154–58, 160–63, 166–70; self-improvement and, 156; suzhi and, 156, 162–63; Woo Park on, 210n7; in Yanbian, 131–37, 153–54

Lee, (Ms.) See Chunja Lee

Lefebvre, Henri, 77

Let the Blue River Run (film): material affluence in, 106–7; on money transformation of relationships, 107–8; waiting and, 105–8

Lim Gwangbin, 53, 63–66, 196n10. See also Uijuro Church

Liu, Xin, 175

loneliness, of pot'ori, 100–101

Lopez, Sarah Lynn, 203n14, 206n6

love: marriage as transaction without, 109; moral and sexual anxiety in, 109, 205n8; remittances as promises of, 116–18; waiting for, 108–12

Maehua Kang: body clock, aging, and ill health of, 93–98; job stability and flexibility importance to, 93; rhythm 2 experience of, 94–95; rhythm 3 experience of, 92–95

Manchuria, 187n3; Japan 1945 retreat from, 36; migration to, 4–5, 62

mangliu (people forced to leave their own land, in China), 130, 139

manual laborer. See dagong

Market Wind (Sijang Param), 8–10

marriage: fake, 14–15, 21, 54, 107, 109, 202n8; between South Korean men and Korean Chinese women, 57–58, 109; as transaction, 109

Marx, Karl: on bodies, 94; on home, 84; on labor, 95, 208n20; on potential of money, 203n13

massage services, of Han Chinese, 145–47

materialism: attitude of obsessive, 2; Korean Chinese migrants contaminated by, 6

Mauss, Marcel, 203n16

Midnight Runners (film), Korean Chinese lawsuit against, 201n6 migrants: Çağlar and Schiller on city relationship with, 206n8; Chinese rural in cities, 130, 139; to Japan, Russia, China, 17, 189n16; South Korea group of Korean Chinese, 3, 16, 52, 53, 61–62

migrant workers, 3; as cheap source of labor, 174; disdain for, 164–65, 173–74; entrepreneurialism encouraged in China, 155; floating population of, 1, 7, 63, 86, 129–30, 145, 155; illegal entry for, 17, 32, 52–53, 59–61; job movement of, 92; Korean dream and South Korea work as, 1, 24. *See also* female workers

migration: abjection and precariousness experiences, 190n24; internal, 125, 127, 129–30, 135, 149; kin-related, 55–59, 201n5, 210n6; Korean Chinese illegal market for, 52–53, 59–61; Korean Chinese reasons for, 48–49; language boundaries in, 135, 165–66; to Manchuria, 4–5, 62; North Korean Wind and, 6–7, 11–13; population regulation and, 197n13; South Korean Wind and, 6–7; Soviet Wind and, 6–7, 13–15, 188n9; turbulence of, 128, 130, 147–48; winds of, 7–8. *See also* transnational migration

mobility: Chu on displacement and, 170–71; as condition of modernity, 80, 102; as economic power symbol, 179; immobility within, 101–2; Korean Chinese non-, 171; Korean Wind and multidimensional, 100. *See also* differentiated mobility

modernity: capitalism in, 170; mobility as condition of, 80, 102

money: backup, 142; Marx on potential of, 203n13; partner conflicts over, 107; relationships and subjectivity reshaped by, 115; rhythm 1 spending anxieties, 82–85, 200n12; Simmel on, 203n13; transnational migration money fever, 102, 114–15; waiting and management of, 104, 112–13, 117–19. *See also* Korean money; remittances

moral and sexual anxiety, of *pot'ori*, 109, 205n8

Munn, Nancy, 198n4

Navaro-Yashin, Yael, 31

neoliberalism: capitalism and, 190n22, 200n17; Seo on, 209n5; F-4 and H-2 visas and, 73–74; Kipnis on, 190n22; in South Korea, 19, 21, 61, 178

new generation, 184–85

non-mobility, of Korean Chinese, 153, 171

North Korea, 33; China economic disparity with, 54; Korean Chinese marriage relationships with, 181–82; Korean War and difficulty entering, 32, 189n17; minimization of Korean Chinese kinship ties, 54, 58, 189n17; political influence on Korean Chinese, 32

North Koreans: persecution of when crossing border, 32; Yanbian restaurant business work by, 182–83

North Korean Wind (*Pukchosŏn Param*), 6–7, 11–13

not-yet-consciousness, Bloch on, 204n20

Oksun Park: arrest and near deportation of, 82; financial burden of meetings and parties, 83–84; return to Yanbian by, 82; rhythm 1 experience of, 79; rhythm 2 experience of, 98; as South Korea undocumented worker, 82; work calendar of, 91; working time pattern of, 90–91

"100 percent Korean Chinese" ethnic talk, 39

one-three-two rhythm, of H-2 visa, 80, 175

Ong, Aihwa, 171

otherness, of ethnicity, 39

Overseas Korean Act (1999): Korean Chinese ethnic solidarity argument against, 62; Korean Chinese unrecognized under, 61–63; Korean Russian and Korean Japanese exclusion from, 63; NGOs' and churches' counterarguments against, 62; overseas Koreans' citizenship, 59–61, 196n9; unconstitutionality of, 69

Overseas Korean Act (2005 revision): amnesty granted by, 23, 66, 102, 105; South Korea on, 65–67

overseas Koreans: Korean Chinese as, 6, 196n8; Overseas Korean Act on citizenship of, 59–61, 196n9

Overseas Koreans Foundation: on South Korea citizenship from family migration, 201n5, 210n6

paper kinship, 58–59, 195n4
param (wind): flow concept in, 7; migration and, 6–7. *See also* China Wind; Korean Wind; post-Korean Wind; South Korea Wind; Soviet Wind
Paramkkot (The windflower) (Xu Lianshun), 52, 63
Park, Alyssa, 188n14
Park, Hyun Ok: on neoliberal South Korea, 19; on territorial osmosis, 4
Park, Woo, 211n7
party-state-market complex, in China, 155–56
patience, Gasparini on waiting and, 116, 203n15
people forced to leave land, 130, 139
peoplehood, of ethnic groups, 39
political economy, South Korea migrant labor and, 3
post-amnesty, 77, 106; H-2 visa and, 53, 72–74
post–Cold War South Korea, China and, 3–4, 49–50
post–Korean Wind: Chinese dream and, 163–66, 176, 178–80; entrepreneurs, not manual laborers, valued, 154–58; Korean Chinese entrepreneur activities, 166–70; after Korean dream, 156–60; migrant returnees at disadvantage, 172–75; proudly staying at home in, 170–72; settled entrepreneurs, 160–63
post-socialist China, South Korea and, 3–4, 49–50
Post-Soviet Social (Collier), 191n26
pot'ori (waiting partner): anxiety and loneliness of, 100–101; romantic betrayal and, 104, 108–9, 205n8; spousal relationships and, 103, 116–18
privatization, in China, 2, 3, 19, 21, 49; *danwei* work unit and, 113, 199n9; economic, 178–79; factory shut down and, 137–41; forbidden in Yanbian, 8
Pukchosŏn Param. See North Korean Wind

Qing Dynasty, Tumen River crossing by Koreans, 34, 192n7

Ran (Ms.), experience of jumping scales, 131–37
remittance-dependent economy: Han Chinese and Korean Chinese interdependency in, 22; of Korean Wind, 147
remittances: development relationship with, 123, 149, 205n1; female worker controlling of, 113–14; financial crisis of 2008 impact on, 123, 147; inability to accumulate, 174; Lopez on, 203n14, 206n6; Mr. Ho experience of, 112–15, 117–18; as promises of love, 116–18; social, 205n1; South Korea economic development and, 60; transformative power of, 112–15, 178; as transnational migration capital, 205n1; Yanji influx of, 125–26. *See also* Korean money
rhythm 1: home defined in, 79–80; Oksun Park experience with, 79, 82–85; one year of unfamiliar home in, 78–80; spending anxieties, 82–85, 200n12; Yanbian time, 80–81; Yanbian unfamiliarity from long absences, 79
rhythm 2, 95–98
rhythm 3: body clock, 92–95; Chunja Lee experience of, 85–88; employment agency, 85–90, 206n7; working time, 90–92
rhythms, 99; designated service and physical labor sectors, 73, 77, 89–90, 195n3, 198n1; female workers in, 78; H-2 visa impact on, 77; Lefebvre on, 77; migration flow and social belonging in, 77; rhythm 1, 78–85, 200n12; rhythm 2, 95–98; rhythm 3, 85–95, 206n7
romantic betrayal, *pot'ori* and, 104, 108–9, 205n8
Russia: Han Chinese move against encroachment of, 34; Yanbian visits from, 21

scales: fixed and fluidity of, 129; *hukou* as marker of, 130–31; internal migration and, 129–30; jumping, 128–31; Smith definition of, 128–29; urban and rural markers of, 129–30

power in, 167–68; development changes 2008–2016 in, 150–52; economic affluence and social stability in, 153; entrepreneur farmer in, 131–37; entrepreneurship in, 153–54; ethnically focused organization in, 42; ethnic comfort and, 46–48; ethnic tensions between Han and Korean Chinese in, 46–48, 136; Han Chinese *dagong* workers in, 145–49; Han Chinese settling in, 20, 22, 79; intense consumption in, 79, 84–85, 123, 126, 140, 147; jumping scales in, 128–31; Korean Chinese 2006–2007 return to, 78–79; Korean Wind and socialism in, 48–50; lack of willing labor in, 141–44; laid-off factory worker in, 137–41; language of, 42, 43, 194n20; location of, 1; market economy confusion in, 8; new social imperative to return to, 4; population and ethnic diversity in, 42; privatization forbidden in, 8; South Korean style of decoration in, 83; Sungchul Park on social split in, 172–73; time management in, 80–81; transition to China Wind, 149

Yanbian University, 44

Yanji: as capital of Yanbian, 123; consumption and rapid urbanization in, 123; downtown district, 124; as ethnic enclave, 125–28, 205n3, 206n8; Korean Chinese identity and, 205n3; Mr. Wang experience in, 125–26; pleasure-centered consumption industries in, 126; remittances influx in, 125–26

Yanji West Market, 9–10, 12, 187n7

Zhang Liu, 195n1

Zheng Panlong, daughter-in-law theory of, 38–39

www.ingramcontent.com/pod-product-compliance
Lightning Source LLC
Chambersburg PA
CBHW020853270326
41928CB00006B/684